Life Insurance
Settlement Options

THE IRWIN SERIES IN RISK AND INSURANCE

BOILEAU, STALNAKER, & LUCK *Life Insurance Agency Financial Management*
BRAINARD *Automobile Insurance*
DICKERSON *Health Insurance* Revised Edition
DONALDSON *Casualty Claim Practice*
FOLLMANN *Medical Care and Health Insurance: A Study in Social Progress*
FRAINE *Valuation of Securities Holdings of Life Insurance Companies*
GREGG *Life and Health Insurance Handbook* Second Edition
GREIDER & BEADLES *Law and the Life Insurance Contract*
HABER & COHEN *Social Security: Programs, Problems, and Policies*
MAGEE & BICKELHAUPT *General Insurance* Seventh Edition
MAGEE *Life Insurance* Third Edition
MAGEE *Property Insurance* Third Edition
McGILL *Legal Aspects of Life Insurance*
McGILL *Life Insurance*
MEHR & CAMMACK *Principles of Insurance* Third Edition
MEHR & HEDGES *Risk Management in the Business Enterprise*
MYERS *Social Insurance and Allied Government Programs*
REDEKER & REID *Life Insurance Settlement Options* Revised Edition
SNIDER *Readings in Property and Casualty Insurance*

Life Insurance Settlement Options

HARRY S. REDEKER, LL.B.

Vice President and General Counsel

The Fidelity Mutual Life Insurance Company

AND

CHARLES K. REID, II, C.L.U.

Associate Director, Company Relations Division

Life Insurance Agency Management Association

REVISED EDITION, 1964

RICHARD D. IRWIN, INC., Homewood, Illinois

REVISED EDITION

First Printing, September, 1964

Second Printing, June, 1965

Third Printing, June, 1967

Library of Congress Catalog Card No. 64–24693

PRINTED IN THE UNITED STATES OF AMERICA

Preface to Revised Edition

This is a completely revised edition of a book first published in 1957. Basically, the statements in the preface to our first edition apply with equal validity to the second.

Here is a summary of the principal changes in this edition:

1. Reorganization of material for more logical presentation.
2. Simplification of explanations.
3. Elimination of unnecessary technical facets of the subject, such as the mathematical structure of settlement options.
4. Elimination of some offshoots of options not commonly encountered.
5. Clarification of pitfalls inherent in the selection of settlement options, particularly related to the life income option, ten years certain.
6. Updating of company practices relating to use of options.
7. Incorporation of recent court decisions and changes in the law, such as revisions of the Internal Revenue Code; new or changed interpretative U.S. Treasury Regulations; changes in provisions for veterans' benefits.
8. Introduction of the time-saving "capitalization and discount" method of calculating insurance needs, as an alternate approach to solution of the revised illustrative case in Chapter 8.

To put together a work such as this, particularly when there are no similar books in existence, takes much more than research, writing, and editing by the authors. This book continues to be a tribute to and a product of people—willing and cooperative volunteers who took time from their busy lives to read these chapters carefully and to make valuable suggestions for their improvement.

As in the first edition, the co-authors each assumed primary responsibility for initial drafts of certain chapters, and both cross-edited all chapters. Most of our friends mentioned in the original preface from the American College, the Fidelity Mutual Life, and the Life Insurance Agency Management Association again gave their full measure of cooperation in the preparation of the second edition.

In the Fidelity Mutual Life, William A. Porter and Martin L. Zeffert, Associate Actuaries, read some of the chapters and gave their counsel on actuarial aspects. Mr. Porter updated the tax examples in Chapter 6.

Richard H. Hollenberg, Second Vice President and Associate General Counsel, Paul L. Wise, Associate Counsel, and Herbert K. Zearfoss, Assistant Counsel, did legal research, added recent statutes and court decisions, and assisted in drafting. Joseph C. Ladd, Vice President—Sales, and S. Bruce Copeland, Second Vice President—Sales Development, read chapters and made suggestions on sales aspects and the practical application of principles to actual cases.

Mrs. A. O. MacFeeters, Manager of the Policy Title Division, carefully checked practices of life insurance companies and made suggestions concerning Chapters 3 and 4. She and Miss Frances Rzucidlo, Assistant Manager of this Division, read every word of galley proof and page proof in all eight chapters and in much of the front and back material as well. Miss Lydia Grayson, Mr. Redeker's secretary, repeated her performance of countless overtime hours in typing, duplicating, assembling, and circulating drafts of all eight chapters and of some of the other material.

In the Life Insurance Agency Management Association, William O. Cummings, Director of Special Services,

Richard N. Ford, Director of Publications, and Don A. Gorsline, Director of Managerial Training, all in the Company Relations Division, reviewed initial drafts and helped edit copy, particularly with respect to programing, the use of options, and the two alternate presentations of the revised case problem in Chapter 8.

We are especially indebted to Mr. Robert B. Proctor and to the Connecticut Mutual Life Insurance Company for permission to use "The Capitalization and Discount Method of Determining the Problem" as the basis for the alternate case solution in Chapter 8. This method was explained by Mr. Proctor in the *Journal of the American Society of Chartered Life Underwriters,* Volume XI, No. 3 (Summer 1957), beginning at page 222.

We followed the pattern of the first edition and requested our friends in life insurance companies to read chapters. We attempted to have each chapter read independently in at least two companies. To all the readers whose names appear under the company listings below, and to others who assisted and who are not specifically identified, our deep and sincere thanks for their suggestions, most of which appear in the book.

Aetna Life Insurance Company (Chapter 2)
    John K. Luther, Director of Training
    E. F. Bassford, Assistant Secretary
    R. J. Peplaw, Assistant Secretary

Connecticut General Life Insurance Company
    Buist M. Anderson, Vice President and Counsel (Chapter 5)
    Alfred S. Moses, Jr., Assistant Counsel (Chapter 5)
    Hugh S. West, Director of Training and Research (Chapters 1 and 8)

The Connecticut Mutual Life Insurance Company (Chapters 1 and 8)
    Robert B. Proctor, Superintendent of Agencies and Training

Home Life Insurance Company (Chapters 1 and 8)
    John W. Langdon, Assistant Vice President

The Mutual Benefit Life Insurance Company (Chapters 3
and 7)
Charles W. Kappes, Vice President and Counsel

New England Mutual Life Insurance Company (Chapter 4)
Vincent V. R. Booth, Vice President and General Counsel
Robert J. Lawthers, Director of Estate Planning Services

New York Life Insurance Company (Chapter 6)
Edwin M. Jones, Assistant General Counsel
George J. Carl, Special Assistant, Settlements and Service
Tax Unit
Harry G. Hohn, Assistant Counsel

The Penn Mutual Life Insurance Company (Chapter 5)
Willis H. Satterthwaite, Vice President and Counsel
Frank W. Hatfield, Assistant Counsel
John S. C. Harvey, III, Attorney

Provident Mutual Life Insurance Company of Philadelphia
(Chapter 7)
Roy G. Shubert, Associate Counsel

The Northwestern Mutual Life Insurance Company
William B. Minehan, Secretary
Theo P. Otjen, Assistant Secretary
William F. Damm, Staff Associate   } (Chapters 3 and 4)
Milton E. Flint, Specialist
William F. Krueger, Supervisor

Melvin C. Teske, Assistant Counsel (Chapter 6)

State Mutual Life Assurance Company of America (Chapter 2)
Henry O. Smith, Assistant General Counsel

We dedicate this edition to our readers, as we did the
first edition. Those of you who are accountants, lawyers, life
underwriters, other representatives of life insurance companies, teachers, or trust officers must interpret and help
apply the principles in this book in actual cases so that life
insurance dollars will do the best possible job for millions
of policyowners, their widows, and their children.

We hope you will respond to our invitation—as you
did after the first edition was published—to send us your

comments for consideration when we prepare the next edition.

Finally, we repeat the word of tribute we expressed in the first edition to our wives, Elizabeth Redeker and Allis Reid, for their sympathetic understanding and their active reading and editorial assistance.

HARRY S. REDEKER
CHARLES K. REID, II

September, 1964

Preface to First Edition

We have thoroughly enjoyed writing this book—and we have learned much in the process. We can only hope that you will find it both interesting and helpful. In presenting it to you, we should like to outline the four objectives we have in mind:

First, we want to give you some idea of what the book is all about. You will have a better understanding of its chapters if you know why the book was written and precisely what the authors hope to accomplish with it.

Second, we know that other texts on this subject will be written in the years ahead. Perhaps the authors of some of those texts may be helped to eliminate a few trial and error steps by knowing just what we did. We believe that the initial plans, the editorial procedures, and the coordination of many skills have an important bearing on the quality of the end product.

Third, we sincerely invite our readers to give us their frank comments. These will be preserved and carefully considered in planning revisions of the book.

Fourth, we want to recognize the significant parts played by members of our unusually large team of willing volunteers. In this wonderful age of automation and atomic power, books are still written only by the labors of people. We wish we could adequately acknowledge the assistance of the many individuals who combined their talents to bring you this book. We must be content with mentioning just those who have been most actively identified with its actual writing, editing or critical reading.

The book is designed to help people who are interested in developing sound life insurance programs. It brings together for the first time the basic concepts and practices essential to the use of settlement options in distributing life insurance proceeds. Briefly, settlement options constitute the various ways in which life insurance proceeds may be disbursed to provide cash or income payments to meet family or business financial needs. Properly used, however, the settlement options also provide a money management service unequaled by any other investment.

This book is devoted chiefly to the proper use of this money management service in life insurance programing. Settlement options are the essential tools of programing, and much has been written about them, as such. However, this material has usually appeared as part of a larger work on life insurance, often with primary emphasis on how to use the guaranteed income rates under the options for the purely mathematical process of determining how far present insurance will go and how much new insurance may be needed. The phase of programing about which the least has been written is that of following through to put into effect a coordinated plan for actual disbursement of life insurance proceeds.

Each of the authors of this book had recently written a booklet to help life underwriters use settlement options more effectively in programing, one published by The Fidelity Mutual Life Insurance Company, the other by the Life Insurance Agency Management Association. The American College of Life Underwriters decided that a textbook on this subject should be included in its educational program. Students, usually life underwriters, participate in this program to learn to serve their policyholders better, and at the same time to prepare themselves to meet the exacting requirements of the qualifying examinations for the Chartered Life Underwriter designation.

Dr. Davis W. Gregg, President of the American College, invited us to collaborate in this joint project. After extensive research, an outline was prepared. It was largely a distillate of the material listed in the Bibliography in Appendix E, and of our ideas of what such a textbook should include. This outline was reviewed critically by officials of the American College, including Dr. S. S. Huebner, President Emeritus, Dr. Gregg, Dean Herbert C. Graebner, and Dr. Jack C. Keir, Director of Educational Publications. The outline was also submitted to the group of life insurance companies identified below. A final outline evolved, which was followed rather closely in the writing of the book.

Next, each author assumed responsibility for an initial draft of four chapters: Mr. Reid for Chapters 1, 2, 4 and 8; Mr. Redeker for Chapters 3, 5, 6 and 7. In addition to extensive cross-editing of each other's chapters, each author had the benefit of expert technical assistance in his own organization.

In The Fidelity Mutual Life Insurance Company, Norman Harper, Actuary, supplied or checked many illustrative figures. Martin Zeffert, Assistant Actuary, helped with the tax examples in Chapter 6. Legal research as well as some actual drafting was done by Richard H. Hollenberg, Associate General Counsel, and by Vincent P. Keesey and Paul L. Wise, both Assistant Counsel. W. Morgan Churchman, Jr., Assistant Manager of Agencies, made some practical suggestions from the field viewpoint. Miss Elsie Ullrich, Agency Secretary, who is in charge of the Company's field publications, contributed valuable editorial suggestions. Mrs. A. O. MacFeeters, Manager of the Policy Title Division, who possesses expert knowledge based on years of supervision of problems covering settlement options, was the "spark plug" that kept the project on its time schedule.

In addition, she and Miss Lydia Grayson, Mr. Redeker's secretary, spent countless hours outside the usual business day typing, duplicating, assembling, and circulating the drafts of his chapters.

In the Life Insurance Agency Management Association, L. W. S. Chapman, Director of Company Relations, and the members of this Division reviewed the basic outline, as did Dr. S. Rains Wallace, Director of Research, and Frederic M. Peirce, Managing Director. The varied backgrounds of these men in life insurance selling, field and home office management, training, writing, research, and management consultation work enabled them to make unusually worthwhile suggestions. Later, Dr. Leonard W. Ferguson, Program Director, and John L. Lobingier, Jr., Director of Public Relations, read the entire manuscript. We are also especially indebted to William O. Cummings, a Company Relations Senior Consultant who contributed much valuable editing of our initial drafts. Last, but by no means least, Mrs. Shirley Wolf and her indefatigable secretarial staff, as well as other members of the Administrative Division and the Company Relations secretaries, performed yeoman service in contributing their skills.

Home office agency and claim executives, law officers, field agency heads and life underwriters in a number of representative companies were asked to review the chapters. Each chapter was assigned more or less arbitrarily to two companies. Our well-qualified friends in many other companies could have been included in this list, but it seemed more practical to limit our requests for criticism and suggestions to a small group of companies of varying sizes. By asking a company to read only one chapter (except in three instances) we felt that a more thorough and immediate reading job could be done. In one company, at least eight key people reviewed the submitted chapter. We wish we could name all the people in these companies who joined in this effort, and whose suggestions were of such great help in preparing the final manuscript. To all of them, our deep and abiding thanks.

Connecticut General Life Insurance Company, Hartford
Connecticut Mutual Life Insurance Company, Hartford
Equitable Life Assurance Society of the United States, New York
General American Life Insurance Company, St. Louis
Home Life Insurance Company, New York
Indianapolis Life Insurance Company, Indianapolis
Lincoln National Life Insurance Company, Fort Wayne
Massachusetts Mutual Life Insurance Company, Springfield
Mutual Benefit Life Insurance Company, Newark
Mutual Life Insurance Company of New York, New York
National Life Insurance Company, Montpelier
New England Mutual Life Insurance Company, Boston
Northwestern Mutual Life Insurance Company, Milwaukee
Penn Mutual Life Insurance Company, Philadelphia
Prudential Insurance Company of America, Newark
Southwestern Life Insurance Company, Dallas
Union Central Life Insurance Company, Cincinnati

We were also privileged to study the programing and settlement option manuals of many of these companies, which we found very rewarding.

The entire manuscript was examined by David A. Ivry, Professor of Insurance, of the University of Connecticut, and most of the chapters by Dr. Gregg and Dr. Keir. Again, their comments were most helpful in drafting the printer's copy.

Finally, a word of tribute to the sympathetic understanding of our wives, Elizabeth Redeker and Allis Reid, in giving us "leaves of absence" from our families during the many months this book was under way, and also for their reading and editorial assistance.

We believe we have set up procedures to produce a text as reasonably complete and accurate as would be expected of a first edition. We now submit it to you—a much larger group of critical readers—to whom we humbly dedicate this book. This dedication is based on our belief that the book will be read principally by people with a sincere interest in making life insurance dollars do a better job for millions of policyowners, their widows and their children—whether the reader be a life underwriter or other member of a life insurance company, a lawyer, an accountant, a trust officer or a teacher concerned with insurance.

Those of you who pass along to us your suggestions will be most welcome participants in the effort to develop progressively better life insurance programing for people served by the readers of future editions.

HARRY S. REDEKER
CHARLES K. REID. II

October 12, 1956

Table of Contents

A. LIFE INSURANCE POLICIES

B. ANNUITY CONTRACTS

C. GROUP INSURANCE

D. GOVERNMENT INSURANCE FOR SERVICEMEN AND VETERANS

CHAPTER 3

THE USE OF SETTLEMENT OPTIONS TO COVER NEEDS

A. CASH FUNDS

CHAPTER 6

TAX ASPECTS OF SETTLEMENT OPTIONS

A. FEDERAL INCOME TAX

CHAPTER 8

PROGRAMING IN ACTION

APPENDIXES

INDEX

Chapter 1

Settlement Options and Life Insurance Programing

A. THE IMPORTANCE OF SETTLEMENT OPTIONS

§1.1 How and why options were developed. The practice of measuring wealth in terms of income instead of capital value, though one of long standing in some older European economies, is a relatively new idea in the United States and Canada. Even today, when the needs of beneficiaries are increasingly expressed in amounts of income, it is still common to think of life insurance and other assets owned by the family head and breadwinner in terms of capital sums.

Life insurance policies are required by law to contain certain standard provisions. They are also permitted by law to include additional provisions of beneficial nature, on a more or less standardized basis. A common provision of insurance laws is that policies may include settlement options under which proceeds may be applied instead of being paid in one sum. The State of New York enacted the first such law in 1906, a comparatively recent date in the history of American life insurance.

However, as early as 1867, at least one company allowed proceeds to be paid in installments over a period of years. In 1883, a company introduced a policy payable automatically to the beneficiary in twenty equal annual installments. During the next few years, a number of companies brought out similar policies or issued riders permitting installment settlement of proceeds as an option. Beginning about 1893, companies often extended the privilege of receiving proceeds in the form of income payable over the beneficiary's entire lifetime.

Following passage of the New York law, similar laws were enacted in other states, and since 1907 most policies have contained settlement options. However, significant growth in their acceptance, both by life insurance men and by the insuring public, did not commence until immediately after the first World War. The idea of life insurance programing based on income needs took shape at that time and began to be reflected in the education and training directed at the life underwriter. This led to the concept of life underwriting as a profession and to intensive training of agents to give specialized advice on utilizing insurance proceeds to the best advantage. In most cases, this meant using settlement options to provide logical and more permanent security for dependents.

The demand for income settlement options, particularly installment options, arose primarily out of the needs for safety of principal and for amounts of income to the beneficiary beyond what could be provided by interest or dividend yields alone. It was recognized that rarely could a family build an estate large enough to allow the family to live on the income, without using principal, even through the creative power of life insurance. The progressive income taxes and relatively lower investment yields of modern times have augmented this age-old problem. The crash of 1929 and the ensuing business depression further crystallized thinking as to needs in terms of income instead of capital, and emphasized the unique dependability of a life insurance program based on settlement options. Passage of the Social Security Act in 1935, and subsequent amendments providing benefits for dependents, focused national attention on family needs for income. Government programs of insurance and pension benefits for servicemen, veterans, civil service and railroad employees, and their dependents, have educated great numbers of people to the concept of income needs. Other factors in the growth of the economy since the turn of this century have contributed in a similar way to public interest in security of income, such as the increase in the use of installment purchase plans and the tendency to budget all expenses on a monthly basis.

§1.2. **Settlement options provide unconditional guarantees.** Funds placed under settlement options are guaranteed both as to principal and interest, and the guarantee is backed by the entire assets of the company. At the same time, depending on the company's investment experience, excess interest may be paid over and above the guaranteed rate. Where a life contingency is involved, there is also a guarantee as to the mortality table used. These guarantees facilitate long-range planning with absolute certainty.

Such unconditional guarantees are possible because the funds of individual policyowners or beneficiaries are not segregated, with the exception of funds set up under recently enacted legislation permitting life insurance companies to maintain separate accounts for qualified pension plans. Funds of individual policyowners and beneficiaries are mingled with the funds of all others involved in the company, and any loss of principal or income is spread over all these assets. Under other similar methods of investing, the individual estate or trust must bear all losses directly. Life insurance is one of the few institutions able to make guarantees. It is the only one providing a guarantee of principal and interest for installments payable over the lifetime of one or more individuals.

§1.3. **A simple and practical income arrangement.** A comprehensive plan of family income can be arranged very simply under settlement options, requiring no investment supervision or added expense. The options provide the only scientific method of liquidating principal over a period of years or a lifetime, without loss of a dollar of capital or a day of interest. For the small estate, especially, they present a more practical arrangement for covering basic family needs than does payment in cash or the use of a trust.

However, to use settlement options, there must be needs which can be met by a more or less fixed schedule of payments to specified individuals. Generally, discretionary power to alter the plan as to time or amounts can be granted only on a somewhat limited basis, and usually must be vested in the payee. On the other hand, basic family needs can be met in most cases by an income plan requiring little or no such discretion.

§*1.4. Options pinpoint needs.* The intelligent use of settlement option tables reduces meaningless capital amounts to periodic income. Both the life underwriter and the client can then understand the problem. Often neither the client nor his potential beneficiaries have ever seen a single sum of money equal to the amount of insurance the family owns. The single sum may, therefore, seem substantial, even though it is barely enough to pay the client's final expenses or to support the family for a year or two.

Applying a conservative interest rate to the family's total capital, including insurance proceeds, will usually result in a pitifully inadequate income. On the other hand, disbursement of this fund at an adequate monthly rate to cover family needs will, in most cases, exhaust the assets long before the need for income has ended. Settlement options are essential in realistically appraising a client's life insurance and other assets in terms of the job they must do for dependents in event of his death, or for himself at retirement.

§*1.5. Options safeguard insurance proceeds.* Settlement options protect life insurance proceeds in many ways. Their inherent guarantees avoid investment losses attributable to market fluctuations. An income program set up before the insured's death may also protect the beneficiary against losses from unwise investments and the recommendations of self-appointed or self-serving advisers.

Most beneficiaries are widows. Many women have proved themselves competent in investment matters, but it must be conceded that most have had little, if any, experience in this field. Indeed, relatively few men have had investment experience, successful or otherwise. Regardless of business ability, the widow usually has a full-time job raising and educating her family. The point is well taken that to give dependents large sums of capital is to add to their problems, whereas to give them income is to help solve these problems.

Closely akin to the investment hazard is the hazard of using proceeds improvidently. It has been said that most men can thrive on adversity but few can endure prosperity. It is unusual for an individual not to be thrown off balance by sudden affluence, and the beneficiary of life insurance proceeds is no exception. Possession of seemingly unlimited cash funds encourages unwise expenditures, including loans or gifts to relatives appearing less well off than the insurance beneficiary. Usually, it is realized too late that such outlays have materially shortened the period of support assured by the proceeds, or have eliminated entirely a lifetime income which might otherwise have been possible. Proper use of settlement options can insure against improvidence while at the same time allowing reasonable flexibility. Indeed, the mere existence of a written plan covering income payments, no matter how flexible, can prove a strong deterrent to using proceeds other than as intended.

Settlement options can also prevent creditors from depriving the family of its means of support. Life insurance proceeds payable to named beneficiaries are usually exempt from creditors of the insured. Many states also protect the cash values of such insurance from seizure during the policyowner's lifetime. However, in most cases, this protection does not apply to creditors of the beneficiary unless proceeds are payable under an optional settlement agreement containing a creditor-protection or "spendthrift" clause. This means a plan of settlement established before the insured's death, for the law does not usually permit a beneficiary to put his or her own money beyond the reach of creditors. Rights of creditors are discussed more fully in Section 5.12.

Finally, settlement options enable the policyowner to direct the ultimate disposition of funds not used by the primary beneficiary. At death of the beneficiary following the insured, any remainder of proceeds received in cash becomes a part of the beneficiary's estate. This may be true as well of proceeds placed under a settlement option by the beneficiary, in lieu of accepting a cash payment. In a typical family situation, the wife is usually the primary beneficiary, and the children would normally inherit such remainders through the estate of their mother. However, this might be affected by terms of the mother's will or by applicable state law. Not only may the policyowner remove any uncertainty in this regard by electing a settlement option, but he can also minimize or even eliminate probate expenses in passing proceeds on to secondary beneficiaries. In addition, he can often arrange for such remainders to be paid to secondary beneficiaries under an income plan suited to their needs.

§*1.6. Settlement options widely used.* As late as 1920, less than 5 percent of proceeds paid by the major companies was applied under settlement options. In 10 years, this had increased to 10 to 15 percent, with some companies reporting as high as 30 percent. The use of settlement options continued to grow steadily, until in the 1950's it was not uncommon to find 50 percent or more of a company's matured endowment and death proceeds payable in this manner.

However, in recent years, the percentage of eligible proceeds placed under options has declined, except in certain large companies which feature programing sales procedures. On the other hand, in 1963 total income payments by companies under settlement option plans exceeded $1 billion for the first time. Total proceeds set aside for payment under income options were more than double the amount similarly set aside 20 years before.

In many cases, income payments under options have been arranged by one sum beneficiaries after the insured's death. But there is evidence that cases involving settlement options elected before death have also increased, as has the volume of proceeds affected by such elections. Moreover, settlement options are being used to an increasing extent for policies surrendered for cash or maturing as endowments during the insured's lifetime.

§1.7.   Rewards and responsibilities.   Properly used, settlement options can be profitable alike to the policyowner, the beneficiary, and the life underwriter. In each case, the profit is not merely in the receipt of more dollars. It also involves a generous measure of personal satisfaction.

Life insurance settlement options constitute a money management service unequaled by any other investment. They enable the insured to provide his family and himself with planned security at minimum premium outlay, with no extra charge for the service. They do this with assured profit to the payee, enhanced by certain tax advantages, and with the peace of mind that can come only from the knowledge that income is assured.

To the life underwriter, selling income through the use of options increases his effectiveness, because he is doing a better job for his clients. Improved quality of business and larger policy sales are but two sources of profit resulting from this practice. The very foundation of the underwriter's ability to develop and hold a true clientele rests on his understanding and proper use of policy settlement options. The accompanying rewards of personal satisfaction mean the difference between a humdrum business life as a salesman of policies and a life full of meaning and purpose and great accomplishment.

Acceptance of rewards and opportunities always imposes certain responsibilities. Obviously the family head has a responsibility for the continued security of his dependents, even after his lifetime. He should have an adequate life insurance estate, properly arranged, and should keep it up to date with changing financial and family conditions. But few men, if any, have the knowledge or can take the time from their own businesses to discharge this responsibility without the life underwriter's help.

Thus, the responsibility of the life underwriter is great. Obviously he has a duty to give his clients wise counsel as to the proper use of settlement options, based on facts. He is also responsible for continuing service to keep their policies up to date with changing circumstances, and for assisting in the settlement of claims.

There is also a broad responsibility to the public at large. For example, to the extent that an underwriter can place more adequate amounts of life insurance, properly arranged, he helps to reduce demands on charitable and governmental sources. Moreover, the way in which each client's insurance is handled has a direct bearing on the acceptance of life insurance by persons within his sphere of influence. This effect is multiplied and influences to some extent the public attitude toward the products and services of life underwriters in general. More than one layman has refused to listen to the story of life insurance or has deferred purchasing it, often with tragic results, because of poor service described by a friend or relative.

A similar responsibility exists toward the underwriter's company and its other agents and policyowners. Unnecessarily complicated settlement plans impose added burdens of cost on all who are involved in the company. Often they lead to misunderstandings that may defeat their original purpose. Settlement plans which have not been kept up to date can cause irreparable damage when death occurs and the beneficiary must accept an income pattern wholly unrelated to current circumstances. The beneficiary, the company, and the cause of life insurance in general suffer as a result of such financial tragedies.

Finally, the life underwriter has a responsibility to himself, to his professional reputation and to his future success. Improper or careless use of settlement options, or well-intentioned promises of service that are not carried out, can make selling difficult and client-building impossible. On the other hand, a job well done in this area will meet a great public demand for competent service. It will lead to real success, not only in dollars but also in the "psychic pay" of personal satisfaction and recognition.

§*1.8. Settlement options and programing.* Recently, over 4,000 family heads were interviewed in a public opinion survey conducted jointly by the Life Insurance Agency Management Association and the Life Underwriter Training Council. The result was a series of reports, "Life Insurance in Focus." Among many findings, this survey indicated clearly that the public wants knowledgeable, sincere agents who will render the kind of service discussed in this book. In particular, families who felt an agent had helped to program their needs and life insurance tended to buy from that agent, to buy in larger amounts, and to indicate willingness to buy again from the same agent.

Income settlement options are the essential tools used in programing life insurance. An understanding of the options is, therefore, a prerequisite to mastering programing techniques. This includes knowledge of what options are available, their uses in meeting family needs, and problems involved in their use, including company practices and tax and legal questions.

At the same time, a knowledge of what life insurance

programing involves is also essential to a complete understanding of settlement options. The various uses of options can best be considered against the background of programing objectives. Accordingly, a brief review of the nature of programing and its essential steps is in order.

B. PROGRAMING THE LIFE INSURANCE ESTATE

§*1.9. Life insurance programing defined.* Programing may be likened to "walking around a client" and looking at him from every angle, in order to appraise all of his needs for life insurance and to meet those needs as efficiently as possible. It is the professional approach to life underwriting. From the point of view of the life underwriter as a professional salesman, it is total needs selling as distinguished from single needs or package selling. The distribution of proceeds may be composed of "income packages," but the total distribution pattern is the actual "sale" that is made in programing.

Programing can be simple or complex depending upon the number of beneficiaries, the contingencies which must be anticipated, and the amounts and types of life insurance involved. A widely used advanced training course states that "programing occurs whenever the life underwriter discusses more than one life insurance need at a time with a client," that is, when any attempt is made to assign priorities to the various needs in a given case. Here, programing is conceived primarily as a method of diagnosing and measuring life insurance needs. In a broader sense, programing also includes arranging the most effective plan for distributing the life insurance estate to cover these needs.

This requires of the underwriter a firm conviction as to the value of all the services performed by life insurance. It calls for a thorough understanding of settlement options and the ability to make judicious recommendations for their use.

Because the ability to do effective programing requires

extensive knowledge and continuous study, there is a tendency to associate this work with complex, time-consuming cases involving persons of substantial means or high income. Experience has proved the fallacy of this concept. The individual of modest means, and especially the wage earner with dependents, also needs the help of skilled advisers in planning his financial future and his life insurance program.

Moreover, programing is basically simple. The fundamental principles underlying it apply equally to the large or small case. It is essentially an attitude rather than a specific procedure, and the attitude of the successful programer must be that of any other professional man. In a very real sense, no case should be too small to warrant his attention nor too large for him to attack. In handling a complex case, many sources of advice and information are available to supplement his own knowledge and experience.

The professional life underwriter's position in this respect is analogous to that of the family doctor. The great majority of the doctor's cases involve very simple diagnosis and treatment, often concluded in one or two brief interviews. Only a small percentage require exhaustive physical examination, protracted study, and possible consultation with colleagues. Yet without his extremely broad knowledge and experience, applied under the basic principles of professional diagnosis and action, the doctor could not solve either type of case. So it is with the professional life underwriter. The scope and complexity of the program he may recommend will vary with the individual case, but all his cases must be approached with the same attitude and receive the benefit of the same knowledge and principles of service.

§*1.10. Programing a part of estate planning.* It was once believed that a will represented the only estate plan needed by an individual. Today, estate analysis or estate planning involves a much broader field. It means a comprehensive survey of all estate assets, liabilities, and related problems. Business interests, capital and income requirements, tax aspects, and many other factors must be considered. A plan must be formulated to cover the entire financial requirements of the client during his lifetime and needs of his heirs after his death.

Life insurance programing is the function of estate planning performed by the life underwriter. In order to perform this function intelligently, the underwriter must take into consideration the size and character of assets other than life insurance. He must determine needs for life insurance to cover tax and other cash requirements. In many cases, he will consult with the client's other advisers, such as his attorney, trust officer, or accountant. Because he often leads a client to consider his overall estate plan, the life underwriter may coordinate activities of such other advisers on the "estate planning team." However, he is not necessarily responsible for developing the entire estate plan.

§*1.11. The nature of the programing process.* Programing means more than diagnosing life insurance needs. It means more than coordinating settlement options. It embraces both the development of an adequate life insurance estate, consistent with the needs of the client and his ability to save, and arrangement of the most effective plan for distributing life insurance proceeds in accordance with the client's objectives.

If a factual analysis of a client's estate is pursued to its logical ultimate conclusion to measure the client's needs for life insurance and future income planning, it differs little from the comprehensive analysis that precedes an overall estate planning procedure. The difference in the comprehensive analysis lies principally in the scope of the recommendations that *follow* the analysis. This book is concerned with the use of settlement options in life insurance programing. Complete estate planning is beyond its purview.

Life insurance programing can consist of
of the following steps:

> Obtaining facts.
> Defining objectives.
> Considering what present insurance can pr
> Determining needs for additional insurance.
> Presenting the recommended program.
> Establishing the final distribution pattern.

Whenever the life underwriter analyzes an estate and
prepares recommendations concerning it, he should be extremely cautious to do nothing that would subject him to a
charge of the illegal practice of law. A life underwriter may
not make recommendations that constitute either giving
legal opinions or rendering legal advice. A helpful discussion of background, danger zones, and ways to avoid unin-
tentional violations may be found in an article, "Cooperation Between Life Insurance Representatives and Lawyers," appearing in the Winter, 1963, issue of *The C.L.U.
Journal,* page 73. The reader's attention is specifically directed to the "expectable consequence test," appearing on
pages 88 and 89, as follows:

> If the expectable consequence of such discussion is
> to motivate the client to consult his lawyer for a review
> of his problems and to seek his advice, it will be in the
> permissive area. However, his presentation will offend,
> despite warnings to consult his lawyer, if it is so defin-
> itive, so final, or so apparently authoritative as to prob-
> ably induce the client to by-pass his lawyer or to regard
> his as a mere scrivener to handle legal details. While
> the life insurance representative will be recognized as
> having the right to make definitive recommendations
> dealing solely with life insurance and the payment of
> policy proceeds, he should still refrain from giving legal
> opinions or legal advice either expressly or by implica-
> tion.

§*1.12. Obtaining facts.* The life underwriter's judgment can be no better than the facts upon which it is based.

Therefore, a clear understanding of the client's situation is essential. This does not mean that the client must be "cross-examined" or that every case requires the elaborate fact-finding treatment needed for analyzing a large and complex estate. But it does mean development of a clear picture of the financial situation, needs, desires, and philosophy of the client regarding the security of his family.

Methods of obtaining and recording facts vary from elaborate, multipage questionnaires to the use of scratch pads or even the back of an old envelope. Most companies provide suitable forms for guiding the fact-finding interview and noting the information obtained. Similar aids may be secured from commercial publishers. Experienced underwriters sometimes design their own forms to fit their individual techniques. The basic objective is the same in any case—to gain a clear understanding of the client's situation and desires. Often the simpler the technique, the clearer the picture.

Many life underwriters explore the client's objectives before seeking specific factual data. Others feel that starting with more or less routine items puts the client at ease and paves the way for a more meaningful discussion of objectives. In general, the following types of information are needed, though the amount of detail will vary with the relative complexity of the case, and the facts will not necessarily be obtained in the order listed:

(1) Full names and dates of birth of family members, including parents, grandparents, or grandchildren where appropriate, together with general information as to their health.

(2) Current status under Social Security, employee benefit plans (such as insurance, profit sharing, and pension benefits), and federal programs for civil service employees, railroad employees, and veterans of service in the armed forces.

(3) General estate assets, including family residences

and personal property, investments such as stocks, bonds, real estate, and interests in closely held businesses. With respect to each type of property, it is important to know whether it is owned solely by the client, solely by his wife, or jointly.

If the assets include an interest in a closely held business, it is necessary to know whether the business is a corporation, partnership, or sole proprietorship. It is also important to know what plans have been made for disposition of general estate assets, such as wills, trusts, or business buy-and-sell agreements.

(4) Potential inheritances that may come to members of the family, as well as gifts of a substantial nature which may have been made by them, either outright or in trust.

(5) Existing life insurance, both personal and business. The policies should be analyzed to determine the kind of insurance, who the beneficiaries are, and how the proceeds are payable. Although it is not always necessary to secure the contracts at the preliminary fact-finding stage, few clients can give reasonably accurate pictures of their holdings without them. In any case, the policies will be needed eventually for planning settlement arrangements. Disability and other health policies should be included.

(6) The names and addresses of other advisers, such as the family lawyer, accountant, and trust officer.

(7) Liabilities, such as outstanding mortgages, notes, insurance loans, and installment-purchase balances. With respect to an outstanding mortgage, it is important to know when it was established, its duration, the rate of interest, and what penalties may be involved in paying back all or part of the principal before its terminal date. Frequently, monthly payments on direct-reduction mortgages include an additional amount to cover insurance and taxes on the property. The client will usually have a statement from the mortgagee indicating such charges. In the case of installment-purchase plans, the monthly installment amount

and the date on which payments terminate will usually be adequate.

(8) Family income from wages, salaries, the client's own business, and investments, including income from any existing testamentary or living trusts. This information is obviously needed to determine the family's standard of living and the client's ability to allocate funds for needed life insurance. It is also important in estimating income which might be expected from sources other than life insurance in event of the client's death.

Because this is highly personal information, the life underwriter may be tempted to approach it indirectly or not at all. Experience has proved that this is unrealistic. All the information required for intelligent programing is quite personal. If the underwriter has established the proper relationship with his client, he should have no difficulty in securing on a confidential basis any pertinent data he needs.

(9) The family's present standard of living. The need for family income after the client's death can be translated readily into a tentative, but specific, amount based on the facts. For example, the underlying objective may be to continue the present standard of living, and the problem is to estimate how much income this will require with the breadwinner out of the picture. The facts might include a reasonably accurate statement as to how much income is now being used to maintain the house or apartment and to support family members other than the client.

In many cases, the client is unable to give such a clear-cut estimate without constructing an elaborate budget. However, the need for family income after death may be estimated more simply. If total income is known, the amount of income tax is also known or can be estimated and deducted. Amounts being set aside for existing life insurance and regular savings or investment programs are known. These can be deducted as items which the family need not continue after the breadwinner's death. Finally, if the client's personal expenses for clothing, transportation to and from work, lunches, club dues, and the like are deducted, what is left constitutes a reasonable estimate of how much income is being spent for the rest of the family. What the client spends to maintain himself may be easier to estimate quickly than what is spent for other members of the family.

(10) The client's specific objectives, which may be expressed in various ways. Often the client is asked to specify definite amounts for the various cash and income needs of his family, such as clean-up and emergency funds, income while his children are dependent, life income for his widow, and so forth. On the other hand, one authority in this field argues that the client cannot reasonably set such dollar objectives in a fact-finding interview, because "he hasn't died yet." True, the life underwriter hasn't either, but his experience with a wide variety of family situations may make him better qualified than the client to suggest specific amounts based on the facts in a given case.

(11) The client's general or intangible objectives. For example, does he view his present residence as a permanent home for his family, or does he feel it is likely to be sold in event of his death? Is he primarily concerned with providing his family as nearly their present standard of living as possible, or is he more concerned with building retirement income? How strongly does he feel about providing all or part of the cost of college education for his children? How does he feel about his future career? What does he think about his earning potential? What are his objectives as to future income?

Is it important to him to leave some ultimate provision for children and grandchildren, or is his main objective to support his widow during her lifetime and his children until they mature? Are there any special or unusual needs or objectives, such as might be presented by a crippled child, or by a child of a previous marriage? Is he interested in giving funds to religious, educational, or charitable organizations during his lifetime, directly at his death, or as final beneficiaries of any remainder funds? Is he concerned with the support of parents or other relatives, either currently or within the foreseeable future?

Such broad objectives give the underwriter a better understanding of the client's problems. Of course, they must be translated into specific amounts consistent with the client's financial situation. But approached from this point of view, the specific amounts usually will be more realistic. They will develop from a study of the facts rather than from the client's offhand opinion during a brief interview.

(12) The client's saving habits as well as his capacity. How much the client can save may be considered as a "fact" to be obtained from him or as a part of the underwriter's recommendations based on analysis of the client's situation.

Some underwriters seek a commitment instead of factual data of the kind discussed in Section 1.13, on the theory that it will make sale of the new life insurance more certain. On the other hand, a commitment may be meaningless until a study of the facts reveals a need for additional coverage. The facts often prove such commitments not only inadequate to purchase needed insurance but also less than the client should reasonably save toward meeting his objectives. Among the important facts to be ascertained are the client's inclination and capacity to save, for the dollar objectives to be established later must be consistent with both.

Obviously, details of any savings or investment program in which the client is currently engaged will be extremely helpful in evaluating what may be set aside for needed life insurance.

§*1.13. Defining objectives.* With the facts in hand,

including the client's basic desires and general objectives, the life underwriter can develop specific objectives and lay out a tentative schedule of cash and income needs. As indicated above, the client may have already set objectives in dollar amounts during the fact-finding interview. However, since these may represent offhand opinion rather than the result of considered study, it is well for the underwriter to review them carefully in the light of the other facts and the intangible objectives. For the purposes of this discussion, it is assumed that no dollar objectives have been set by the client. Thus, the life underwriter's first step toward a recommended program is to translate the client's desires as he understands them, in the light of all the facts, into specific terms.

For example, the clean-up or estate clearance fund must be adequate to cover debts, final expenses, and possibly taxes and administration costs. Present debts are known. Final expenses may be estimated from published reports of actual estates in various services available to the life underwriter. The part health insurance benefits might play in defraying such expenses may be considered. If the general estate is significant, estimates of administration expenses may be obtained from similar sources. If death taxes are anticipated, they may be calculated on the basis of the existing taxable estate, but the final estimate must wait until any recommendation for additional insurance to fill other needs is determined.

The amount and duration of any outstanding mortgage are known facts. If a separate mortgage fund is desired, the amount is therefore known. A similar fund may be set up as an objective for a client who does not own a home. For example, home ownership may be a major current objective toward which the family is saving. In event of the client's death before this is realized, it may be entirely logical to provide the family cash funds with which to carry out the objective. As a matter of fact, the amount of capital required to produce income for renting equivalent space may be greater than the purchase price of a suitable home. In determining the amount of such a fund, the life underwriter will be guided by what the client has in mind as to price range.

Next, considering the factors outlined in items (9), (10), and (11) of Section 1.12, a reasonable family income objective can be determined. This can be refined further in terms of the amounts needed during the initial readjustment period, the children's dependency, the gap during which Social Security will provide nothing, and the widow's life income.

This pattern will be subject to modification, usually downward, as the final recommendations are developed. In most cases, the income must drop substantially for the widow's lifetime after the children are grown, in order to keep the program within the client's ability to save. The relative priority of other needs will also affect final recommendations as to family income.

Similarly, tentative objectives can be set up for other needs, such as funds for college education, income for other relatives, or retirement income, depending on the client's interests and the facts in the case. Though a number of steps are suggested above, along with a number of facts to be considered in defining objectives, it must be remembered that the complexity of this process and the time involved depend entirely on the individual case. Many clients, even in relatively high income brackets, have extremely simple estates, with little or no property other than life insurance. Hence, defining the objectives will often prove a simple task requiring very little time.

§1.14. Considering what present insurance can provide. The next step in programing is to determine how far present life insurance, Social Security benefits, and other sources of principal and income will go toward meeting objectives. This is sometimes called "spending present insur-

ance" in conjunction with other sources of funds, to find
out what gaps or needs are not covered.

Knowledge of settlement options is basic to this step,
particularly options involving payments of principal and
interest. A simple income graph or chart may be constructed, similar to the examples shown on pages 232 and
243. Income from Social Security and other sources beyond
the control of the client is entered on the chart, together
with benefits from special insurance contracts such as family income policies. Remaining insurance is then "spent"
under appropriate options consistent with family needs.
The result will be a picture of what might be expected from
present resources in relation to needs and objectives.

Alternatively, the capitalization and discount approach
described in Section 8.9 may be used to estimate quickly,
but accurately, to what extent present resources fall short
of meeting objectives.

At some point in the programing process, existing policies must be examined in detail. Obviously, the amount
and type of each contract must be ascertained. The kind
of contract will have a bearing on retirement provisions as
well as on provisions for dependents. Occasionally, a settlement option agreement already in effect for an existing
policy will fit in with the final recommended distribution
pattern. More often, changes in the beneficiary designation
and settlement plan will be found necessary. Sometimes errors will be found, particularly in names of the insured or
beneficiaries. The policy may lack certain optional features
which can be added on request.

Many life underwriters record essential policy data on
a checklist form covering the various contract features. As
the program develops, reference can be made to the checklist much more easily than to the policies themselves. In
addition to amount and type of policy, typical items may
well include the policy number, age at issue, premium and
how paid, present beneficiary and settlement option desig-

nations, disability and accidental death features, who owns the policy and whether it has been assigned, dividend accumulations or paid-up additions, outstanding loans, and any aviation or other special-hazard restrictions.

Changes made as a result of programing work can also be entered on the checklist to form a simple, permanent record of what has been done. This kind of record can also help save time in subsequent periodic reviews of the program.

§1.15.   *Determining needs for additional insurance.* When the insurance needs have been determined and it is known how far present insurance will go toward filling these needs, consideration must be given to additional insurance required to complete the plan. This involves not only the amount but also the type of policy or policies that should be purchased. Thus, the relationship between family needs and retirement objectives must be considered, along with the client's ability to increase his premium outlay.

"How much life insurance should a man own?" is a question frequently asked by laymen. The underwriter who has handled a large number of programs may find that the situations of his clients fall into relatively few well-defined patterns. Often, the simpler cases which involve primarily life insurance and Social Security benefits are susceptible to "programing by formula." Here, all major elements of the program may be expressed as a percentage of the client's annual income. But in the last analysis, the questions of how much and what type of life insurance a particular man should own must be answered: "It all depends." It depends on all the *facts* in that particular case.

One approach is to select the additional policy or policies so as to provide what is needed in event of death, at a premium outlay within the client's ability to save, letting the chips fall where they may as to retirement benefits. Taken literally, this may often result in excessive use of term insurance. A study of most situations will reveal needs for more additional life insurance than can be afforded on any plan. There is, therefore, a strong temptation to use temporary, low-premium plans and to gamble heavily on the client's future ability to convert term policies. But the need for death benefits, the relative importance of retirement objectives, and the ability to save must be considered together. They are not isolated problems. In fact, all facets of programing are interrelated.

Many factors in this consideration are not entirely mathematical in nature. The age of the client and the progress he has made in his life work may give some clue as to what might be expected of him in the future. It may appear that he has reached the limit of his potential and that his earnings probably will not increase substantially. If so, perhaps more weight should be given to building cash and retirement values in the new insurance, even at the expense of filling desirable but not urgent protection needs. A similar approach may be indicated if the time between the client's current age and anticipated retirement is relatively short.

On the other hand, the client may be a young business or professional man of outstanding ability or with an assured future—if he lives. Liberal use of term insurance or policies combining permanent coverage with term riders may be completely justified in such a case. However, it is especially important here that the life underwriter review the program frequently. The passage of time enhances the ever-present hazard of "too little and too late" attention to retirement objectives.

The ages of other family members and the condition of their health are also important factors. Needs for insurance may be extremely important where the wife is not in good health or there is an invalid child to be supported for life. Quite different problems are presented if the wife is young and healthy, or if there are no children and none likely in the future. In the last situation, however, the fact that the wife will grow older and less able to find employment, as well as the possibility that children may be born or adopted, dictate commonsense caution against an all-out retirement program with minimum insurance.

An important consideration in determining the kind of additional insurance to recommend may be the types of policies already owned. If, for example, these are predominantly on high-premium or endowment forms—and the need for protection is great—the required additional insurance may have to be recommended on a plan which places major emphasis on protection. Conversely, a program already top-heavy with term or term combinations can be brought in balance by adding higher-premium plans consistent with the client's needs and ability to save.

Often, the need for insurance on other members of the family is overlooked in the effort to cover the breadwinner's life adequately. Until this objective is reached, the need for insurance on the wife or children may be deliberately ignored. However, all objectives must be viewed as relative and considered in the light of facts in the individual case. Moreover, the recent public opinion survey referred to in Section 1.8 shows clearly that people are interested in considering needs for insurance on all family members.

It is true that a husband, because of earning capacity, could meet the expenses incident to his dependent wife's death without nearly so much difficulty as she would encounter in replacing him as a provider. On the other hand, the inflation of values in recent decades, the gradual reduction in federal estate tax exemptions, and the concept of splitting estates and income for tax purposes have pointed up the economic need for insuring the wife to prevent undue loss to future generations.

Whether or not taxes are a major consideration, failure to insure the wife at least to the extent of an adequate clean-up fund may have serious consequences for young children. For example, her premature death may require savings or other funds intended for the children's higher education to be used instead for meeting clean-up expenses of her estate. Moreover, the cost of providing a housekeeper or other person to care for the children may prevent the father from accumulating or rebuilding educational funds. Certainly, insurance on the wife should be considered as a primary need when the first child is born, if not before.

Similarly, the immediate economic effects of a child's death can usually be overcome by the father's earning ability. But if there are two or more children, the expenses resulting from long illness and the untimely death of one child may actually deprive the others of educational advantages which might otherwise have been possible. Insurance is generally desirable for children for a variety of reasons. Aside from the need to accumulate funds for higher education, often better handled by insurance on the father, the principal reason is to provide the young child with a low-cost or paid-up cornerstone for his future estate. However, the immediate need for such insurance, at least for clean-up purposes, becomes an important consideration in planning for a family with more than one child.

In thinking about how much the client might reasonably save for new insurance, it will be helpful to review the process suggested in Section 1.13 for defining income objectives for dependents. Usually a spread will be found between net income (after taxes and present insurance premiums) and living expenses for the whole family. This might be called "discretionary income" which can be spent as the family chooses. Some of this spread may be going into an employee benefit plan or pension fund, changes in which may not be possible or desirable. Part may be represented by luxury purchases which, when the facts are presented clearly, the client may be happy to reduce in order to adopt the recommended program. Other savings or investment programs may be consuming a portion of discretionary income. Frequently, an objective analysis will indicate that all or part of such savings should be diverted to new insurance, at least for the immediate future.

Often, however, the facts reveal no spread at all between necessary living expenses and net income. There are cases in which no additional life insurance should be recommended, no matter how great the need may appear. But the fact remains that such cases are rare, except perhaps in very low income brackets.

Considerable progress has been made in programing and needs selling since the turn of the century. Despite this progress, underwriters and agencies using the program approach report consistently that few of their new clients have existing programs. In about 80 percent of their cases, the facts reveal substantial needs for additional life insurance and the ability to pay for it. The essence of a sound programing job certainly lies in this step of determining needs for additional life insurance and the amount and type of insurance to be purchased.

§*1.16. Presenting the recommended program.*   In some cases, presentation of the recommended program may be viewed as the last step, following establishment of the final distribution pattern described in Section 1.17. On the other hand, the final distribution pattern will depend not only on the client's basic objectives and family situation, but also on how much insurance and property he actually owns. Hence, many underwriters prefer to settle first the question of how much of the recommended additional insurance the client will actually buy.

It has been said that when all the facts are known, there can be no disagreement. While this may not be literally true, it is a fact that most laymen have never looked at their financial situations objectively and are not likely to on their own initiatives. They do act when a sound life insurance program is presented, based on intelligent and objective analysis of all pertinent facts.

A good program presentation moves along in a smooth progression of logical steps. Whether it is to be a one-interview sale or a sale requiring several interviews, the presentation should include:

(1) Getting the client's agreement to all facts that affect his program.
(2) Establishing in the client's mind his basic objectives.
(3) Pinpointing and emphasizing the problems that must be solved before the client's objectives can be accomplished.
(4) Presenting the best practical solution to these problems that the life underwriter can devise.
(5) Closing the sale.

The first four steps are based on sound reasoning. The fifth step, the close, sometimes follows easily and naturally; usually, however, a client's decision to act is dictated more by emotion than by logic. Logic tells him he should buy, but most of the time it takes dramatic motivation to convince him that he should buy now. And this, of course, applies to the program sale as much as to any other.

Programing is an important service to the buyer, but it is also a sales procedure to the life underwriter. Nearly always, if a sale is not completed, the service has not been rendered. No program, however thoughtfully and skillfully designed, will solve the problems of a client or his family unless it is funded with enough of the right kind of life insurance.

For that reason, the professional life underwriter prepares his close as carefully as he plans every other step in his program presentation.

§1.17. Establishing the final distribution pattern. Income guaranteed by the settlement options is used in the mathematical process of determining how far present insurance will go and how much new insurance may be needed. This process may result in a general or tentative pattern for distribution of the total proceeds.

However, development of a final plan for disbursing proceeds must take into account a number of additional factors. For example, primary, secondary, and final beneficiaries must be selected, and a settlement plan determined for each class. The need for flexibility after the insured's death must be appraised, as well as the extent to which it can be provided. Life insurance payments must be coordinated with other sources of cash and income. There may be tax considerations or the question of using a life insurance trust. Individual company practice governing the use of settlement options may influence the selection of policies to meet certain needs.

Settlement options are widely used in the purely diagnostic process of measuring needs. Yet, the most neglected phase of programing is the use of options in developing a coordinated plan for actual disbursement of life insurance proceeds. It would seem logical that the underwriter should make sure that settlement plans are kept up to date as to policies in his own company and in others. He would work closely with the client's attorney, trust officer, accountant, and other advisers to assure that settlement plans for life insurance and instruments governing distribution of other assets are coordinated at all times. Records would indicate where to obtain documentary evidence of births, marriages, divorces, deaths, and adoptions, or such evidence would be kept on file.

Information in the life underwriter's record of a given case should enable him to handle disability or "living death" claims as well. It should enable him to revise the program of a disabled client to reflect his new situation.

Similarly, in event of the client's death, the life underwriter should be able to set up a new program for dependents. Such a program would not only reflect provisions made for the family by the original client but also objectives of the "new" family.

All these functions of the life underwriter are related to setting up a distribution pattern for life insurance proceeds at death of the family head. They are also related to the rewards and responsibilities discussed in Section 1.7. Most of the thoughts in this book are devoted to the use of settlement options in establishing plans for the efficient distribution of life insurance proceeds.

Chapter 2

Settlement Options in Life Insurance and Annuity Contracts

§2.1. Introduction. Settlement options are usually designated in the contract by number or letter, depending on individual company practice. The order in which they appear in the policy also varies with the company. Moreover, each company has adopted rules governing the use of its options, which can be discussed in this book only in a very general way.

Most individual life insurance policies today provide for settlement under one of the first five alternatives described below in Sections 2.2 through 2.6—cash or one sum, Interest Option, Fixed Period Option, Fixed Amount Option, Life Income Options. Additional options are often provided or may be secured on request. Some or all the options may be available for other forms of policies, such as group insurance and certain annuity contracts.

A. LIFE INSURANCE POLICIES

§2.2. Cash or one sum. Strictly speaking, cash is not an "option" in most cases, because life insurance policies usually specify one sum settlement in the absence of some other direction by the policyowner. However, for this very reason it may be regarded as an option "selected" by

30

default—operative only because some more appropriate arrangement was not considered by the insured or his advisers.

Certain policies are written as "income contracts" with death or retirement benefits payable in installments unless otherwise directed. In these cases, which include U.S. Government and National Service Life Insurance, if a cash payment is desired, it must be elected in advance of claim. In the more usual case, proceeds are payable in cash, but the beneficiary may elect one of the interest or installment options.

In most companies, there are a number of disadvantages to the one sum settlement, *even for proceeds intended to be made available in cash,* notwithstanding the beneficiary's right to elect an income option in lieu of cash. The chief drawback is lack of protection against the so-called "common disaster" or the much more common "short-term-survivorship" situation.

Generally, a standard "common disaster" or "delayed payment" clause may be available, but such provisions cannot give full protection against the contingency. They may also have undesirable estate tax consequences. This problem is discussed more fully in Section 7.7.

Another disadvantage of a cash settlement is that it generally affords no protection against creditors of the beneficiary. Such protection can usually be arranged in connection with the income options, if elected before the insured's death.

A third disadvantage, found in the procedures of only a few companies, is that a beneficiary who elects an income option instead of taking a cash settlement may not be permitted to designate contingent beneficiaries or even to redesignate contingents originally named by the policyowner. In such cases, any proceeds remaining in the company's hands at the primary beneficiary's death must go to the estate of that beneficiary.

The limited nature of most policy provisions covering options may present a fourth disadvantage. Usually these provisions merely grant the insured or beneficiary the right to have proceeds settled under "one of the optional modes of settlement" instead of being paid in cash. Rarely does the policy grant any specific rights to a contingent beneficiary. Relatively few contracts specify that proceeds may be split into separate funds and each fund applied under a different option, or that proceeds may be settled initially under one option, with another to take effect at some future time. Although it is the practice of most companies to permit many arrangements not specifically granted by contract, such company practices are generally more liberal respecting income settlement plans adopted by the policyowner before death than for those requested by a beneficiary entitled to a one sum payment. Moreover, a settlement agreement prepared before death has the added advantage of protecting the beneficiary against any future changes in company practice.

Finally, a one sum settlement may result in the beneficiary losing interest on the proceeds between the date of the insured's death and the date on which a settlement option is elected or a cash settlement accepted. In practice, a number of companies allow interest only from the date of receipt of proof, or the date of election of the settlement option. Others allow interest from the date of the insured's death only if the beneficiary elects a settlement option within a specified time. However, when the settlement option has been elected for the beneficiary by the policyowner, the great majority of companies appear to allow interest from the date of the insured's death, even if the beneficiary delays in filing proofs of death. Loss of interest may seem a minor disadvantage, but it can be important to the beneficiary if the proceeds are large in amount.

Nothwithstanding these important disadvantages of the cash or one sum settlement, it is the simplest way to pay proceeds intended to be used in cash. This is also true when it is desirable to give the beneficiary a free choice between electing settlement options and otherwise investing or using the funds. Under most policies, however, the only way to satisfy these objectives without the disadvantages of a one sum settlement is to use a settlement option agreement which delegates to the beneficiary as much flexibility as company practice allows. A substantial proportion of the settlement agreements now in force are of such nature.

Almost a decade ago, one major company conducted an exhaustive study of the settlement plans attached to all its policies. Among other things, it was found that if the one sum settlement provisions of the insurance policy could be worded so as to eliminate the usual disadvantages, the number of requests for settlement option agreements before death of the insured could be reduced substantially, with obvious savings in time and money to the policyowner, the agent, and the company. As a result, this company introduced a new series of policies, the one sum provisions of which are designed to accomplish just this objective.

In essence, the policies issued by that company provide that, in the absence of an election by the policyowner, any proceeds payable in one sum: (1) will earn interest from the date of death until withdrawn in cash or applied under a settlement option, for a period not to exceed one year; (2) may be placed under any settlement option or options by a primary beneficiary or, with certain limitations, by a contingent beneficiary; (3) are protected from creditors of the beneficiary, to the extent permitted by law; (4) are covered automatically for common disaster or short-term-survivorship situations; (5) may be assigned by a third-party owner within a specified period of time after the insured's death. In addition, the primary beneficiary may designate contingent beneficiaries, unless the policyowner has specified that those designated by him cannot be changed.

This arrangement is based on the theory that primary

and contingent beneficiaries should be able to exercise substantially the same rights as the policyowner may exercise in advance for them. This system eliminates the need for electing an option in advance, when the primary purpose of such an election is to overcome the disadvantages of the usual one sum settlement provision, while still making proceeds fully available in cash. More recently, a few other companies have provided "automatic" settlement option arrangements similar to that just described.

Under most contracts, a one sum settlement is not generally recommended for personal life insurance, except where a relatively small policy is involved or where payment is to be made to an estate, trust, or business entity

§2.3. *Interest Option.* The proceeds remain with the company, and only the interest is paid to the beneficiary. In most cases, the interest cannot be accumulated or compounded, but must be paid out monthly, quarterly, semiannually, or annually, commencing at the end of the first such period.

The majority of companies pay excess interest (sometimes called "dividends" or "surplus interest") declared above the guaranteed minimum rate at the end of each year; the minority use it to increase the periodic payments.

There are legal limits to the length of time the principal may be kept intact, as is explained in Sections 5.6 and 5.7. Often, further limits are imposed by company practice, such as the lifetime of the first beneficiary, or 30 years, whichever is the longer. Guaranteed interest rates vary slightly between companies. Older policies may guarantee a higher rate than newer issues in the same company.

For each $1,000 of proceeds held by a company, the Interest Option yields interest payments at the rates indicated in Table I on page 35.

A guaranteed interest rate commonly encountered under the Interest Option in policies currently issued is 2½ percent per annum, with excess interest of from 1 percent to 1½ percent generally being declared, bringing the total distributive rate in the majority of companies to a figure of 3½ percent to 4 percent per annum.

If the settlement option agreement provides for interest payments more frequently than annually, as it generally does, the actual interest payments are made according to a table or according to factors expressed in the policy. A company whose guaranteed interest rate is 2½ percent per annum can pay $25 on $1,000 of proceeds only at the end of the year. Not only does the principal amount left with the company earn interest, but the interest accruing from day to day earns interest as well. If payment is made more frequently, a discount factor must be applied to reflect the earlier payments and the corresponding loss of interest earnings on the accruing interest. Thus, the monthly equivalent of interest at the rate of 2½ percent per annum is not 1/12 of $25.00 or $2.08, but is $2.06.

TABLE I

INTEREST PAYMENTS

Rate	Annual Payment	Monthly Payment
2.0%	$20	$1.65
2.5%	25	2.06
3.0%	30	2.47
3.5%	35	2.87

The Interest Option is the most flexible of all the options and, therefore, one of the most widely used. Basically, it assures the beneficiary freedom from investment worries while guaranteeing both principal and interest. Moreover, depending on individual company rules and, in some cases, applicable state laws, the beneficiary under this option may also enjoy:

(1) The right to withdraw all or any part of the principal at any time, or to make partial withdrawals up to a specified aggregate portion of the fund, or to withdraw up

to a stated amount in any one year, or to withdraw fractional portions at specified ages of the beneficiary, as the policyowner may desire. Usually, any reasonable combination of limiting factors may be set up in connection with rights of withdrawal, or the fund may be held without any withdrawal privileges if directed by the policyowner. In this connection, some companies guarantee a lower rate of interest on withdrawable funds than on nonwithdrawable sums.

(2) The right to name the payee of any balance at the primary beneficiary's death, or the right to change the contingent beneficiaries previously designated by the policyowner. This "power of appointment" appears to be most frequently requested when it is desirable to qualify proceeds for the federal estate tax marital deduction, as explained in Section 6.7.2. In such cases, the power is often limited to a right to the wife as primary beneficiary to name her estate as contingent beneficiary, and thereby to nullify any contrary provisions of the settlement agreement.

Company practices in allowing such powers of appointment appear to apply in like manner to other settlement options.

(3) The right to elect another settlement option or combination of options at a later time, when the beneficiary's income needs may have changed. The majority of companies will permit change to the Fixed Period or Fixed Amount Options at any time at rates of income guaranteed in the policy, and almost half the companies will allow the beneficiary the same right as respects change to a Life Income Option. The other companies impose some limit on the privilege of changing to a Life Income Option, such as requiring that the change must be made within a specified period, such as one year after the insured's death or after the right accrues to the beneficiary, if income rates stated in the policy are to be assured. Obviously, policies owned by

a client must be read carefully, and the practices of individual companies ascertained.

(4) An automatic or mandatory change to another option at some specified later date or age, or on the happening of an event, such as entry of a child into college. Most companies will permit such automatic change from either the Interest Option or the Fixed Amount Option (described in Section 2.5), without limitation, except possibly to require that the amount of proceeds at the time of change be $1,000 or more.

(5) Protection from most creditors under a spendthrift clause in the policy, which is also available for the other options explained below.

§*2.4.* *Fixed Period Option.*   This is one of the two options based on the fundamental concept of liquidating principal and interest in an orderly fashion over a period of years, without reference to a life contingency. The other is the Fixed Amount Option, which is discussed in the next section.

The Fixed Period Option is used when it is desired to pay proceeds in equal installments over a definite period of time. Depending on the company, the period may run as long as 20, 25, or 30 years. The amount of proceeds, the period of time, the frequency of payment (annually, semi-annually, quarterly, monthly), and the guaranteed rate of interest determine the amount of each installment.

The guaranteed payment is calculated in advance. Excess interest, if any, is usually credited at the end of each year. In some companies it is paid in one sum; in others it is applied to increase basic income.

Proceeds of a typical policy guaranteeing 2½ percent interest under this option would provide the income shown in Table II on page 38.

Unlike the Interest Option, payments under the Fixed Period Option commence immediately rather than at the end of the first payment period. For this reason, as shown in Table II, payments made more frequently than once a year will aggregate more in the year than the corresponding annual installment. This effect is the opposite of that found under the Interest Option.

The Fixed Period Option is valuable when the most

TABLE II

GUARANTEED INSTALLMENTS PER $1,000 OF PROCEEDS

(2½% Interest)

No. of Years Payable	Annually	Semiannually	Quarterly	Monthly
1	$1,000.00	$503.09	$252.32	$84.28
2	506.17	254.65	127.72	42.66
3	341.60	171.86	86.19	28.79
4	259.33	130.47	65.43	21.86
5	210.00	105.65	52.99	17.70
6	177.12	89.11	44.69	14.93
7	153.65	77.30	38.77	12.95
8	136.07	68.46	34.33	11.47
9	122.40	61.58	30.88	10.32
10	111.47	56.08	28.13	9.39
11	102.54	51.59	25.87	8.64
12	95.11	47.85	24.00	8.02
13	88.83	44.69	22.41	7.49
14	83.45	41.98	21.06	7.03
15	78.80	39.64	19.88	6.64
16	74.73	37.60	18.86	6.30
17	71.15	35.79	17.95	6.00
18	67.97	34.20	17.15	5.73
19	65.13	32.77	16.43	5.49
20	62.58	31.48	15.79	5.27
21	60.28	30.33	15.21	5.08
22	58.19	29.27	14.68	4.90
23	56.29	28.32	14.20	4.74
24	54.55	27.44	13.76	4.60
25	52.95	26.64	13.36	4.46
26	51.48	25.90	12.99	4.34
27	50.12	25.21	12.65	4.22
28	48.87	24.59	12.33	4.12
29	47.70	24.00	12.04	4.02
30	46.61	23.45	11.76	3.93

important consideration is to provide income for a definite time—for example, during the readjustment period immediately after the insured's death, or while the children are in school, or during the college years. In most companies, the policyowner may give the beneficiary the right to commute, or discount, all remaining unpaid installments and receive a one sum payment, but this is about as much flexibility as the Fixed Period Option affords.

Companies almost universally prohibit partial withdrawals under the Fixed Period Option. Probably the principal reason for the prohibition is a practical one, since a special calculation would be required after each partial withdrawal to reset the remaining installments to a reduced amount.

Apparently, companies are seldom requested to permit election to change from the Fixed Period Option to another settlement option or to provide for automatic change to such option at a later time. Possibly the reason for absence of such requests is based upon the fact that a Fixed Period Option arrangement is usually regarded as a permanent one to satisfy a particular need, whereas the Interest Option is often a temporary or interim arrangement.

Because the period of time selected is the primary factor in determining the amount of income available, a policy loan which is outstanding at the insured's death will reduce the amount of each installment but will not affect the number of installments. Conversely, any dividend accumulations or paid-up additions payable with the proceeds will operate to increase the beneficiary's income but will not lengthen the income period.

In many rate books and in compends and loose-leaf services, fixed period tables are provided in two forms—one showing income per $1,000 of proceeds and the other showing the amount of insurance needed to produce $10 per month for various periods of time. Generally, these tables are much easier to use and make for fewer mistakes.

Table III below is an example of the amount-needed form, which will be found especially helpful in planning.

TABLE III
AMOUNT OF PRINCIPAL NEEDED TO PROVIDE GUARANTEED INCOME FOR VARYING DURATIONS
(2½% Interest)

Months of Income	Monthly Income $10	$25	$50	$100
12	$ 119	$ 297	$ 593	$ 1,187
24	235	586	1,172	2,344
36	348	868	1,737	3,473
48	458	1,144	2,288	4,575
60	565	1,413	2,825	5,650
72	670	1,675	3,350	6,698
84	773	1,931	3,861	7,722
96	872	2,180	4,360	8,718
108	969	2,423	4,847	9,690
120	1,065	2,661	5,322	10,650
132	1,157	2,893	5,785	11,574
144	1,247	3,119	6,237	12,469
156	1,336	3,339	6,679	13,351
168	1,422	3,554	7,109	14,225
180	1,506	3,764	7,529	15,060
192	1,588	3,969	7,938	15,873
204	1,668	4,169	8,338	16,667
216	1,746	4,364	8,728	17,452
228	1,822	4,554	9,108	18,215
240	1,896	4,740	9,479	18,975
252	1,968	4,921	9,841	19,683
264	2,039	5,097	10,195	20,390
276	2,108	5,270	10,539	21,079
288	2,175	5,438	10,876	21,752
300	2,241	5,603	11,204	22,422
312	2,305	5,762	11,524	23,048
324	2,367	5,918	11,836	23,672
336	2,428	6,070	12,140	24,281
348	2,487	6,219	12,437	24,875
360	2,545	6,364	12,727	25,445

§2.5. Fixed Amount Option. Here, the *amount* of income is the controlling factor, rather than the period of time over which the proceeds and interest are to be liquidated. For example, it may be specified that payments be made at the rate of $100 per month, $75 per month, $25 per month, or at any other rate, until the principal and interest thereon are exhausted. As with the other options, annual, semiannual, or quarterly payments may be stipulated if desired.

The Fixed Amount Option is basically similar to the Fixed Period Option; in fact, they represent virtually the same idea expressed in different ways. For this reason, the income tables for the fixed period plan may be used in calculating amounts and periods of time for the Fixed Amount Option.

Usually, the guaranteed interest factor is the same, in a given policy, for both the Fixed Amount and the Fixed Period Options. This is why tables for the Fixed Period may be used in calculating the amount and number of payments under either of these two options. However, under the Fixed Amount Option, any excess interest is usually credited to the unpaid balance as earned and operates to lengthen the income period.

As a rule, income tables for this option do not appear in policies, but may be found in the company rate book and in the compends and services. A typical example of such a table is Table IV, page 42.

Obviously, this table does not have the same potential for income measurement and presentation on a graph as do the fixed period tables. However, it can be useful in demonstrating to a client how long present insurance will provide a given income, as well as in estimating roughly how much insurance will be needed to do a particular job. For example, to estimate the amount of insurance necessary to produce $100 per month for eight years, on a 2½ percent interest basis, a rough interpolation can be made along the horizontal line for $100 of monthly income. The period just under eight years is six years, nine months, in the column headed $7,500, and that just above eight years is nine years, three months, in the vertical $10,000 column.

TABLE IV

Length of Period for Which Monthly Income Provided By Varying Principal Sums

(2½% Interest)

Desired Monthly Income	$1,000 Yr.-Mo.	$2,000 Yr.-Mo.	$3,000 Yr.-Mo.	$4,000 Yr.-Mo.	$5,000 Yr.-Mo.	$7,500 Yr.-Mo.	$10,000 Yr.-Mo.	$12,000 Yr.-Mo.	$15,000 Yr.-Mo.	$20,000 Yr.-Mo.
$10	9- 3	21- 5								
15	5-11	12-11	21- 5							
20	4- 4	9- 3	14-11	21- 5						
25	3- 5	7- 3	11- 5	16- 1	21- 5					
30	2-10	5-11	9- 3	12-11	16-11					
40	2- 1	4- 4	6- 9	9- 3	12- 0	19- 8				
50	1- 8	3- 5	5- 3	7- 3	9- 3	14-11	21- 5			
60	1- 4	2-10	4- 4	5-11	7- 7	12- 0	16-11	22- 7		
70	1- 2	2- 5	3- 8	5- 0	6- 5	10- 0	14- 0	18- 5		
75	1- 1	2- 3	3- 5	4- 8	5-11	9- 3	12-11	16-11	21- 5	
80		2- 1	3- 2	4- 4	5- 6	8- 8	12- 0	15- 8	19- 8	
90			2-10	3-10	4-10	7- 7	10- 6	13- 6	16-11	
100			2- 6	3- 5	4- 4	6- 9	9- 3	12- 0	14-11	21- 5
125			2- 0	2- 9	3- 5	5- 3	7- 3	9- 3	11- 5	16- 1
150				2- 3	2-10	4- 4	5-11	7- 7	9- 3	12-11
175				1-11	2- 5	3- 9	5- 0	6- 4	7-10	10-11
200					2- 1	3- 2	4- 4	5- 6	6- 9	9- 3

Since eight years is just halfway between these two time periods, $8,750 of principal is indicated, which is halfway between $7,500 and $10,000. (The actual amount needed is only $8,720, but the difference is of little consequence for practical purposes.)

In most situations, the Fixed Amount Option has many practical advantages over the Fixed Period Option, because it is a great deal more flexible. Not only can the policyowner specify varying amounts of income to be paid at different times, but in most cases he may also give the beneficiary unlimited or partial withdrawal rights similar to those available under the Interest Option. Usually, the Fixed Amount Option can be set up to provide regular installments to a certain date or until a certain age has been attained by the beneficiary, at which time any unpaid balance can be applied under another option. Often such balance may be applied under the Life Income Option, subject to the possible limitations on such changes discussed in Section 2.3, covering the Interest Option. Obviously, the longer the insured's death is deferred, the larger will be the amount available for the second option at the specified date or age.

Because the amount of each installment is the controlling factor under this option, the effects of excess interest, dividends, or loans are quite different from those outlined for the Fixed Period Option. Here, dividend accumulations or additions payable with the proceeds, together with any surplus interest declared while installments are being paid, lengthen the period of time but do not affect the amount of each installment. On the other hand, loans outstanding at the insured's death, or withdrawals of principal by the beneficiary along the way, shorten the income period. Where a definite cutoff date has been specified, on which the fixed income is to cease and the unpaid balance is to be distributed in some other way, these plus or minus factors will, of course, increase or decrease the sum available on the cutoff date.

Because of the nature of this option, there is usually a special rule governing minimum installments in addition to the general rules covering payments. This rule specifies a minimum monthly, quarterly, semiannual, or annual installment per $1,000 of initial proceeds placed under the Fixed Amount Option. Often, at least $50 or $60 per year is required to be paid out for each $1,000 of proceeds. Sometimes, the minimum is as high as $10 per month. This is in keeping with the purpose of the option to exhaust both principal and interest within some definite period of time.

§*2.6. Life Income Options.* These options, sometimes called annuity or continuous installment options, are peculiar to life insurance companies. No other financial institution makes such an arrangement with its clients. These options provide for orderly liquidation of the capital sum, with interest, over the lifetime of the payee.

Life Income Options are often described as "life insurance in reverse." By means of life insurance, an estate is created on the happening of an event, namely death, the time of which cannot be foretold accurately for any individual. On the other hand, the life income liquidates an estate by regular payments spread over a person's entire lifetime, the span of which, again, cannot be foretold for any individual.

The life income or annuity plan is the only way an individual can be positive that he will not live longer than his funds will last. Thus, while life insurance spreads the risk of "dying too soon," the annuity spreads the risk of "living too long." Though the latter concept is more often associated with retirement, the hazard of outliving one's funds applies equally to the beneficiary of life insurance proceeds paid at death.

The amount of each installment depends on the type of annuity selected, the amount of proceeds, the rate of interest assumed, the age of the payee when the income commences, and the sex of the payee. In some older contracts, sex of the payee is not a factor; the same income is paid to males and females of the same age. Because female annuitants, on the average, actually live longer than males of the same age, such older contracts are especially valuable in providing life income for female beneficiaries, as compared with more recent issues.

Life Income Options providing income for an individual lifetime are commonly arranged under the three plans described below—the Life Income Option, the Refund Life Income Option, and the Life Income Option with "Period Certain." However, not all are found in every policy, though in many companies those not shown in the contract may be added on request.

1. *The Life Income Option.* Installments are payable only as long as the payee lives, with no return of principal guaranteed. Because no principal return is guaranteed, the straight life annuity income option provides the largest life income per $1,000 of proceeds for a given payee.

If the payee dies before receiving in installments a total amount equal to the principal sum, in effect, the balance of his principal is used to continue payments to other annuitants in the group who live beyond the point where total income they have received equals their original principal. This is what is meant by "sharing the risk" of living too long, of outliving one's funds.

Most people hesitate to take this risk, despite the high rate of annuity income, because they have relatives or other objects of their bounty to whom they wish to leave any funds they do not need for themselves. Obviously, this form of life income would normally be impractical for a widow with young children, as it affords the children no protection in case of the early death of their mother. There is also a possibly unfavorable public relations aspect if a beneficiary dies after receiving one or two annuity payments and there is nothing left for any contingent payee,

2. *Refund Life Income Option.* Installments are payable as long as the primary payee lives, but if this payee dies before receiving an amount equal to the principal sum, the balance is paid to a second payee. If the option provides for the balance to be paid in cash, it is called a "cash refund life income." There is another plan, known as the "installment refund life income." Under this plan, if the primary payee dies before receiving an amount equal to the principal, the installments are continued to a second payee until the sum of *all* the installments paid equals the original amount of principal. However, the second payee may be given the right to commute the unpaid installments.

Since the amount of income from a given principal sum varies with the age of the primary payee when the payments begin, the period of time required for the payee to receive an amount equal to the principal sum also varies. Thus, the older the payee, the larger the payments, and hence the shorter the period before the refund guarantee is exhausted. In programing some situations, this may make planning for contingent beneficiaries more difficult; in others, the automatically decreasing certain period of the refund annuity might prove quite helpful.

3. *Life Income Option with Period Certain.* Installments are payable as long as the primary payee lives, but should this payee die before a predetermined number of "years (or months) certain," the company will continue the installments to a second payee until the end of the certain period, or pay their commuted value in some other specified way. Usually the certain period runs for 5, 10, 15, or 20 years, or the equivalent number of months. Most policies contain only two or three alternative periods, the most usual being 10 and 20 years, but often the others may be obtained by special request.

Sometimes, policyowners are confused by the term "years certain" and do not realize that installments are guaranteed to the *original* payee for life, whether that means 100 years or more, or only one month, a point it is wise to emphasize in explaining this option to clients. This option is frequently used for death benefits, because it assures the desired income for life while still providing reasonable protection for contingent beneficiaries.

4. *Mathematics of Life Income Options.* The mathematical concepts underlying the Life Income Options are essentially simple. The basic principles are the same as those which govern life insurance and annuity rate-making.

For example, the "life annuity due" used in net level premium calculations is the exact counterpart of the straight life annuity option, since in both cases a life contingency is involved and the first payment is immediate. However, different mortality tables are employed because annuitants, on the average, live longer than insured lives of the same age.

The life income or annuity options involving a refund or period certain feature are based on familiar concepts. Actually, they represent a combination of two options—the Fixed Period Option for the period certain, followed by a straight life annuity, without refund, the commencement of which is deferred to the end of the period certain. Naturally, mortality and discount factors are taken into account in calculating the deferred life annuity.

For example, the period certain for a Life Income Option, 20 years certain, could be calculated as a fixed period income for 20 years. Then, to calculate the ensuing life annuity income, the first payment is assumed to be made 20 years hence, at the payee's then attained age, if the payee is then living, instead of immediately and based on the present age.

Table V, page 48, is a typical rate table for the Life Income Options. As noted above, however, most contracts do not show so many alternatives.

TABLE V

MONTHLY LIFE INCOME PER $1,000 OF PROCEEDS—AT VARIOUS AGES

($2\frac{1}{2}\%$ Interest)

Age Male	Female	Life Income Only	5 Years Certain and Life	10 Years Certain and Life	15 Years Certain and Life	20 Years Certain and Life	Install- ment Refund
25	30	$3.08	$3.08	$3.08	$3.07	$3.05	$3.01
30	35	3.27	3.27	3.26	3.24	3.22	3.17
31	36	3.31	3.31	3.30	3.28	3.25	3.20
32	37	3.36	3.36	3.34	3.32	3.29	3.24
33	38	3.41	3.40	3.39	3.36	3.33	3.28
34	39	3.45	3.45	3.43	3.41	3.37	3.32
35	40	3.50	3.50	3.48	3.45	3.41	3.36
36	41	3.56	3.55	3.53	3.50	3.45	3.40
37	42	3.61	3.61	3.59	3.55	3.50	3.44
38	43	3.67	3.66	3.64	3.60	3.54	3.49
39	44	3.73	3.72	3.70	3.65	3.59	3.53
40	45	3.79	3.78	3.76	3.71	3.64	3.58
41	46	3.86	3.85	3.82	3.77	3.69	3.63
42	47	3.93	3.92	3.88	3.82	3.74	3.68
43	48	4.00	3.99	3.95	3.88	3.79	3.74
44	49	4.08	4.06	4.02	3.95	3.84	3.80
45	50	4.15	4.14	4.09	4.01	3.90	3.85
46	51	4.24	4.22	4.17	4.08	3.95	3.91
47	52	4.33	4.31	4.25	4.15	4.01	3.98
48	53	4.42	4.40	4.33	4.22	4.07	4.04
49	54	4.51	4.49	4.42	4.29	4.12	4.11
50	55	4.61	4.59	4.50	4.37	4.18	4.18
51	56	4.72	4.69	4.60	4.44	4.24	4.26
52	57	4.83	4.80	4.69	4.52	4.30	4.33
53	58	4.95	4.91	4.79	4.60	4.36	4.42
54	59	5.07	5.03	4.90	4.69	4.41	4.50
55	60	5.20	5.15	5.01	4.77	4.47	4.59
56	61	5.34	5.28	5.12	4.86	4.53	4.68
57	62	5.48	5.42	5.23	4.94	4.59	4.77
58	63	5.64	5.56	5.35	5.03	4.64	4.87
59	64	5.80	5.72	5.48	5.12	4.70	4.98
60	65	5.97	5.87	5.61	5.21	4.75	5.08
61	66	6.15	6.04	5.74	5.30	4.80	5.20
62	67	6.34	6.22	5.87	5.39	4.85	5.31
63	68	6.54	6.40	6.01	5.48	4.90	5.44
64	69	6.75	6.59	6.16	5.56	4.91	5.57
65	70	6.97	6.79	6.30	5.65	4.98	5.70
70	75	8.32	7.95	7.07	6.05	5.14	6.48

The rates shown are based on guaranteed interest of $2\frac{1}{2}$ percent per annum. In some companies, different interest rates are used in calculating the period certain income and the deferred life annuity, such as $2\frac{1}{4}$ percent for calculating the first and $2\frac{1}{2}$ percent for the second. In such cases, income during the certain period will usually be on the same basis as the Fixed Period Option in the same policy.

Where a refund or period certain guarantee is involved, excess interest may be payable in addition to the income at the guaranteed rate. Usually, this applies only during the period certain and is handled like excess interest on the Fixed Period Option.

Very little flexibility is afforded by the Life Income Options. About one-fourth of the companies will permit commutation and withdrawal of the present value of installments certain if authorized by the insured or if requested by a beneficiary to whom the proceeds were payable in one sum but who instead elected the Life Income Option. In such cases, the beneficiary may be entitled to resumption of the life income at the end of the certain period, which presents obvious problems as explained in Section 3.10.4.

§2.7.　*Joint and Survivorship Life Income Option.* The joint and survivorship option, which provides income for two lives, is a variation of the Life Income Option. It is not always included in the original policy or available in all companies. If at the death of the first payee, the second payee is still living, installments are continued during the latter's remaining lifetime.

In some cases, payments are continued in the same amount to the second payee, and the option is known as "joint and survivor" or "joint and last survivor." In others, at the death of one payee, installments are reduced to three-fourths, two-thirds, or one-half the original amount, and the reduced income is continued for the second payee's remaining life. Such options are usually identified as "joint and three-fourths," "joint and two-thirds," and the like. In companies which do not offer such step-down joint options, a similar result may be approximated by using a level joint and survivor option for part of the proceeds, with other parts settled on one of the other Life Income Options for each payee.

A few companies provide joint and survivor options with a certain period of 10 or 20 years. These guarantee that if both payees die before the certain period ends, installments will be continued to the end of that period to a contingent payee, or commuted and paid in a single sum.

The joint and survivorship option is most useful in providing for parents or for the retirement income of the insured and his wife. In the latter case, it is applied at retirement age to the proceeds of a matured endowment or retirement income policy, or to the cash value of any other permanent form of insurance.

§*2.8. Special purpose options.* Though almost any desired pattern of income can be obtained by using the various options described above, either singly or in combination, some companies provide options which are designed to meet a specific need or to serve a particular purpose. For example, a number of companies offer a separate "educational plan option." This often provides a fixed-dollar income during 9 or 10 months of each college year, with a modest "graduation present" in cash after the final installment. There may also be additional cash payments at the beginning of each semester, to provide for tuition and travel expenses.

If the policy is on the life of a parent, interest is usually paid between the insured's death and the beginning of college. Sometimes, however, regular installments of principal and interest commence immediately, according to an ascending scale during elementary school, high school, and college. The various types of installment and cash payments may be keyed to specific dates, stipulated ages of the child, or proof that he has entered school, such as "an accredited college, university or other institution of higher learning."

A less common example of special purpose options is one designed to provide a definite monthly income for a period of 10, 15, or 20 years after the insured's death, at the end of which time a principal sum is paid. The arrangement is such that when this option is applied to a given amount of proceeds, each monthly installment is 1 percent, 1½ percent, or possibly 2 percent of the principal sum payable at the end of the income period, as desired. The final principal payment may usually be settled under one of the regular policy options. As a practical matter, this special purpose option merely makes a regular policy of any type into a "family maintenance policy," insofar as settlement of proceeds is concerned.

As in the case of joint and survivor options, special-purpose options are derived from the basic options. Educational settlement plans are merely the Fixed Period or Fixed Amount Options expressed in a different form. Part of the proceeds may be settled under the Fixed Period Option, with annual or semiannual installments to provide tuition and travel money. Part is paid under the Fixed Amount Option, calculated to run 9 or 10 months in each college year, instead of the usual 12 months, with accumulated interest earnings on this part held for the graduation present. For simplicity, all these provisions are sometimes expressed in a single settlement option, along with possible use of the familiar Interest Option, which may precede the installments.

§2.9. *Settlement by mutual consent of the company and the policyowner or beneficiary.* Notwithstanding the extremely wide variety of distribution plans offered by the various settlement options or combinations of options, a rare situation may be encountered in which the standard options do not seem to fit. To meet this problem, most companies include in their policies some such clause as: ". . . or proceeds may be payable in any other manner mutually agreeable to the company and the policyowner or payee."

Actually, if the facts in such a case are submitted to the company, the home office frequently can suggest using the regular options in a way which may not have been apparent. If not, the company may be willing to set up a special settlement plan, within reasonable limits.

§2.10. Special policies, based on settlement options. Some policy forms are designed for automatic settlement in the form of income, or part income and part one sum, to meet specific needs. In effect, these policies are, in themselves, miniature programs or parts of programs. They are constructed by applying one or more of the income options to a specific need and then working out the amount and type of insurance required to satisfy that need on the desired basis. The resulting special policy is usually sold in "units" for easy adaptation to the problem of a given client. Thus, a family income policy may be sold in units of $10,000 face amount, with a minimum sale of a quarter unit, while an educational policy unit might be $5,000, with a minimum of a half unit.

Some of the principal contracts based on settlement options are discussed in Sections 2.11 through 2.14.

§2.11. Family income policy. This type of policy is a combination of reducing term insurance with a basic policy having a level face amount, settled in such a way that if the insured's death occurs before the tenth, fifteenth, twentieth, or other specified anniversary of the policy issue date, a fixed monthly income will be paid until that anniversary date. At that time, the face amount of the policy will be paid in one sum or may be applied under one of the settlement options. The amount of reducing term insurance is so calculated that, when it is settled under the Fixed Period Option for the period from the insured's death to the date specified for payment of the policy's face amount, the resulting income will make up the difference

between monthly interest payments on the deferred face amount and the fixed family income installments stipulated by the policy.

As an example, a certain $10,000 20-year family income policy (with $15,085 reducing term) issued January 1, 1964, provides that if the insured dies before January 1, 1984, an income of $100 per month will be paid until that date, at which time the $10,000 face amount will be payable. On a 2½ percent interest basis, if death occurred immediately after issue of the policy, this contract would work out as follows:

Monthly interest at 2½ percent for 20 years on $10,000 deferred face amount: $2.05 per $1,000 (first payment immediate instead of at end of month as in §2.3)	$ 20.50
Monthly installments for 20 years from $15,085 term insurance, at Fixed Period Option rate of $5.27 per $1,000	79.50
Total monthly income to January 1, 1984	$100.00

Obviously, the later the insured's death occurs, the shorter will be the period of income. Accordingly, the term element in such a policy reduces each month until it reaches zero at the end of the specified family income period. Such a policy is often useful in mortgage cancellation arrangements.

Though construction of the policy is based on regular settlement options, substantially as in the above example, the insuring clause of the contract generally mentions only the total monthly family income and the face amount, with specific provisions as to when and how each will be paid. The rate of interest assumed for both parts of the total income is usually the same. Ordinarily, it is that specified for the Fixed Period Option in the policy, even though the Interest Option in the same policy may guarantee a lower rate.

Based on this general principle, various types of family income contracts are offered today. In addition to the popular 10, 15, and 20 year plans, some companies offer income periods running to the insured's age 60, 65, or even 70. In a few cases, *any* period of income may be selected, provided it is not less than 10 years and will not run beyond the insured's age 70. Monthly installments may be at the rate of $10 per $1,000 face amount, as in the foregoing example, or at the rate of $15, $20, or more per $1,000. Some companies include a small amount of level term insurance, payable before the family income payments commence. Thus, a $10,000 family income policy might provide an initial cash payment of $2,000 for clean-up or readjustment purposes.

A substantial number of companies offer contracts similar to family income but with one important difference. The face amount is payable immediately on the insured's death, and the reducing term element is therefore calculated to provide the entire income for the stated period. This arrangement offers more flexibility in the use of settlement options, because there is no tie-in between the face amount and the family income installments. It is also an easier arrangement to explain to a beneficiary.

Another variation consists of reducing term without any base of level insurance. This policy provides only a fixed monthly income to a specified date, if death occurs before then. The last two plans are usually given names other than family income but are based on similar principles.

To an increasing extent, family income plans are made up by adding a term rider to some regular form of level insurance. Once limited to ordinary life, today the base policy may take almost any form, ranging from certain types of term at one extreme to endowment and retirement insurance contracts at the other. It is also fairly common practice to allow the commuted or discounted value of the income payments, together with the face amount, if any, to be paid in one sum or under one of the regular options in the policy.

§*2.12. Family maintenance policy.* Here, the basic concept is also that of deferring payment of the policy's face amount, with a fixed monthly income payable during the period of deferment. Commonly, a 10, 15, or 20 year term rider is added to a base policy, as in constructing a family income policy, but the rider is level rather than reducing term. This enables the stipulated family maintenance income to run for a stated period after the insured's death, rather than just to a specified date.

A typical $10,000 family maintenance contract provides that if the insured dies within 20 years after the date of issue, an income of $100 per month will be paid until 20 years after the date of death, at which time the $10,000 face amount will be paid. Assuming 2½ percent interest, such a contract would contain a level "supplementary term" rider in the amount of $15,085 and have a total commuted value, including the face amount, of $25,085. It will be noted that these values are the same as the corresponding initial values in the family income policy example.

Family maintenance policies or riders are also available in a variety of combinations, though not so numerous as for family income. Rates of income are usually $10 or $15 per $1,000 of face amount, occasionally more, but income periods usually do not exceed 20 years. Today, family maintenance riders can be attached to many base policies. However, terminology has not been standardized, and the names assigned to family maintenance contracts and riders vary widely among the companies.

§*2.13. Retirement income policy with insurance.* Essentially an endowment contract maturing at a specified age, usually between 50 and 70, the "retirement income" policy differs from a standard endowment because of the way in which the maturity value is determined. Ordinarily, the maturity value of a "unit" is the amount needed to produce a life income, 10 years certain, of $10 per month at the stated retirement age. In most cases, the face amount of such a unit is $1,000, which is considerably less than the maturity value.

For example, Table V, page 48, shows that each $1,000 of principal will provide $6.30 per month for life, 10 years certain, to a male, age 65. On this basis, a retirement income contract having a face amount of $10,000 would develop a cash value of $15,873 to produce a retirement income of $100 per month at age 65, 10 years certain and for life. The death benefit before maturity would be the face amount or the cash value, whichever is greater.

For a female policyowner, $17,825 would be required at age 65 to provide $100 per month for life, 10 years certain, according to the same table, because of the greater life expectancy. For this reason, the premium charged women for a given retirement income unit of $1,000 face amount and $10 per month income is higher than for men of the same age.

In some companies, the face amount and maturity cash values more closely approximate each other. A $1,500 unit may be designed to provide $10 per month at the stated retirement age, or, conversely, a $1,000 unit may provide only $5.00 per month at retirement.

Some policies, while designed to provide $10 per month life income at a stated retirement age, indicate optional maturity dates from five or more years before the stated age to five or more years after. In effect, the early retirement option merely places the reduced cash value available at the earlier age under the Life Income Option, to yield a smaller income than would be paid at maturity. This usually can be done with any such policy, or for that matter with any permanent form of contract. The option to defer maturity is especially advantageous, for, without incurring any adverse federal income tax consequences, the retirement income increases rapidly with each year of deferment. Three factors operate to produce a substantially larger income—the increased age of the insured, the additional premiums paid, and the longer period of compound interest.

A few companies provide a deferred maturity option without continuing premium payments. Interest is accumulated and compounded on the maturity cash value, which places a larger fund under the increased life income rate for the later maturity age. Where this option is not available, deferment can often be arranged by placing the maturity value under the Interest Option, to be followed by one of the Life Income Options at a specified later age. However, because interest will be paid out rather than accumulated, the ultimate life income will not be as large under this plan as under the special deferment option. There may also be some tax disadvantage to such a plan.

Though the Life Income Option, 10 years certain, is often used to determine the maturity value, other forms of the Life Income Option are sometimes employed. Regardless of the basis on which the maturity value is constructed, however, retirement income policies with insurance customarily contain a full complement of regular settlement options. As in other standard contracts, these can be applied to death benefits and, in most cases, to cash or maturity values.

One thing not standard is the name by which such a contract is known. Perhaps no other policy has been described in such varied terms, many of which are also used for quite different contracts. The same name may be used by one company for a policy with insurance and by another for one without insurance. It is important to study the terms of any contract, but it is especially so in working with retirement policies. By whatever name they are known, these policies have been used extensively in connection with pension trusts and H.R. 10 self-employed retirement plans.

§*2.14. Survivorship or reversionary annuity.* Though called an annuity, this is actually a life insurance policy, the death benefit of which is based on the Life Income Option, without refund. It is usually written in units of $10 monthly income, payable for life to a named beneficiary or "annuitant" if that person survives the insured (sometimes called the "nominator" or "purchaser"). The contract terminates without value on the death of the named beneficiary, whether before or after the insured. *The beneficiary cannot be changed.* There is no cash value in event of lapse, but usually there is a reduced paid-up annuity value, expressed in dollars of monthly income. This paid-up value terminates at the beneficiary's death. However, largely because of the development of modern family income policies and other low-cost, high-benefit plans, such survivorship annuities are rarely issued.

B. ANNUITY CONTRACTS

§2.15. Types of annuities and relationship to settlement options. Annuity contracts may be classified as either immediate or deferred. They may also be classified as single premium annuities or annual premium annuities. It will be apparent that an immediate annuity is usually a single premium annuity. However, a deferred annuity may be issued on either a single or an annual premium basis.

Annuity contracts bear a close resemblance to the various types of Life Income Options found in life insurance policies. Indeed, they were the forerunners of this group of options, and are based on the same mathematical principles.

Of course, an expense charge is included in the premium for an annuity contract. Thus, a given amount of cash proceeds will normally produce a larger income under one of the Life Income Options than under a similar single premium immediate annuity, if both are based on the same mortality table and interest assumptions, and contain identical refund features.

However, largely due to improved interest earnings in recent years, some companies now offer immediate annuities on a more favorable basis than Life Income Options in policies they issued five or ten years ago. In such cases, the policyowner or beneficiary may be permitted to apply policy funds under the more favorable annuity rates, net of all expenses including commissions, either by company practice or, in a few cases, by policy provisions. The practice of many companies requires that a Life Income Option settlement must produce a better income than that which could be provided on the date of settlement if the same amount of policy proceeds were applied as a single premium under an immediate annuity contract.

Annual premium deferred annuities without insurance are usually called retirement income or retirement annuity contracts. They are usually issued in units of $100 annual premium. The death benefit before retirement is normally a refund of total premiums paid or the cash value, whichever is greater.

The cash value provides the income at retirement, often on an optional basis as to age and as to refund or joint income features. In many cases, regular settlement options are also included for use with either the cash value or the death benefit.

This type of annuity contract is commonly used in connection with pension trusts.

Some companies also offer single premium deferred annuities without insurance, which provide a death benefit equal to the cash value or the premium paid, whichever is greater. Usually, these policies contain standard settlement options.

C. Group Insurance

§2.16. Settlement options in group policies. Originally designed to furnish cash proceeds, modern group insurance is sometimes payable in installments and may provide some settlement options. In most cases, options provided in the master contract are limited to fixed period or fixed

amount installments. In practice, other options may be made available in some cases, sometimes depending on the amount of insurance involved.

The trend in recent years toward larger amounts of group insurance on individuals has contributed to more liberal practices regarding settlement options. Sometimes, the settlement option rates will be those effective when the option is selected or when it becomes operative, but often the rates will be based on options in use on the issue date of the master contract. Companies often reserve the right, in the master contract, to change settlement option provisions on any policy anniversary.

The Revenue Act of 1964 provides that premiums paid by an employer on group insurance coverage in excess of $50,000 per employee is taxable as income to the employee. It will be interesting to observe the impact this change may produce on group insurance sales and on settlement option practices on group policies.

D. GOVERNMENT INSURANCE FOR SERVICEMEN AND VETERANS

§2.17. General description of settlement options. National Service and U.S. Government Life Insurance policies contain settlement options similar to those found in commercial contracts. However, only the Fixed Period and Life Income Options are offered, the latter with guaranteed installments for not less than 10 years. The Interest Option is not available, nor are any of the joint Life Income Options.

Cash is definitely an option which only the insured may select. If no option is selected by the insured, the beneficiary or contingent beneficiary, as first taker, may elect an option, but payments must be spread over a minimum of three years. Where the insured has selected an income option, the beneficiary may change this selection after the insured's death, provided the period of guaranteed installments is not shortened.

Cash surrender values cannot be applied under any option. However, the maturity proceeds of an endowment policy may be paid to the insured in installments over a period of from 3 to 20 years. Life Income Options are *not* available to the insured in any case.

§*2.18.   U.S. Government Life Insurance.*   The sale of new USGLI was terminated for servicemen on active duty on October 8, 1940, and for veterans of World War I on April 25, 1951.

Four settlement options are available in policies now in force: No. 1, One Sum; No. 2, Fixed Period, 36 to 240 months; No. 3, Life Income, 20 years certain; No. 4, Life Income, 10 years certain. Income options guarantee 3½ percent interest, and Life Income Options are based on the American Experience Table of Mortality, with the same rates for males and females. Since this table assumes a mortality substantially higher than that experienced today, annuity returns based on it are exceptionally high.

At death of a beneficiary while receiving income, any unpaid guaranteed installments will be paid to the estate of that beneficiary unless otherwise directed by the insured.

§*2.19.   Regular participating National Service policies.*   The sale of these contracts was terminated on April 25, 1951, but a substantial number are still in force.

The four settlement options available are slightly different from those in USGLI: No. 1, One Sum; No. 2, Fixed Period, 36 to 240 months; No. 3, Life Income, 10 years certain; No. 4, Refund Life Annuity. For age 69 and over, option 3 is substituted automatically for option 4, to keep the certain period at not less than 10 years. Guaranteed interest is 3 percent, but the life incomes are on the same mortality basis as in USGLI.

Unlike USGLI, at the death of a payee not entitled to cash settlement, unpaid guaranteed installments will be continued to secondary beneficiaries. The final payee will be the estate of the *insured,* unless otherwise specified by the insured.

On the other hand, if the insured selects the one sum option and the beneficiary elects an income option instead, any remainder will be payable to the beneficiary's estate. In such cases, contingent beneficiaries cannot be named or renamed.

§*2.20. "Modernized" National Service policies.* These contracts were available on a renewable, nonconvertible term basis to persons serving in the armed forces after June 26, 1950, and discharged before January 1, 1957. They are still available to discharged persons having service-connected disabilities which render them unable to buy insurance at standard rates, subject to Veterans Administration regulations. Since January, 1959, these term policies have been convertible to any of the usual NSLI forms, but only on the nonparticipating "modernized" basis as to premiums, settlement options, and the like. They may also be exchanged for a five-year convertible term plan, renewable to age 50, at a reduced premium. Later, other NSLI policies became available to disabled veterans on a limited basis. Also, holders of NSLI may now convert their policies to a modified life plan.

Settlement options are similar to those in regular NSLI, except that the interest factor is $2\frac{1}{4}$ percent, and the Annuity Table of 1949 is used for the Life Income Options, with different rates for males and females.

§*2.21. Servicemen's (gratuitous) indemnity.* This insurance was automatically granted in the amount of $10,-000, less any other government insurance in force, to persons on active duty from June 27, 1950, until January 1, 1957, when it was repealed by Public Law No. 881, Eighty-fourth Congress, Second Session. However, beneficiaries may be encountered who are receiving payments from this source.

No settlement options were available, the only form of payment being in monthly installments of $9.29 for each $1,000 of insurance, for a fixed period of 10 years.

Chapter 3

The Use of Settlement Options to Cover Needs

§*3.1.* *Introduction.* Basic family needs and suggested options for meeting them are presented here in the order that they are often considered in a life insurance program. These needs differ in individual cases, and there can be many variations in each category. However, a program that covers the needs in their broader aspects will yield more readily to normal changes in the family picture than will one which attempts to embrace every possible contingency.

An intelligent insurance program combines the settlement options offered by the various companies into a comprehensive distributive pattern tailored to fit the major needs of the individual client. If ready-made settlement plans are applied to every client's situation, the inevitable result will be inadequate or improper coverage of one or more important contingencies. Accordingly, various methods of using the settlement options to cover broad types of family situations are discussed in this chapter.

A. Cash Funds

§*3.2.* *Using options for funds payable in cash.* There are at least three principal types of funds which must be made available in the form of ready cash to meet various contingencies. These are the clean-up or estate clearance fund, the mortgage cancellation fund, and the emergency fund. Cash funds are often regarded as synonymous with a one sum settlement. However, a one sum settlement is not generally recommended for personal life insurance policies, for the reasons given in Section 2.2, unless the amount is small or the beneficiary is an estate, trust, or business entity. Admittedly, a minority, contrary view reasons that a one sum settlement saves time in the field for agents, saves administrative handling of advance endorsements or recordings in the home office, and gives beneficiaries more flexibility than might be given under a settlement option agreement. Proponents of this view accomplish their stated objectives either by liberal practices concerning elective rights by beneficiaries, or by the "automatic" settlement option arrangements described in Section 2.2. The reader's attention is directed to Section 3.6, in which are discussed some hazards inherent in excessive flexibility.

Thus, proceeds to be made available in cash will normally be retained or paid under one of the settlement options. Before considering the various cash needs, it may be helpful to state three general principles concerning proceeds to be made available in cash.

(1) A settlement option is usually a better arrangement than a one sum payment. The Interest Option with an unlimited right to withdraw proceeds will make the proceeds available in cash but will avoid the disadvantages of a cash payment, as explained in Section 2.2. There may be a psychological advantage in the fact that the beneficiary under such option must take affirmative action to secure cash, as contrasted with the necessary affirmative action under a one sum settlement to *leave* the proceeds with the company until needed.

(2) Whenever the Interest (or other) Option is used with the unlimited right of withdrawal, it is usually good

practice to request inclusion of the right to elect any other option in the policy at any time, to the extent that such right is permissible under company rules. Such all-inclusive right may preserve for the beneficiary the benefit of favorable income rates in the policy if all the funds are not needed in cash and it should prove desirable to have any balance contribute additional income. If such right is not specifically included, and if change to some other option is requested by the beneficiary after the insured's death, it will sometimes be available only on income rates offered in current policy issues, which may be less favorable than those in the particular policy. There are some objections inherent in this type of settlement option arrangement when used as a regular income fund rather than as a cash fund, as is explained in Section 3.6.

(3) The choice of beneficiaries should normally be determined by the purpose of each cash fund, and the beneficiary designation in each case should be coordinated with the wills and other instruments governing the family estate plan. The basic design of a general settlement plan for cash funds has been indicated by the first and second principles. Application of the third principle to each of the three major types of cash funds is discussed in Sections 3.3, 3.4, and 3.5.

§*3.3. Clean-up or estate clearance fund.* Obviously, the expenses of last illness and burial may be sizable in amount and should be paid within a reasonably short time. Funds must also be available to probate the insured's will or to take out letters of administration if there is no will. Various other costs of administration must be paid from time to time. The decedent may leave a number of unpaid debts. Periodic income tax installments are often substantial. Definite periods are prescribed within which death transfer taxes must be paid to the federal and state governments. These are just some of the items which may require immediate cash.

Unless adequate cash or its equivalent is provided, a forced sale of nonliquid assets may reduce their value sharply. Special circumstances often have a direct bearing on the amount of cash required. However, for estates of less than $100,000, a good rough estimate is 15 percent of the gross estate, not including insurance payable to named beneficiaries, with perhaps a minimum of $2,000 to $5,000.

It is generally agreed that life insurance is the ideal source of clean-up funds. Proceeds may be made available in several ways to meet this need. The individual circumstances and objectives in each case will help determine the manner of settlement.

1. *The wife (or husband) as primary beneficiary.* In many cases, the general estate assets are modest. The wife is the sole recipient of such assets and is named primary beneficiary of the life insurance. The purpose of the clean-up fund can be served adequately by holding a stated portion of the proceeds under the Interest Option for the wife, subject to the full right of withdrawal and the right to elect other options.

However, if the wife is named primary beneficiary of the clean-up fund, it is important that the insured's estate, rather than minor children, be named contingent beneficiary. Otherwise, where moneys are payable to a minor, a court might not allow the proceeds to be used for obligations of the insured's estate. Generally, the funds of minors must be used for their exclusive benefit and cannot be expended for any other purpose.

It is sometimes felt that this is actually a reason for naming children as contigent beneficiaries for the clean-up fund, on the theory that a man is more interested in his offspring than in his creditors. However, the insured's obligations must be met, even if they exhaust all assets in the hands of his executor or administrator. In modest estates, even the family silver and heirlooms intended for the children may have to be sold. In the long run, it may be better for the children to have the clean-up fund revert to the insured's estate, if the wife does not live to use it, so that non-liquid assets need not be sold at distress prices.

However, if the insured's estate is named as contingent beneficiary, this designation is sometimes made operative only if the wife predeceases the insured or dies within a stated period after his death. Otherwise, if the wife should die many years after the insured, any unused portion of the fund would cause his estate to be reopened, which could be a costly process. Moreover, after the expiration of six to eighteen months, it can be assumed that administration of the insured's estate will be closed or virtually ready to be closed, and that the clean-up fund is no longer needed for that purpose.

A settlement option agreement prepared to carry out the following request will solve this problem and meet most clean-up needs satisfactorily:

> Hold proceeds under the Interest Option with interest payable monthly (or less frequently if required by company rules) to my wife, if living, otherwise in equal shares to my surviving children, subject to the right to withdraw all or any part of the proceeds at any time, and to the further right to elect any other option in the policy at any time (in accordance with company rules), provided that if my said wife predeceases me, or survives me and dies within six months [or one year, or some other desired period] after my death, pay the proceeds or any remainder thereof to my estate, instead of to the contingent beneficiaries named above.

2. *The insured's estate as primary beneficiary.* Another way is to provide for payment of the clean-up fund directly to the insured's estate. This method is entirely logical, as the estate has primary responsibility for debts and expenses which the clean-up fund is designed to cover, and the insured may want to relieve his widow of details of administration. He can accomplish the latter purpose by

naming as executor in his will a trust company or some individual other than his wife.

This arrangement may be especially appealing where the widow is to receive only a portion of the estate rather than being its sole distributee. In such case, she might be reluctant to use her insurance funds to clear an estate that she must share with others. Even where she is the principal beneficiary of general estate assets, the estate is often named as beneficiary of the clean-up fund if death transfer taxes are sizable. If it seems desirable, an additional clean-up fund may be provided for the widow's own use, which can be settled under the Interest Option.

Life insurance proceeds payable to the estate will be subject to expenses of administration and state death transfer taxes, a result frequently avoided if a beneficiary other than the estate is named to receive the proceeds. However, where policy proceeds are payable to named beneficiaries and thereby do not pass through the estate for probate purposes, the modern trend is to permit the executor and the attorney for the estate to base their fees in part on such life insurance proceeds, especially where tax returns and other services and responsibilities are necessitated by the existence of the insurance.

The settlement options usually are not available to the estate. Statutes protecting cash values from claims of the insured's creditors usually do not apply if the estate is named as beneficiary. Accordingly, all the factors in a given case must be weighed to determine whether the proceeds should be payable directly to the estate or made available to the widow.

3. *Payment to the estate under the Interest Option.* In some cases, the advantages of the Interest Option may be combined with direct payment, or rather accessibility, to the estate. Some company practices permit proceeds to be retained under this option, with interest payable to the *estate of the insured* for a limited period, such as from one

to two years after the insured's death. During this limited period, the executor has the right to withdraw principal as needed.

The wife or other individuals are named as secondary beneficiaries to receive whatever funds have not been withdrawn by the executor, often under a specified interest or installment arrangement. The secondary beneficiaries may begin to receive their payments at the end of the stated period of time, or at an earlier date if the executor releases his interest in the fund under a provision to this effect in the settlement agreement.

This plan has received some company acceptance in recent years, and it is often recognized as an exception to the general rule prohibiting use of settlement options by executors or trustees. The usual objections to designation of an estate as beneficiary probably apply to this plan.

4. *Use of a life insurance trust.* Instead of making the clean-up or estate clearance fund payable to the widow or the insured's estate, it may be paid to the trustees under a life insurance trust. This approach may be especially useful where the amount required to clear the estate is large. In such a case, the cost of administering the trust may be less than the state death transfer taxes and administration expenses that would be incurred by paying proceeds directly to the estate. Moreover, the proceeds are protected against possible claims of creditors.

Under this arrangement, liquid funds for estate settlement costs are made available to the executor through a provision in the trust authorizing the trustees to lend money to the estate or to purchase estate assets. Thus, the trust may come to hold assets formerly held by the estate. In effect, this procedure is somewhat analogous to a widow paying the obligations of her husband's estate out of a clean-up fund payable directly to her.

The relative advantages and disadvantages of trusts and settlement options are compared in Section 7.5.

§3.4. *Mortgage cancellation or permanent home fund.*

This is really another facet of the clean-up fund. A family is normally obliged to live on a reduced income after the death of the family head. Cancellation of any outstanding mortgage will help to bring basic expenditures within the limits of the reduced income. It usually requires less insurance to do this than to produce monthly income equal to the regular mortgage payments, and considerably less than would be needed to provide for rental of equivalent space. On the other hand, if the mortgage has no prepayment privilege, the Fixed Period or Fixed Amount Option may be chosen to make the mortgage cancellation fund available in the manner in which it must be paid out.

Where home ownership is a family objective that has not yet been realized, a permanent home fund may be indicated. For most families, the concept of home ownership is preferable to renting on a long-term basis. Again, it will usually take less insurance to set up such a fund than to provide the additional income needed to continue in a rented home or apartment.

Also, the concept of a permanent home fund may be more realistic where a present home will be sold in any event, because of the cost of maintaining it or because of the size of the mortgage.

If the home is titled in the insured's name, his estate may be the logical beneficiary of the fund. On the other hand, if the husband and wife own the home jointly, or if the wife is expected to purchase a home, this fund should normally be payable to her under the Interest Option, with the right to withdraw proceeds or elect other options.

Both primary and contingent beneficiaries should be determined not only with regard to how the home is titled but also in the light of the family's desires in case the children are orphaned. The children may be of such an age that the family feels it would be logical for them to remain in the home in this event. If so, the estate of the last survivor of the husband and wife might be designated as contingent beneficiary, because the jointly owned home would also fall into the estate of the last survivor, and the mortgage would become an obligation of that estate. In most cases, particularly where the children are still young, it may be obvious that retaining the home for their use would be impractical. In such cases, the children may be named contingent beneficiaries of the insurance fund, and the funds can be handled for their benefit as discussed in Section 3.13. The home would then be sold through the estate that happens to receive it.

If an estate is to be primary beneficiary or contingent beneficiary, a suggestion should be made to the family attorney that he consider incorporating in the insured's will provisions to authorize the executor or trustee to pay off the mortgage and to retain the home for use of the wife or children. If the family presently lives in a rented home, the will might authorize purchase of a home for the benefit of the wife or children, possibly being guided by their wishes. The attorney should also consider provisions to authorize sale of the home by the executor or trustee. Obviously if a present home is jointly owned, appropriate provisions should also be considered for the wife's will.

§*3.5. Emergency funds.* The third principal need for cash funds is to provide for unforeseeable emergencies in addition to regular family maintenance requirements that will be met by an interest or installment arrangement. Depending on the requirements of the individual case, an amount such as $1,000, $5,000, or more may be made available annually for emergency purposes.

There are many ways to provide emergency funds. In some cases, it may be wise to set up a separate policy for this purpose, payable under the Interest Option. In others, this contingency may be covered by withdrawal rights under policies allocated primarily to income needs and settled under the Interest Option or the Fixed Amount Option. In such cases, however, it should be made clear that excessive use of the withdrawal privilege may seriously reduce or eliminate future income.

Withdrawal privileges may be given to the widow, children, or other beneficiaries. Such privilege may be without limitation, or a specified limit may be prescribed each year. A withdrawal limitation is sometimes expressed in the form of an overall or aggregate amount. For example, a beneficiary may be given the privilege of withdrawing not more than $1,000 per year, with the aggregate of the withdrawals never to exceed the sum of, say, $15,000. Sometimes the withdrawal privilege is on a cumulative basis, for example, to the extent that a permissible amount is not withdrawn in a particular year, the amount available in a future year or years may be increased.

Another variant is to permit substantially larger withdrawals during the first year or two following the insured's death. For example, a widow may be given the right to withdraw not more than $5,000 during the two-year period after the insured's death and not more than $500 during any one year thereafter.

Whatever method is used to fix these limits, care should be taken that the available sums are sufficiently large to cover all anticipated debts or expenses that may be incurred in the particular case. For example, the possibility of assessment for a substantial income tax deficiency may make it wise to give the widow a much larger withdrawal privilege than would normally be deemed necessary. Otherwise, inability to satisfy a tax lien might result in the attachment of periodic income, which could deprive the family of all or part of its maintenance for a long period of time, as explained in Section 5.13.

B. REGULAR INCOME FOR THE FAMILY

§*3.6. Types of income needs.* Basic family needs for income fall naturally into several categories. These may be classified generally as readjustment, dependency period, "Social Security gap," and widow's life income. While each of these needs relates to a distinct period in the family's economic life, they also overlap in some respects.

A different settlement option or combination of options may be indicated for each need. However, a settlement plan intended primarily for one period may often contribute income to another. For example, interest on funds held for later use during the Social Security gap will help to fill readjustment and dependency period needs meanwhile. Accordingly, each of these needs must be considered in relation to the other income requirements.

A very popular settlement option arrangement today is to hold the proceeds under the Interest Option, with the right on the part of the wife as primary beneficiary to withdraw principal at any time or to elect any other settlement option. Manifestly, this arrangement offers maximum flexibility. If the life insurance field man or other counselor is present after the insured's death to guide the beneficiary in making the proper election, and if she follows the advice, this arrangement may offer distinct advantages over a more precise installment arrangement, particularly where there has been a significant change in the family picture over the years and the prearranged installment agreement has not been changed to meet it.

Several objections are inherent in this kind of arrangement when it is intended to provide long-range regular income for the family, as opposed to a short-term cash fund. First, it offers a temptation, coupled with unbridled opportunity, for dissipation of funds by a beneficiary who may have had little or no experience in money management. Even if the beneficiary would not dissipate funds in her own behalf, she can be prey for designing relatives who would "borrow" part or all of the funds, or for others who would scheme to obtain the moneys from the widow through get-rich-quick ideas.

A second objection is that a knowledgeable life underwriter who analyzes the insured's estate at a later time can point out the dangers inherent in the Interest Option-all privileges arrangement and imply lack of knowledge or carelessness on the part of the underwriter who first suggested the plan.

The third objection is a psychological one: the Interest Option-all privileges arrangement tends to keep the insured's mind focused on the face amount—probably more money than he has contemplated at any one time. He may not be so receptive to later suggestions for additional insurance to cover needs as he would have been had the life underwriter "spent" his insurance estate under an installment arrangement tailored to his particular needs.

For these reasons, installment arrangements designed to fulfill the client's specific needs seem preferable to holding the proceeds under the Interest Option with the right on the part of the wife as primary beneficiary to withdraw principal at any time or to elect any other settlement options.

§*3.7. Readjustment income.* The need for readjustment income is based on the assumption that few husbands can leave their families as much income on a permanent basis as they provided while living. Yet it is just as hard to stop or drastically reduce family living expenses overnight as it is to stop a speeding train within a few yards. Provision should be made for a period of gradual adjustment, during which income will normally be larger than may be available for the family on a more permanent basis. This extra income may be provided on a level basis or may involve one or more intermediate steps.

When the head of the family dies, critical, important, and long-range problems almost invariably confront the widow. Should she seek employment? Should she take a refresher course to prepare herself better for the business world? Should the family move into a smaller home? How long can the family carry its fixed charges? Can the older children continue in college?

The widow should not be forced to decide these and other important questions during the period of emotional stress following her husband's death. Moreover, her decisions should not be colored by a shortage of income for accustomed obligations.

Even with an adequate clean-up fund, there are often monthly commitments, such as certain installment purchases, which cannot readily be settled in one sum. Mortgage payments may have to be continued, for a short time at least, while the family adjusts to a new life and decides on final disposition of the home. If the home is rented, there may be rent to be continued to the end of the lease or until the property can be sublet. The total income during the readjustment period should be as near as possible to what the family has enjoyed in the past.

Where income from general estate assets is a factor in providing for the client's family, it must be remembered that this income may be interrupted during probate and settlement of the estate. Ordinarily, this may take six to eighteen months, although litigation, tax debts or disputes, the absence of a will, or other factors could greatly extend the time. Accordingly, the greater the proportion of readjustment income that can be provided by life insurance, the more certain the insured can be of an orderly transition and readjustment for his family.

How long a period should be provided for readjustment will depend on the facts in each case. It has been suggested that the length of time should be related to the ultimate drop in family income to be expected by the end of the period. In general, the greater the drop, the longer the readjustment period should be, so that successive step-downs may be less severe.

Once the amount and duration of readjustment income are determined, the actual settlement arrangement may take various forms. The Fixed Period Option may be used to provide one or more years of extra income, but it lacks the flexibility that may be needed to meet some of the variables indicated above. The Fixed Amount Option is, therefore, a better choice in many cases. It is especially helpful where a step-down income is desired or where the extra readjustment income is to come from a large policy allocated primarily to other income needs.

If, for example, $350 per month is needed from life insurance during a two-year readjustment period, and it is necessary to step this figure down to $150, this can be done in various ways under the Fixed Amount Option. Here are three illustrative plans:

First, provide $350 per month to the widow for two years, and $150 per month thereafter until the proceeds are exhausted.

Second, provide $350 monthly for the first year, $250 monthly during the second, and $150 thereafter. Though less will be paid out in total income during the two years, this plan avoids the abrupt transition of the first one.

Third, specify $150 per month from the date of the insured's death, but also give the widow a limited withdrawal privilege so that she can make up the desired additional income during the first two years.

§*3.8.* *Dependency period income.* The dependency period for minor children starts at the insured's death, runs through the readjustment period, and continues until the children become self-supporting. In many cases, Social Security payments will cover a sizable portion of this need, at least before the children reach age 18. On the other hand, families in the middle or upper income brackets may find that this source represents only a minor portion of the total income needed. The families of medical doctors and of a few other groups may even be excluded from Social Security benefits, except to the extent that credits may have been earned in previous military service or "covered employment."

Often there are other sources of income during the dependency period. Interest will be payable on life insurance proceeds retained for later use, such as educational or life income funds. Family income or family maintenance policies or additional term insurance to serve a similar purpose may be in the program. In some cases, income from general estate assets may be a factor. There may be compensation or pension benefits arising from employment or from previous military service. Nevertheless, most situations call for additional dependency period income from life insurance specifically allocated to this need.

The dependency period may run for a decade or two. Care must be taken not only to provide adequate income, but also to select the proper settlement option or options. The settlement plan must be tailored to fit the major needs and objectives of each family. It may be better to guarantee a reasonable standard of living for a limited period of years, during which the widow may adjust herself to her new situation, than to set up a wholly inadequate income spread out over her entire lifetime.

Dependency period income is often provided under either the Fixed Period Option or the Fixed Amount Option. The latter is usually more attractive for several reasons. Partial withdrawals may be permitted for emergencies without affecting the level of income. Similarly the monthly income is not subject to reduction because of policy loans. Dividend accumulations or surplus interest earnings will tend to offset the effect of withdrawals or loans, again without affecting the level of monthly income.

The Fixed Amount Option is especially useful where proceeds are more than adequate to cover the entire dependency period, or may become so with the passage of time. Each year the insured lives, the dependency period becomes shorter, and the amount of unused proceeds becomes larger, assuming no new additions to the insured's family. He may specify that the monthly income be increased through withdrawal privileges or otherwise, as each child attains age 18, to offset the reduction in Social Security benefits or to provide funds for educational expenses, as explained in Section 3.14. Or he may direct that any proceeds remaining on a certain date be settled under another option, such as the Life Income Option. Depending on company practice, the widow may be given the privilege of making such changes in the original distributive pattern, instead of making the changes mandatory.

§*3.9. Social Security gap fund.* The period between the youngest child's eighteenth birthday and the attainment of age 62 by the widow is the period during which no Social Security benefits are payable. This interval is known as the Social Security "blackout" or "gap" period. At the same time, children are normally ready for advanced education at this age, and their expenses are likely to increase.

Often proceeds used to fill the gap are held under the Interest Option until the youngest child is 18. Obviously, the interest payments will provide income for the readjustment and dependency periods, but the amount of such income cannot be known until the size of the gap fund has been determined. For this reason, the Social Security gap fund should be one of the first *income* needs to be considered in calculating a tentative program for meeting the client's objectives.

Assuming the gap fund is held at interest until needed, the Fixed Period Option may be well suited to distributing the proceeds during the gap. However, because this option is usually payable over whole years, it must provide income either for more or for less than the exact number of months involved. The insured will be well advised to select the fixed period so as to extend beyond the widow's sixty-second birthday rather than falling short of it. She will have to reapply for Social Security benefits at that time anyway, and any overlap will minimize the possibility that insurance payments may cease before her Social Security claim has been processed.

The Fixed Amount Option may also be used. In fact, it may be preferable where proceeds are available in excess of the amount needed to bring the gap income up to the widow's Social Security payments after age 62. The excess can be applied in part to increase the fixed income during the gap as well as to produce an increase in life income after the lifetime Social Security benefits start. While the excess could also be placed under the Life Income Option at the *beginning* of the gap period to accomplish much the same result, the widow would often be too young then to justify commencement of that option, as explained in Section 3.10.1.

A family income policy can be a good vehicle for income during the gap. The face amount can be settled under the Fixed Period or Fixed Amount Options at the end of the family income period. The result will usually be entirely satisfactory, even if the family income installments continue beyond the youngest child's eighteenth birthday. In some cases it may be desirable to provide for the commuted value remaining on such date, or on the date of the insured's death, if later, to be settled under the Fixed Period Option for the appropriate number of years, if such an arrangement is permitted by the company. If the amount is large, the commuted value may be so applied to the extent required to fill the gap income need, with any balance used under the Life Income Option, as explained in Section 3.10.

Where the Life Income Option is not involved, it is usually possible to give the widow as much flexibility as may be desired prior to commencement of the gap income. In any event, consideration should be given to granting her the privilege of electing the gap income at an earlier date if the only living child under age 18 should die before reaching that age. Should this contingency occur, Social Security benefits would cease until she became eligible for her lifetime benefit at age 62.

§*3.10. Widow's life income.* Chronologically, the

widow's life income is considered in a program following the end of the dependency period. In projecting estimates and allocating proceeds, the insured's estate has long since been settled. The family has passed through its period of readjustment. The dependency of minor children is no longer a problem. Now an ideal arrangement, in the usual case, is an income that the widow cannot possibly outlive.

In most cases, this later life income cannot be provided in adequate amount from interest payments under the Interest Option. Few persons can accumulate enough life insurance or other property to cover basic needs without expending principal. Here the Life Income Option can serve its most useful function. In no other way can a specified, regular income be guaranteed to a widow, no matter how many years she may live. As stated in Section 2.6, life insurance spreads the risk of "dying too soon," and the Life Income Option spreads the risk of "living too long."

However, there are four or five important points to be considered before specifying a Life Income Option. First, the death of the insured may not be the proper date for commencement of the Life Income Option. Second, extremely adverse consequences may result in individual cases from use of the "10-year-certain period." Third, it may be unwise to compel a beneficiary to accept a Life Income Option at a stated time irrespective of the facts and circumstances at that time. While the Life Income Option is highly recommended as a settlement option, its use at certain times or in certain circumstances may be highly questionable. Fourth, should a commutation privilege be incorporated in the arrangement? Fifth, is there a significant probability that the insured and his beneficiary may die in a common accident or common disaster?

Finally, if there is no need or desire to preserve some values for contingent beneficiaries, request should properly be made to the life insurance company for a straight life annuity—either as a policy option or as an extracontractual arrangement—to give the beneficiary the maximum possible guaranteed life income. Such annuity will yield a larger income than that provided under either the 10-year-certain Life Income Option or the 20-year-certain Life Income Option. However, the insured should understand that all values under the policy will cease on the death of the beneficiary for whom the annuity is provided.

1. *Very young beneficiaries.* Age 50 or 55 is, perhaps, the minimum age at which commencement of the Life Income Option is attractive. At younger ages, the return seems not to justify the shrinkage in the amount available for contingent beneficiaries under the period certain or refund feature. Approximately the same amount of income as under the Life Income Option can be provided by combining three options, while at the same time preserving more principal intact for a much longer time. Commencement of the Life Income Option can thereby be deferred to an age when danger of shrinkage is substantially lessened because of the smaller proportion of proceeds attributable to the deferred annuity feature at later ages, as discussed in Section 2.6. The principle of this arrangement is to place a major portion, such as two-thirds, of the proceeds under the Interest Option for, say, 20 years, after which this portion of the proceeds is paid to the beneficiary under the Life Income Option, 20 years certain. The remaining portion of the proceeds—one-third in this case—is paid to the beneficiary in installments for 20 years under the Fixed Period Option.

The exact percentages will depend on the interest guarantees in the particular policy and the age of the beneficiary when the life income is to commence. Company actuaries can supply the percentages readily, or the computation can be made from a rate book. The dollar income for the beneficiary will closely approximate the income that would have been paid by the immediate commencement of the Life Income Option. However, the option combination arrangement retains intact some guaranteed amount for contingent beneficiaries during the following 20 years —a spread of 40 years as compared with 20 if the Life Income Option commenced immediately at the insured's death.

For example, suppose that an insurance program, after providing clean-up funds, dependency period income, emergency funds, and a portion of the life income, calls for an additional monthly life income of about $90 for the wife, age 36. Here are two plans for accomplishing this objective, based on settlement options in policies currently issued by a typical life insurance company:

PLAN A

Purchase $28,000 of insurance and place it all under the Life Income Option, 20 years certain and continuous, to provide a monthly life income of $90.16
At the end of the first 20 years following the insured's death, *the refund feature will have reduced to zero.*

PLAN B

Purchase $30,000 of insurance—*only $2,000 more* than under Plan A—and combine the Interest Option, Fixed Period Option and Life Income Option as follows:

	Monthly Income	
	First 20 Years	*After 20 Years*
$22,000 under the Interest Option for 20 years	$45.32	
Then change this $22,000 to the Life Income Option, 20 years certain		$91.96
$8,000 under the Fixed Period Option, 20 years	$42.16	
	$87.48	$91.96

The figures shown in Plan B are based on the particular company's 2½ percent *guaranteed rate* of interest under the Interest Option. If a higher *distributive rate* is assumed, such as the 3½ or 4 percent rate currently in effect in many companies, the $28,000 of insurance required in Plan A will be more than sufficient to produce all the needed income, when distributed in the manner of Plan B.

Deferment of the Life Income Option in this manner does not *guarantee* that the children or other contingent beneficiaries will receive any of the proceeds. It merely *increases the possibility* of their receiving some proceeds by slightly reducing, in most cases, the primary beneficiary's income. In some cases, it may be impractical or even impossible to use a deferment plan. For example, government policies have no Interest Option. This fact, coupled with their unusually liberal life income rates, suggests the immediate use of a Life Income Option in most cases.

2. *Selection of proper period certain.* Another method of preserving values for children or other contingent beneficiaries, without seriously reducing the widow's life income, is to select a longer period certain under the Life Income Option.

As discussed in Section 2.6, there are really two portions of proceeds under the Life Income Option. One portion provides a Fixed Period Option for the period certain, and payments under this portion are guaranteed even if the beneficiary does not live. The other portion provides a deferred life annuity, payable to the beneficiary only if she outlives the period certain. There can be no refund on the latter portion. The portion of proceeds required to provide the deferred annuity is much more substantial at the younger ages because of the likelihood that the beneficiary will survive the guaranteed period. Conversely, a much smaller portion of proceeds is required by the deferred annuity at the later ages because of the probability that payments will be made for shorter periods.

Here are some figures from settlement options in policies currently issued by a typical life insurance company, based on $1,000 of proceeds:

Age of Female Beneficiary When Life Income Option Commences	Monthly Life Income		Percent of Proceeds Required for Deferred Annuity	
	10 Years Certain	20 Years Certain	10 Years Certain	20 Years Certain
35	$3.35	$3.28	64%	38%
45	3.82	3.67	59	30
55	4.53	4.18	52	21
65	5.57	4.73	41	10
75	6.98	5.12	26	3

It will be observed that for a female beneficiary 55 years of age, 52 percent of the proceeds may be required to provide the deferred annuity feature under the Life Income Option if the 10-year-certain period is chosen. Stated another way, if the female beneficiary under a $10,-000 policy is 55 years of age at the insured's death and lives to receive just one monthly payment under the Life Income Option with a 10-year-certain period, contingent beneficiaries will receive, on a one sum basis, only $4,800 less the payment of $45.30 already made to the primary beneficiary—a shrinkage of $5,200! If the 20-year-certain period is used in the same circumstances, only 21 percent of the proceeds is required to provide the deferred annuity and the shrinkage is only $2,100.

Facts such as these will be a compelling deterrent against recommendation of the 10-year-certain period under the Life Income Option in most cases, and will alert the insured to consider seriously the propriety of using the Life Income Option on any basis in the case of beneficiaries of very advanced years or in poor health. Settlement plans which involve no possible shrinkage because of the deferred annuity feature may be a better arrangement for those beneficiaries who are old or ill. Certainly the policy-owner should understand the possibility of shrinkage under the Life Income Option and also the importance of selecting the proper period certain. Here, the responsibility of the life underwriter looms very large.

3. *Elective versus mandatory commencement.* Where permissible under company rules, the beneficiary may be given the right to elect the Life Income Option at a future date or age instead of making its commencement mandatory. In this way, the proceeds can be left under the Interest Option if the Life Income Option seems inadvisable at the date the right of election accrues to the beneficiary.

4. *Commutation privilege.* Many companies will not include in a life income settlement the privilege to take down in one sum the commuted value of installments certain. Partial commutation is impracticable and usually cannot be granted under the Life Income Option, and a full withdrawal privilege seems wholly inconsistent with the philosophy of a life income.

Of course, the portion of proceeds attributable to purchase of the deferred life annuity feature has no value that may be reduced to a one sum basis. However, it has a value that should not be terminated simply because a commutation privilege is granted and exercised as respects the installments certain. Accordingly, the companies that permit granting of such commutation privilege will, if the privilege is exercised, generally give to the beneficiary a deferred life annuity certificate. This certificate provides for life income payments to the beneficiary if she outlives the period certain. It may be most difficult to locate such beneficiary many years later to resume payments under the deferred annuity feature. Practical considerations like these prompt the majority view that a commutation privilege may not be incorporated in a settlement option agreement that provides a life income, as explained in Section 2.6.

A commutation privilege may be requested simply to qualify the proceeds for the marital deduction under the federal estate tax law, as explained in Section 6.7.2. Such qualification may be achieved as effectively by granting the beneficiary the right to name her estate as contingent beneficiary, in the manner suggested in Section 6.7.2.

5. *Common disaster.* The common disaster or short-term survivorship hazard may in some cases raise a question of the advisability of making the Life Income Option operative automatically from the moment of the insured's death. If the beneficiary dies soon after the insured's death, the proceeds will be substantially less than the full proceeds that will be paid if the beneficiary dies before the insured.

This contingency is easily handled by a delayed payment provision, as explained in Section 7.7.2. In larger estates where marital deduction is a factor, it is important that the beneficiary's right to income payments not be made contingent on her surviving any special period. Therefore, in such a case, a better plan would be to use the Interest Option instead of a delayed payment clause, with the Life Income Option to commence after a stated period, such as 30 or 60 days. Since interest payments will not commence until at least one month after the insured's death, nothing would be payable to the estate of the beneficiary who died within a month after the insured. The requirements for marital deduction qualification could be met by a right to the beneficiary to name her estate as contingent beneficiary, as explained in Section 6.7.2.

C. INCOME FOR CHILDREN

§3.11. Considerations affecting provisions for children. In designing settlement plans for children, there are at least five principal considerations: (1) providing for children while the surviving parent is living, (2) maintenance income for children as contingent beneficiaries, (3) funds for educational expenses, (4) the vehicle for payment during minority, and (5) ultimate disposition of each child's share of principal.

§3.12. Provision for children while surviving parent is living. While the widow is living, all income is normally payable to her, and the insured is usually content to leave the children's support and education in her hands. However, if there is ample life insurance to carry the family through the dependency period, to fill the Social Security gap, and to provide adequate income for the widow's remaining lifetime, any balance of the insurance proceeds may be made available in some manner for the primary benefit of the children. Often this balance is set aside for the expenses of higher education, or for some other purpose that is important to the children's future.

In large estates, it may be desirable to allocate some income directly to children as a means of reducing the family's income tax burden.

In some instances the life insurance is not sufficient to meet all the basic income needs, and the policyowner cannot purchase additional life insurance. So much of the proceeds are required to cover the dependency period that the amount remaining when the children reach college age can provide *either* for a modest life income to the widow or for the children's education, but not for both. The question of priority may be decided by the policyowner in considering the insurance settlement plan, or the decision may be left to the widow's discretion.

§*3.13. Income for children as contingent beneficiaries.* After the deaths of both the insured and his wife, suggestions of life underwriters vary widely as to the proper method of providing income for children. Proceeds remaining under the Interest Option may be retained for the children, subject to the same rights and privileges granted to the widow. At times, guaranteed installments payable to the wife under the Fixed Period, Fixed Amount, or Life Income Options, or under family income or family maintenance policies, are continued to the children in equal shares. Another arrangement sometimes observed is provision for payment under the Life Income Option to the wife, but if the wife dies before the insured, payment of the proceeds to the children under the Fixed Period Option in the same number of guaranteed installments as specified for the

Life Income Option. Under this arrangement, if a life income, 20 years certain, is selected for the wife, a fixed period of 20 years might be specified for the children. As an alternative, the Fixed Amount Option could be used for the children on an equivalent basis, with the added advantage of the greater flexibility this option affords. Some option other than Life Income should normally be specified for the children in event of the wife's death before the insured.

Actually, none of these installment plans may be as practical as they seem. The needs of minor children are not easily projected after the widow's death, because there are apt to be very significant changes in the family picture. It may be difficult or impracticable to keep the home together for the children. It may be necessary for the children to separate in order to find room with various relatives. The complexities multiply in attempting to project living costs when the children are ultimately ready to attend college.

Often settlement agreements that endeavor to carry out specific income estimates are quite complicated. Moreover, to the extent that these estimates cannot be increased at the discretion of a guardian or trustee, the minor children may be chained to an inadequate income during times of inflation. A more practical approach, having simplicity and flexibility, is to retain each child's share at interest with the full right to withdraw that share or to elect any other settlement option in the policy. Objections to this arrangement are pointed out in Section 3.6, as respects long-range, regular income needs, when the wife is named as primary beneficiary. However, a different factual situation is presented during minority, when control of the funds is placed in a guardian or trustee, as discussed in Section 3.15.

Under such an arrangement, the child's guardian prior to age 21 may elect precisely the type of settlement that seems best suited for the child when the need arises, with the power to change the arrangement from time to time. The guardian has a responsibility to provide all adequate funds for the minor child's necessaries. The fact that the guardian must usually render a regular accounting to the court which appointed him and also secure court approval in exercising privileges under the settlement agreement provides an added safeguard. On the other hand, a responsible trustee can often be named in the agreement, to function without the necessity of complying with the formalities of having a guardian appointed, as explained in Section 3.15.5. This approach may provide added flexibility and also reduce costs. The trustee generally has more latitude in his ability to make withdrawals or to elect appropriate alternative options without seeking court approval. Various channels for administering and providing income or cash for minors are discussed more fully in Section 3.15.

§*3.14.* *Educational funds.* Life insurance has long been recognized as an ideal medium for accumulating funds to guarantee young people the benefits of higher education. Sometimes an endowment policy on the child's life is issued for this purpose, but insurance on a parent's life is usually preferable. As a rule, the father is insured, but sometimes the situation calls for placing the insurance on the mother. Because the type of insurance may have a bearing on the design of settlement plans for such funds, some practical aspects of these two general approaches are considered briefly before discussing appropriate modes of settlement.

1. *Who should be insured?* Insurance on the father's life will often prove more economical than a juvenile endowment. To be fully effective, the accumulation of an educational fund should be protected against the premature death or disability of the adult who is making the deposits. To protect a juvenile endowment against these hazards requires the addition of a "payor" rider, which often makes the total premium larger than would be needed for an equivalent endowment policy on the father's life. Moreover, the policy on the father's life guarantees the full face

amount of the fund immediately in event of his death, to earn interest until needed. In contrast, a payor rider merely waives further payment of premiums on the juvenile endowment, and the full amount of the fund is not available until the stated maturity date of the policy.

Insurance on the father's life is also more flexible. Any permanent form of policy plan may be used, whereas in the case of insurance on the child, an endowment is usually needed. If a parent cannot afford a policy which will accumulate the entire fund by the time it is needed, at least he may be able to purchase a lower-premium policy on his life to guarantee his child's education if he dies too soon. When the child is ready for college, the cash value of such a contract will provide a part of the needed fund. Meanwhile, the father may be able to convert the policy to an endowment plan and thereby build up the full amount.

Similarly, the educational fund may be incorporated into a larger policy on the father's life, which can cover other needs as well. In this case, the cash value at college age may be sufficient to provide for all expenses. If it should prove undesirable to surrender the policy at that time, the cash value can be borrowed as needed and the loan repaid in convenient installments after the child's support is no longer an item in the family budget. This approach offers considerably more flexibility than use of an endowment on either life.

Flexibility can be very important from still another standpoint. Most parents want to treat their children equitably. While this may not always mean absolute equality in all things, it usually applies to funds left to or for the children at death. The man who rushes home from the hospital to arrange a $5,000 to $10,000 juvenile endowment at age 18, to provide part or all of the cost of the education of his firstborn, may be in for some extra financial shocks when the stork makes his second and third or even fourth visit!

Obviously, insurance on his own life would be far

easier to adjust to the new situation if he cannot afford duplicate or triplicate complete plans. For example, he might purchase low-premium contracts to protect the later children until he can afford more substantial savings. A guaranteed-purchase feature could also be included, under which the father could purchase additional insurance coverage on the option dates without evidence of insurability. If unable to afford new insurance, he could at least arrange to divide the proceeds of the first contract so as to give each child the same start toward a college education.

It is not surprising that juvenile endowments are often changed to lower-premium plans long before they have served their original purpose. Indeed, there are many leading underwriters who feel that insurance on a child, when it can be afforded without depriving the entire family of needed protection on the father's life, should always be on a life plan of some sort, or possibly a very-long-term endowment, so as to be of permanent value to the child when he or she reaches an age to be self-supporting.

2. *Educational settlement plans under insurance on the father's life.* Educational funds are normally payable to the wife as primary beneficiary, and most clients prefer to give their wives complete discretion in handling such funds. A popular arrangement is to retain the educational fund under the Interest Option, with rights to withdraw principal and to elect other options. After the wife's death, special educational provisions need not be set up if each child's share of proceeds is retained at interest, with full withdrawal privileges and the right to elect other options. The child's guardian or a named trustee will be able to elect the proper educational plan when the child is ready for college, as suggested in Section 3.15.

On the other hand, some insureds strongly prefer to set definite provisions for monthly interest or installment payments during minority and equally definite provisions for payments during college. Often general maintenance income is provided for the child under the Interest Option or the Fixed Amount Option until the child furnishes evidence that he or she is enrolled as a student in an institution of higher learning. Thereafter the child's income is increased under one of the installment options. Monthly installments are sometimes specified for nine or ten months of the college year, with much larger installments for tuition payments in the months of August and February, as outlined in Section 2.8. Opinions differ as to whether the child should be gainfully employed during the summer months or should receive maintenance payments on a full 12-month basis.

The settlement agreement frequently provides that the remaining balance of the child's share be paid to him in one sum upon graduation. Good draftsmanship also suggests a mandatory payment or a withdrawal privilege after a specified age, such as 25, to cover the possibility that the child may never attend college. Otherwise, if a "proof of enrollment" provision is included, the child would be restricted to interest income during his or her entire lifetime.

In any event, any definite pattern should be kept as simple as possible. Normally flexibility should be provided by adding rights to withdraw principal or elect other options. Even if the insured in a given case is unwilling to grant such privileges to the widow as primary beneficiary, he should be willing to provide them for funds payable to minors, because of the court-supervised guardianship or trusteeship which would then come into play. It is impossible to make precise estimates for college expenses and other purposes many years ahead. An unlimited arrangement can be simpler than a precise plan, it is much more flexible, and it avoids many objections inherent in a fixed pattern.

3. *First things first.* Proper handling of educational funds is especially important for several reasons. On the average, college graduates earn far more than those whose

educations are terminated earlier. This fact reinforces the normal desire of parents to give their children the best possible start in life.

However, for this very reason, educational funds or educational policies are sometimes given undue priority in building a life insurance program. They are often purchased even before there is enough insurance to feed the children over the years they must wait to enter college. The life underwriter has a serious responsibility to help his clients put first things first, and when educational funds are in order, to help set them up on a sound, flexible basis.

§*3.15. The vehicle for payment during minority.* Some state statutes permit a life insurance company to make payments directly to a minor after a specified age, such as 15 or 18. In the absence of such enabling provisions, there are several vehicles which may be chosen for payments during minority.

1. *Administration by a guardian.* The client may depend on a court to appoint guardians if he dies while the children are still minors. This means separate legal proceedings—a separate petition for each child. Some initial expense is entailed, and the law may compel the guardian to give bond for double the amount of proceeds, with an annually recurring bond premium. Guardians must obtain specific court approval for many acts, and must periodically file an accounting with the court. The insured may not dictate the court's selection of the guardian. While some recent laws provide that the guardian named in a will has control over life insurance proceeds payable to the minor, other state laws have contrary provisions. Seemingly more attractive procedures are available than that of relying on a guardian.

2. *A formal trust.* The insured father may enter into a formal trust agreement naming a corporate trustee, with perhaps one or more individuals as cotrustees. This is a popular procedure in larger estates, and even in those of

more modest size when there is other property to be administered for the minor, such as cash in bank, securities, and real estate. However, the cost of creating and administering the trust may not be justified where a relatively small amount of insurance is the chief asset to be administered.

3. *An individual trustee named in the policy.* A third procedure, suggested by some companies, simply names an individual as trustee in the settlement agreement. If no trust powers are specified, a court could decide that a "dry trust" had been created—that is, one which is not enforceable. In such a case, the court might prohibit the continued holding of funds by the trustee and direct their transfer to a guardian to be appointed by proper court proceedings. If the trustee under the dry trust had already dissipated the funds, the insurance company might be required to pay them again to a guardian, on the theory that the company should have known better than to pay proceeds to such a trustee.

The companies suggesting this procedure probably do so on the theory that the amounts involved are frequently quite small and therefore the practical business risk is slight. In fact, company rules often limit use of this procedure to a stated maximum of proceeds, such as $5,000. Since the funds are normally used for the minor's benefit, there is probably little likelihood that the company would have to make payment a second time. From a strictly legal point of view, however, the procedure seems vulnerable.

4. *A trustee named in a separate brief trust agreement.* This procedure is very similar to the third method described above. The difference is found in a brief specimen trust agreement which accompanies the beneficiary papers. The policyowner is told to consult his attorney for preparation of the actual trust agreement to be executed. No problems arise if both the trust agreement and the beneficiary papers are signed by the policyowner. However, there is understandable delay while the policyowner consults his at-

torney and the lawyer does the necessary research. The policyowner may die during this interval. He may sign the beneficiary request, mail it to the company, and then die before executing the trust agreement. Complications akin to those described under the third procedure could then arise.

5. *Trustee under specific trust provisions in the settlement agreement.* These considerations have led an increasing number of companies in recent years to adopt still another procedure. The trustee is named in the settlement option agreement as a vehicle for payment, with a couple of extra sentences stating that the trustee shall hold and expend the moneys for the benefit of the minor until age 21 and then pay him any unexpended funds. Usually the Interest Option is specified, with rights to withdraw principal or elect other options. This procedure is illustrated in the following provision used by one company:

> Regardless of any provision herein to the contrary, any sum payable as herein provided to any of said children during such child's minority shall be paid to JOHN DOE, brother of the insured, as trustee for such child. In the event said brother shall fail to serve or shall cease to serve as trustee for such child, because of death or otherwise, any sum payable as herein provided to such child during minority shall be paid to RICHARD DOE, nephew of the insured, as successor trustee. If the right to withdraw proceeds or elect other options is granted a beneficiary during his minority, such right or election shall be exercisable by said trustee. All sums payable to said trustee shall be held and expended for the maintenance, support and education of such minor beneficiary in the discretion of the trustee, except as may be otherwise provided in a separate trust instrument, and when such beneficiary shall attain the age of 21 years, the trustee shall pay over any unexpended funds. As respects any payment made to said trustee the Company shall be under no liability to see to or be responsible for the proper discharge of the trust or any part thereof, and

any such payment to said trustee shall fully discharge the Company for the amount so paid. If the trustee designated above shall for any reason fail to serve or cease to serve as trustee, a successor or substitute trustee shall be appointed by a court of competent jurisdiction. The Company shall not be charged with notice of a separate trust instrument, a change of trustee, the death of such beneficiary, the termination of the trust, or of rights under the trust, until written evidence thereof is received at the Home Office.

There appear to be definite advantages in this new procedure where modest insurance proceeds represent the principal or only asset to be administered for the minor. It is simple, it involves no expense, and it eliminates most formalities. However, it may be contended that this procedure makes it easy for the insured to bypass his lawyer. The particular company whose clause is quoted states it recommends that such agreement be reviewed by the insured's lawyer and that the lawyer should advise whether this procedure, or one of the others, should be adopted. Moreover, this procedure is applied only during minority and cannot be followed where a separate trust agreement is actually in effect. In such a case, this company follows the procedure described in Section 3.15.2.

§*3.16. Ultimate disposition of children's shares.* Fewer problems are presented in this category. Essentially there are two questions: how and when to distribute each child's share of principal to him; and how to distribute shares of deceased children.

1. *Distribution to children at or after maturity.* A policyowner will often be content to have a child's share paid outright to him on attaining age 21. Another popular method is to distribute the share in specified fractions, for example, one-third after attaining ages 21, 25, and 30. Principal may be distributed in the form of mandatory payments, or the child may be given the right to make withdrawals after attaining the specified age or ages. Obviously

the withdrawal privilege method affords greater flexibility as the child is not compelled to accept and invest money for which he may have no immediate need.

Deferment of some or all of the principal until a later age than 21 is predicated on the theory that amounts withdrawable at early ages are most likely to be dissipated. Indeed, it is not unusual to deny full withdrawal privileges to daughters and restrict them to a life income at, say, age 45 or 50. Such a provision gives the daughter some degree of financial independence and may prevent a designing husband from gaining control of her share of principal. For a son, on the other hand, a right confined to election of the Life Income Option may defeat a worthwhile purpose, such as the opportunity to make an attractive business investment, or to purchase a home upon marriage. Customarily, sons are given full control of proceeds, though such control may be deferred for some time after attaining majority.

2. *Distribution to children of children: per stirpes or per capita?* These are formidable, legalistic phrases. They arise mostly in the construction of wills, and the law books are filled with decisions that attempt to determine which type of distribution was intended. To illustrate the problem, assume that an insured has provided that the proceeds of his policy shall be paid to his children, John, William, and Mary, and to surviving children of a deceased child. Suppose John and Mary die before the insured. John leaves four children surviving him. Mary has no children. How shall the proceeds of the policy be divided at the insured's death?

Per stirpes means "by branches" of the family. A per stirpes distribution gives the share of the deceased child to his children. Accordingly, under a per stirpes distribution, William would take one half the proceeds and John's surviving children would divide the other half among them.

Per capita, on the other hand, means "by heads." A per

capita distribution will give one share of the proceeds to each beneficiary. On a per capita basis, William and each of John's four children would receive one fifth of the proceeds.

Per stirpes distributions are more popular. It is most important that the written request for the agreement accurately reflect the distribution desired by the policyowner, and that such distribution be clearly set forth in the life insurance settlement option agreement.

D. SPECIAL PURPOSE FUNDS

§3.17. *Provision for aged relatives.*   There are a number of special circumstances which, though encountered less frequently than basic needs, present strong motivations to a particular client. For example, he may wish to provide for one or more aged relatives. Often such provisions are not essential to the maintenance requirements of the older person, and therefore are completely secondary to the needs of the client's immediate family. On the other hand, especially in the case of parents, the client may be the sole or chief source of support. Failure to provide for an aged dependent may result in thrusting an unfair burden on the client's brothers and sisters, or on his widow. Obviously, the probabilities favor the client surviving his parents, but the possibility that he will not must be considered.

Where there is such a primary need, if the older dependent lives with the client, his or her requirements can be included in the overall estimate of family income to be payable to the widow. However, a direct provision is usually preferable. For example, the client's mother may be willing to accept support from him but might feel uncomfortable about taking funds from income provided for her daughter-in-law and grandchildren.

If the client owns a U.S. Government or National Service policy, a relatively small allocation of such insurance will provide a substantial life income for the older person, because of the unusually liberal annuity guarantees in these policies. A very old commercial contract may produce similar results.

Where there is adequate insurance for both primary and secondary needs, it is a simple matter to allocate a policy or a portion of proceeds to the older person. A popular settlement plan is the Interest Option, with either an unlimited or a limited withdrawal privilege. Another plan provides payment to the relative under the Fixed Amount Option, with or without a withdrawal privilege.

In any case, the widow and children normally should be named to receive any proceeds remaining at the death of the relative. The extent to which such remainder may be added to the major part of the life insurance and dovetailed into the distributive pattern for the family depends on that pattern and the company rules involved.

§*3.18. Christmas, birthday, and anniversary gifts.* The policyowner may request the company to pay a stated amount to a beneficiary each Christmas, or on a particular date each year to commemorate some birthday, anniversary, or other special event. Another method is to give the beneficiary the right to withdraw a limited sum at any or all of these times each year. Such arrangements usually can be worked out under company rules. There may be much sentimental gratification to a particular policyowner to contemplate that the beneficiary will think of him pleasantly each year at this very time.

§*3.19. Payments to charities.* Many policyowners prefer to name religious, charitable, or educational institutions as beneficiaries, particularly after the deaths of all members of their immediate families. A charitable organization, such as a school, church, or hospital, is almost certain to be in existence after the family has passed on. Moreover, the policyowner may want to be sure that any proceeds not used for his immediate family, however small, will be applied to worthwhile purposes rather than distributed to remote heirs of little concern to him.

Generally, any payment to such charitable organization

must be made in one sum, except in very unusual circumstances which may be recognized by the company as warranting an income option. Each charitable organization should be clearly and properly named and identified. Many charitable provisions in both wills and life insurance policies have failed to fulfill their purpose because of careless beneficiary designations. It is well to check whether the particular charity is incorporated. If it is not, special provisions may be needed to carry out the wishes of the policyowner in naming his beneficiary. The charitable group or association must be one that is legally capable of giving the insurance company a release for receipt of the proceeds. In this respect, it is well to consult an attorney—preferably one who is interested in the particular charity.

E. COORDINATING SETTLEMENT OPTIONS WITH INCOME FROM OTHER SOURCES

§*3.20. General estate assets.* It is important to know whether general estate assets are of such character and in such amount that income from them will be a significant factor in the overall picture. This is especially true with respect to long-range considerations, such as the dependency period for minor children. Depending on the nature and amount of general estate income, the insurance income may be lessened so that the two sources can be projected as a level amount for a longer time.

Where the anticipated general estate income appears significant, a lawyer or trust officer should be consulted to determine the fair figure to use as the estimated income from this source, and also for expert advice as to whether the use of a trust is desirable. Moreover, the large estate owner usually has problems that require analysis and recommendations under a comprehensive estate plan.

§*3.21. Other sources of income.* Whether or not there is a general estate of any consequence, there may be income from various sources other than investments to take into account. Social Security benefits are found in most situations today. Tables are readily available to the life underwriter for estimating survivor benefits and retirement income from this source.

Many employees who are not entitled to Social Security benefits are covered under special acts. For example, railroad employees receive similar benefits under the Railroad Retirement Act. Moreover, time spent in covered employment under the Social Security Act is taken into account when computing benefits for railroad employees.

Permanent employees of the federal government, who are also currently excluded from Social Security coverage, receive retirement benefits for themselves and survivor benefits for their families under the Civil Service Retirement Act.

In addition, a great many persons may be entitled to servicemen's and veterans' benefits by reason of their identification with the armed forces of the United States. Payments for themselves or their families may be an important factor in evaluating needs and setting up the life insurance program. Certain of these benefits may be interrelated with Social Security. For example, persons now on active duty are fully covered under this act, like other employees. Also, service between September 16, 1940, and January 1, 1957, earned special "military credits" which may have a lasting effect for veterans of such service.

In recent years, considerable impetus has been given to fringe benefits for employees. Many private employers provide liberal insurance and pension benefits under company plans. Individual death benefits may also be provided by employers for particular key employees. The estate of the client may be entitled to receive payments under an agreement for the purchase of his interest in a small business when he dies. He may be presently entitled to principal and income under either a testamentary or living trust set up by some other person. If the principal and income are not presently payable to the client, or a member of his family, there may be a definite expectancy of payments at some future time.

The alert underwriter must be constantly on the lookout for facts of the type discussed in this section, so that decisions will be based on a complete and true estate picture.

F. IMPORTANCE OF FLEXIBILITY

§3.22. The effect of inflexibility.   Many cases are seen in which the entire program is set up to furnish precise income for virtually all purposes except the clean-up fund. If such a program is not scrupulously kept up to date, a lapsed policy, a heavy loan outstanding at the insured's death, or a change in economic conditions can result in real hardship for the family. Even if it is reviewed frequently and conscientiously, such a "tight" program becomes "frozen" on the insured's death. Often there is little or no provision for adjustment to meet the many emergencies and changes in the family picture that are bound to occur.

Some of the greatest hardships resulting from inflexibility are perhaps most often found in settlement plans which provide adequately for college or other deferred needs, but lack even minimum provision for more immediate requirements. Such a settlement option agreement was involved in the case of *McLaughlin* v. *Equitable Life Assurance Society of the United States,* 112 N.J. Eq. 344, 164 Atl. 579, decided in 1933 by the highest state court in New Jersey. The "educational fund agreement" provided for retention of the proceeds under the Interest Option until the son had attained age 18, after which they were to be paid in installments over a four-year period. The insured died while the son was many years younger than 18, leaving no general estate and apparently without other life insurance. The child's guardian attempted to obtain a court order directing payment of $25 weekly from the insurance fund for the much-needed maintenance and support of the son. The court ruled that the settlement provision, containing no permissive withdrawal clause, constituted an unchangeable contract between the insured and the company, and that the court could not consider evidence of what the deceased insured might have intended.

Similar reasoning was adopted by the Michigan Supreme Court in the case of *Pierowich* v. *Metropolitan Life Insurance Co.,* 282 Mich. 118, 275 N.W. 789 (1937). After a divorce, the insured changed the beneficiary from his wife to his two sons, aged eight and ten. A settlement option agreement provided that each son's share of the proceeds should be retained, and that interest should be compounded annually under each share until the son attained age 21, when the principal plus the compound interest accumulations were to be paid to him in one sum. The insured died six months later. The mother as guardian sought to obtain from the proceeds such funds as the court might find necessary to maintain and educate the children properly. The mother stated she was without funds for this purpose. The court said: "The disposition of the property has been fixed by contract, and this court cannot alter the terms thereof even in view of the changed now existing conditions."

Except as this problem may be solved by a statute like Section 17 (2) of the New York Personal Property Law, an insured can cause undue hardship to his family by committing errors of inflexibility such as these just described. The New York statute provides that where life insurance proceeds are retained by the company under an agreement to credit the interest, and the beneficiary is destitute of means of support or education, the court may order a suitable sum applied for the support and education of such beneficiary from the interest credited or to be credited. Since the principal may not be invaded under this statute, the law is obviously very limited in its application and its potential relief. Moreover, provisions of this type are not common under statutes of other states.

§*3.23. Two kinds of flexibility.* This chapter has shown numerous examples of how basic family needs can be met by settlement options in a practical and flexible manner. On the other hand, there are certain needs which require definite, regular income of a type that permits of little flexibility after the income starts. For example, once payments commence under the Life Income Option or under certain forms of special policies, the die is cast. To a certain extent, this is good, because the beneficiary is assured a basic income that will be unaffected by adversity or by the temptation to withdraw principal in anticipation of future payments.

The underwriter's problem in this regard is twofold. First, he must help his client maintain a balance between settlement provisions that can be partially or completely flexible and those which must necessarily provide little or no room for adjustment. Second, he must assume the responsibility of reviewing the program with the client at regular intervals, such as each year or two. Families grow and change. Accordingly, a life insurance program is not built in a day, but rather evolves over the years. It will change both as to amounts and as to the settlement options applied to the policies covered by the program. It is the underwriter's job to keep the program as fluid as possible, both before and after his client's death.

Chapter 4

General Rules and Practices
Governing Use of Settlement Options

§*4.1.* *Introduction and scope of this chapter.* The preceding chapters indicate the wide variation in company practices relating to use of the settlement options. In substance, the settlement provisions of many contracts merely grant the insured, or the beneficiary of a one sum settlement after his death, the right to elect just one of the settlement options in lieu of cash, with payments to commence immediately. Rarely do contracts spell out the right to elect more than one option or the right of a contingent beneficiary to select an option.

In practice, the companies have recognized that the requirements of many policyowners could not be met by strict adherence to the letter of the settlement option provisions in their policies. Accordingly, in recognition of their obligation to render a complete service, companies generally permit arrangements extending far beyond contractual rights.

In these circumstances, it cannot be expected that the practices of the various companies will be uniform. It is manifestly impossible to set forth all these varying practices within the confines of a single chapter, or, for that matter, within a complete textbook. Even a summary of the practices would mean little, because they are constantly changing, and furthermore, up-to-date information is available elsewhere. This chapter covers some of the problems the life underwriter frequently encounters, and the range of company practices on these problems.

The life underwriter working on a particular case should consult one or more of the loose-leaf or annually revised compends or services published for this purpose, such as Diamond Life Bulletins, Flitcraft Compend, Settlement Options by Flitcraft, Handy Guide, Little Gem, or Research and Review Advanced Underwriting Service. Flitcraft's Settlement Options is particularly useful in giving precise answers on the more usual settlement option practices of more than 100 life insurance companies. Of course, the companies themselves are the logical source of such information, as well as the most reliable. However, the type of publications mentioned above will answer most of the life underwriter's questions in a given case, at a considerable saving of time and effort.

A. Who May Elect Options and Receive Income

§4.2. In general. The owner of a life insurance policy usually possesses, among other "incidents of ownership," the right to specify that proceeds shall be payable under one of the settlement options. Also, an option generally may be elected after the insured's death by a beneficiary entitled to a one sum payment.

Most policies are issued on the application of the person to be insured, who becomes the policyowner. Many contracts are also issued on the basis of third-party ownership, under which someone other than the insured applies for the insurance, has absolute ownership of all the rights in the policy, and usually pays the premiums. Such contracts are often found in business insurance cases involving either a buy-and-sell agreement or key man insurance. They are also found in family situations when a wife may own insurance on the life of her husband or a child on the lives of his parents, or vice versa.

Ownership of a policy, whether originating in the insured or in a third party (the company and the insured being the other two parties), usually may be transferred by an assignment or by an instrument in the nature of an assignment. Contracts may also be owned jointly by two or more owners. For ownership transfer, companies usually provide forms which are keyed to the needs of a particular policy. Ownership provisions are described more fully in Section 5.10.

Application of the general rule that a policyowner may select settlement options varies considerably in practice. Whether a settlement option arrangement can be elected in a given case may depend on whether the policyowner is a natural person or an entity, such as a corporation, partnership, trust, or an estate. Many policies provide that the payee under a settlement option must be a natural person who will receive payments in his or her own right. Some policies state that an assignee may not elect a settlement option. Election of options under assigned policies is further discussed in Section 5.9.

§4.3. *The insured as owner.* Much of the material in Chapters 2 and 3 covers settlement plans set up by the insured for payment of death benefits to the beneficiary. The insured may also use the settlement options for payments to himself, assuming of course that he is the owner of the policy.

Under most endowment policies, the insured may have the proceeds at endowment maturity retained under settlement options for his own benefit. Indeed, the Internal Revenue Code today encourages the election of installment options by giving many such arrangements a tax advantage over a one sum maturity settlement. The various types of retirement income policies discussed in Chapter 2 are usually written to mature automatically under one of the Life Income Options, subject to the insured's right to select some other arrangement.

Most often, the insured may also place the cash surrender value of a policy under the settlement options. However, this right will not always be found in the policy contract, particularly if the contract was issued some years ago. In such cases, the company will usually be willing to add this privilege by amendment.

In some cases, the amendment states that the insured may use the settlement options already contained in the policy. In others, the amendment may include similar or additional options for the insured's use, with different rates than those in the original policy. The rates may be those appearing in new policies being issued at the time of the amendment, or they may be similar to rates in earlier policies. Sometimes the original policy, or amendment at a later date, may require that the policy be in force for a certain length of time, such as five or ten years, or that the insured attain a minimum age, such as 50 or 55, before the options can be used for his benefit.

§4.4. *An individual as beneficiary.* If the policy is payable in one sum to a natural person taking in his or her own right, the contract usually provides that the beneficiary may elect an income option in lieu of cash. Where a settlement option agreement has been set up before death of the insured, an individual beneficiary may be able to elect a different option or combination of options, but only to the extent that such election is specifically permitted by the agreement or in the policy itself. However, in certain instances, company practice may extend to a beneficiary privileges which are not specifically contained in the agreement. For example, if the settlement option agreement in force at the time of the insured's death grants an unlimited right of withdrawal to the beneficiary, companies will often allow the beneficiary to elect any other option, just as if the policy were actually payable in one sum. In some cases, an option granted to such a beneficiary would be based on current rates in effect for new policies being issued at the time of election, as explained in Section 2.3.

In a one sum settlement, the beneficiary is given reasonable time to decide whether to take the one sum or to settle all or part of the proceeds under a settlement option. What is considered reasonable will vary considerably from company to company. Sometimes, the proceeds will remain idle, without drawing interest, until the beneficiary decides what to do, although the modern trend is to allow interest from the date of the insured's death. A number of companies will allow interest from the date of death only if the election is made within a specified time after death, as explained in Section 2.2.

While the primary beneficiary of a one sum settlement can usually work out acceptable arrangements to meet his or her own needs, such a beneficiary sometimes may not select options for contingent beneficiaries. In many such cases, the primary beneficiary cannot designate contingent beneficiaries. Companies may insist that any balance of proceeds at the primary beneficiary's death must be paid to his or her estate.

In contrast, a settlement option agreement executed before the insured's death usually can name contingent beneficiaries, even though it may allow the primary beneficiary complete freedom as to withdrawal of proceeds and change of options. Such an agreement may also grant the contingent beneficiaries the right to elect settlement options, or the agreement may at least specify settlement options for such beneficiaries.

§4.5. *An individual owner other than the insured.* In general, an individual who owns a policy on the life of another may elect settlement options in the same manner that an election might have been made by the insured. In fact, the policy clause or instrument indicating such ownership frequently states that all rights and privileges are vested in the "owner." Such an owner is often the primary beneficiary as well, and may elect options in that capacity after the insured's death. During the insured's lifetime, the owner can normally elect options for his or her own benefit or name other beneficiaries and elect options for them.

In some cases, notwithstanding the transfer under an absolute assignment of all the incidents of ownership, the assignee may be prevented by contract provision from electing an income option. In other cases, the assignee may be permitted to select an option for the insured or for a beneficiary other than himself. It is important to consult the precise provisions of the policy to determine the extent to which an individual owner other than the insured may elect settlement options. Company practices and policy provisions vary substantially in this area.

§*4.6.* *Corporations and partnerships as owners.* A corporate owner may usually elect settlement options for individual beneficiaries to the same extent as the insured or other individual owner. In addition, a corporation other than a trustee may sometimes elect to have proceeds retained under certain of the settlement options for its own benefit. Normally the use of options must be identified with a legitimate business purpose other than the mere desire to make an investment. Even then, the election may be limited as to the type of option available, or as to the period of time during which income will be paid to the corporation. As an example of a business purpose, a corporation may wish to fund an obligation to pay a retirement income to a retired insured or to continue the insured's salary to his dependents for some period after his death. If a policy on his life maintained by the corporation is simply turned over to him, the entire value of the policy may be taxed as income to him in the year of retirement. The same result may follow if the employer elects an option under which the insurer is obligated to make payments directly to the employee or his beneficiary. Accordingly, the corporation may request that the income payments under the policy be paid to it, without legally coupling these payments to its retirement income obligations to the employee.

A few companies will permit a corporate or partnership owner or beneficiary to use options other than the Life Income Option for its own benefit, without inquiring into the purpose of the election. However, in most cases which do not involve funding an obligation to an employee or his family, the corporation or partnership will normally desire a one sum settlement.

§4.7. *Trustees as owners.* Whether a trustee as owner or beneficiary may elect a settlement option depends in large measure on the terms of the agreement under which the trust is created and the rules of the company whose life insurance policy is involved.

The trustee's authority to elect a settlement option may be found in a specific provision in the trust agreement, or in a general provision that investments need not be confined to those classed as "legal" investments for fiduciaries. In absence of such authority, there is serious question whether a trustee may elect a settlement option, except as a court may follow the conclusion of *Latterman* v. *Guardian Life Insurance Co.,* 280 N.Y. 102, 19 N.E.2d 978 (1939), discussed in Section 5.8, that settlement options are not "investments."

A far more significant question is the practice of the life insurance company. As a general rule, trustees are not permitted to use settlement options. Trustees, whether corporate or individual, properly charge reasonable fees for their services. Normally, these services include a responsibility for investing the trust principal to produce income for beneficiaries of the trust. It has been suggested that life insurance companies should not absorb any part of the cost of making trust investments by permitting trustees to use settlement options.

At the same time, trustees as owners or named beneficiaries of life insurance policies are often permitted to elect settlement options for the benefit of specific trust beneficiaries. The practices of companies differ considerably regarding the election of an option by or for the benefit of a trustee. The purpose of such an election may make a difference in the company's decision. As discussed in Section 3.15, some companies will permit payments due a minor beneficiary to be paid to a trustee for the minor without the formality of a separate trust agreement.

In a qualified pension or profit-sharing trust, ownership of any life insurance or annuity policies used to fund a plan is usually vested in the trustees. Therefore, the trustees must elect any settlement option involved in providing retirement income to an employee, or income for the benefit of the employee's beneficiaries in event of his death before retirement. Usually, the trustees will honor a request from the employee in this regard, subject to the terms of the trust, the terms of the policies, and the practice of the life insurance company. Some qualified trusts or plans (and some policies issued under them) may reserve directly to the insured or annuitant the right to change beneficiaries or elect settlement options for such beneficiaries.

§*4.8.*   *Executors, guardians, committees, and other fiduciaries.*   Since the duty of the personal representative of an estate is to liquidate the assets of the decedent, it is doubtful whether he may elect an option unless the policy or settlement agreement expressly provides for such election. However, executors or administrators may sometimes elect options for payment to an individual, and may derive limited direct benefit from options in certain types of business insurance cases. In many instances, the insurance company would require a court order before permitting a personal representative to elect a settlement option.

Of course, when ownership in a policy on the life of someone other than the decedent is involved, the personal representative not only has the right, but also the duty, to transfer it in accordance with the provisions of the will. In such a case, the insurance company will often require a copy of the court's order for distribution before completing the transfer.

Life insurance benefits payable directly to minors or persons who are legally incompetent normally must be paid to a guardian, committee, or trustee. In turn, any rights the ward may have to elect settlement options in lieu of a one sum payment, to withdraw funds, or to change options under an existing settlement agreement, must usually be exercised by the fiduciary. Again, the insurance company may require a copy of the authorizing court order.

The extent to which options can be so elected involves not only the practices of individual companies but also the law of the state having jurisdiction. For example, statutes in some states permit minors over a specified age to enter into certain direct transactions with life insurance companies. These legal aspects are covered in detail in Section 5.8.

§*4.9. Business insurance cases.*   Life insurance is frequently used to fund buy-and-sell agreements disposing of closely held business interests at death. The essence of such a transaction is that the insured agrees to sell his interest in the business at the time of his death to the purchaser named in the buy-and-sell agreement. The purchaser of that interest may be the partnership or corporation, or the individual partners or shareholders themselves. In some instances, such a buy-and-sell arrangement is used in sole proprietorships.

The insurance is taken out to fund part or all of the purchase price to be paid for transfer of the decedent's business interest. However, since in many cases the insurance proceeds will be used ultimately to guarantee security for the decedent's family, there may be a strong desire to utilize settlement options for their benefit. Various methods have been used to satisfy this desire. Some of them have created serious legal and other problems.

One method that may accomplish this purpose satisfactorily is to name the insured's estate as primary beneficiary, the insured's wife as contingent beneficiary, and, perhaps, the insured's children as second contingent beneficiaries. The Interest Option with full withdrawal privileges may be elected for the insured's estate as primary beneficiary. If the executor does not withdraw the proceeds during a stated period, such as 18 months, the proceeds then become available for the succeeding beneficiaries under whatever settlement arrangement is specified. The stated preliminary period is designed to give the executor opportunity to withdraw any proceeds needed to satisfy claims of creditors of the decedent. If such creditors are not satisfied, there is a danger that they can pursue the business interest in the hands of the purchasers. The decedent's will, then, should instruct his executor not to withdraw the proceeds unless other suitable assets are unavailable to pay creditors.

In some instances, the attorney may suggest what appears to be a still better arrangement—that is, to name the purchaser of the business interest as primary beneficiary, with the decedent's estate as first contingent beneficiary and the widow as second contingent beneficiary. The purpose of this suggestion will be to assure the purchaser of complete protection, especially to obtain the proper credit toward his cost basis for federal income tax purposes. The Interest Option can be specified in the manner suggested above. However, since the purchaser's withdrawal privilege is included primarily to satisfy an income tax technicality, the period during which it may be exercised can be very short, such as 30 or 60 days following the insured's death. For the same reason, the purchaser can actually release his interest immediately after the insured's death. As soon thereafter as the executor is satisfied that there are no unpaid creditors of the decedent, he too can release the interest of the estate and thereby start the income arrangement for the insured's family.

The use of settlement options in business insurance cases may not be practical in some cases because of company limitations or prohibitions, or because of objections the attorney may see to the arrangement in the light of the facts. This subject is somewhat complicated and requires careful study by an experienced lawyer. Some companies publish informative booklets that discuss the tax and other problems under buy-and-sell arrangements.

B. BASIC RULES ON USE OF OPTIONS

§4.10. Minimum amount requirements. As a rule, not less than $1,000 may be placed under a settlement option. If the proceeds of a policy are split into two or more funds for use with different options, this minimum usually applies to each fund. Similarly, it applies to the share held for each beneficiary. Thus, a policy large enough to meet the rule in providing income for a widow might have to be paid in one sum if several children become payees as contingent beneficiaries. In a number of companies, this minimum has been increased in recent years to $2,000.

A minimum installment is often specified in the policy. Ten dollars is the usual figure, with policies reserving the right to make payments less frequently than specified in the settlement agreement to equal or exceed this minimum figure. Many companies have set a minimum of $20 or $25 per installment per beneficiary.

As mentioned in Section 2.5, usually an additional requirement in connection with the Fixed Amount Option is disbursement of a minimum amount per year for each $1,000 of proceeds initially placed under the option. The minimum may be expressed as $5.00 or $6.00 per month per $1,000, or as a percentage, such as 4, 5, or 6 percent per year. The purpose of this rule is to assure that all proceeds and interest will be paid out in a reasonable period of time.

§*4.11. Time limitations.* Company rules limiting the length of time that proceeds will be retained under a settlement option are applied primarily to the Interest Option. Under the various Life Income Options, payments will be made over the entire lifetime of one or more persons. Generally, guaranteed payments under the certain-period provisions of such options are limited to periods of 20 years or less, except in the case of a Refund Life Income Option elected at a very young age. Fixed period or fixed amount installments usually are not provided for more than 30 years, though the formula minimum in the latter may permit a slightly longer period.

The Interest Option presents a different problem, because the company may be directed to hold proceeds intact without right of withdrawal by the beneficiary. If such a right is provided, the beneficiary might not exercise it fully during his or her lifetime. Without some rule, a company might conceivably be requested to hold proceeds at interest forever, or at least to the fullest extent permitted by law.

Most companies are willing to retain proceeds at interest for the lifetime of a primary beneficiary or until the death of the survivor of joint primary beneficiaries. Some companies will extend this period for the lifetime of a contingent beneficiary as well, but many will not. Frequently, a limit of 30 years after the death of the insured is specified for proceeds retained at interest for a contingent beneficiary. However, this is often expressed as "30 years or until the prior death of the contingent beneficiary," so as to require payment in one sum to second contingent beneficiaries. In a few cases, the maximum retention for a contingent beneficiary is related to the age of that beneficiary, such as 21, 25, 30, or 35.

Closely related to time limitations are rules governing payment of installments or interest to successive beneficiaries or classes of beneficiaries. As indicated above, interest payments usually will not be continued to a third beneficiary. However, family income or family maintenance installments are more often permitted for third beneficiaries, particularly if the beneficiaries are children, or the parents or other aged relatives of the insured. This is also true in the case of fixed period or fixed amount installments.

§*4.12. Privileges of withdrawal, commutation, and change of option.* The extent to which various privileges may be given beneficiaries in setting up a settlement option agreement is discussed in Chapter 2, in connection with each type of income option. In general, considerable flexibility can be provided under the Interest Option and the Fixed Amount Option, and very little under the Fixed Period and Life Income Options. A number of companies will permit commutation and withdrawal of the income installments under family income and family maintenance policies. Often, a settlement option may be elected for payment of all or part of such one sum value. However, a number of companies will not permit any such change in these contracts.

Where a privilege of withdrawal is incorporated in the settlement option agreement, the maximum limits may usually be set by the person electing the settlement option. Whether withdrawals are to be unlimited, restricted to a certain amount per year or to an aggregate amount, whether the limited yearly amounts are to be cumulative or noncumulative, are questions with which the companies usually are not concerned themselves, except as necessary to avoid unduly long and complex agreements. However, companies have found it necessary to establish their own rules as to the frequency of permitted withdrawals and as to the minimum amount of each withdrawal. The minimum which may be withdrawn at any one time ranges from $10 to as high as $500, but most companies specify $100. A few have no minimum requirement. Some companies limit withdrawals to a stated number, such as three, four, or six per year, but few enforce such a rule in cases of demonstrated emergency.

Most policies reserve the right to delay cash withdrawals under the settlement options for a period of up to six months. The provision is similar to that governing withdrawals from savings accounts, building and loan associations, and other deposit institutions. It is also similar to the right reserved by life insurance companies in connection with loan and surrender values. It is intended to protect the institution against a "run" in case of panic or severe depression, and, therefore, the rule is rarely invoked in ordinary circumstances.

As discussed in Chapter 2, provisions may be included in many settlement agreements for a change from one option to another, either automatically at a specified time or on the happening of a certain event, or at the option of the beneficiary. The Interest Option and Fixed Amount Option afford the most flexibility in this regard, but it is often possible to incorporate such provisions in electing the Fixed Period or Life Income Options. In these, such provisions are more often available with respect to settling the commuted value of unpaid installments certain payable to contingent beneficiaries.

The rules governing changes from one option to another vary perhaps more widely among the different companies than do those governing other practices. What might be expected is set forth in more detail in Chapter 2, which describes the various types of options and their characteristics. Certain of these rules are also amplified in Chapter 3 in connection with specific uses of the various options.

Generally speaking, more flexibility can be provided for primary beneficiaries than for contingent beneficiaries, and usually considerably less for second contingent beneficiaries. Also, with some companies, more flexibility can be written into an agreement set up by the policyowner in advance than can be obtained by a beneficiary electing settlement options after the insured's death. This is particularly true of rights to change options or to designate or change contingent beneficiaries.

§*4.13. Income rates in policy versus current rates.* One of the most important guarantees a policyowner purchases concerns the income rates for settlement option payments. Because of this guarantee, the minimum amount of income which will be available from the policy at a given time, either for a beneficiary or for the insured himself, is known exactly in advance and will not be changed as a result of fluctuations in the economy.

On the other hand, this guarantee often relates only to the election of a specific settlement option at death, at maturity of an endowment, or on surrender of the contract. Where a beneficiary is given the privilege of changing from one option to another, and particularly from the Interest Option to the Fixed Period Option or Fixed Amount Option, the great majority of companies will permit the change at any time at rates of income guaranteed in the policy. Almost half the companies will allow the beneficiary the same right as respects change to a Life Income Option. As explained in Section 2.3, the other companies impose some limit on the privilege of changing to a Life Income Option, such as requiring that the change must be made within a specified period, for example, one year after the insured's death or after the right accrues to the beneficiary, if income rates stated in the policy are to be assured.

Most companies will guarantee rates of income in the policy under settlement option agreements providing for a change in options if the change is to occur automatically, without control by the payee. At least one company provides that rates for the Life Income Option will depend on how long after the policy issue date the income is to

commence. This is accomplished by means of an age adjustment table which adds or subtracts years from the payee's
age, based on the calendar year in which the income is to
start. This formula is designed to provide that the sooner
the life income commences, the higher the rate of return
will be. The "adjusted age" is then applied to the standard
Life Income Option tables in the policy.

The companies are not arbitrary in imposing these
limitations. They reason that the actuarial computations
under the Life Income Option are based on the assumption
of an average mortality experience with no element of selection on the beneficiary's part. If an unlimited right of
change is available to the beneficiary, it is conceivable that
beneficiaries in poor health would tend to refrain from
electing the Life Income Option, whereas all healthy ones
would tend to make the change to it. Should this happen,
there is possibility of loss to the company. The various de-
grees of limitations in their practices reflect the extent to
which the companies are concerned with this danger of
adverse selection. Company practices may also depend on
the extent of their exposure to the election of policy guarantees which are unrealistically high as measured by current standards.

Company practices also vary widely with respect to
adding to a policy options which were not included when it
was issued. Generally, such additional options include joint
and survivor annuities and other variations of the Life Income Options. Some companies will add these to old policies on the basis of the rates in effect when the policy was
issued. In many cases, however, these options are added on
the basis of current rates in effect at the time they are requested to be endorsed or attached to the policy. For this
reason, many life underwriters automatically request such
options in applications for new contracts.

Sometimes, the income rates available to the insured
at retirement are related to a policy provision permitting

the contract to be converted or exchanged for another form having a higher cash value. Such policies may provide that income rates guaranteed by the old policy will apply only to the portion of the cash value originally provided by that policy. Current income rates are applicable to any additional cash value developed by the new contract. However, a number of policies issued in recent years provide that income rates in the old policy will apply to the full cash value of the converted contract.

§4.14. Proceeds from additional accidental death benefits. Some policies state that accidental death benefits will be payable under the same settlement plan selected for the regular proceeds. This will result in increasing the income under most of the options, but it usually operates to extend the period of income under the Fixed Amount Option. Other policies provide that in the absence of any special instructions, accidental death benefits will be paid in one sum. Usually in such cases, the beneficiary may elect to receive the additional benefits under an option. With some companies, payment of the additional death benefit will depend on what is requested when the settlement option is elected.

Sometimes, the policy provisions are not clear. In *Liner* v. *Penn Mutual Life Insurance Co.,* 286 App. Div. 517, 145 N.Y.S.2d 560 (1955), the company contended that accidental death proceeds should extend the period of monthly installments under the Fixed Amount Option. The court sided with the beneficiary, ruling that the specified installments should be doubled in amount.

In a family income or family maintenance policy, this additional insurance will increase the income installments only slightly, because the only additional payment during the installment period will consist of interest paid on the extra funds. The final face amount or the income provided by it under a settlement agreement would normally be increased.

The contingency of accidental death is somewhat remote. However, the possible effect of such added payments should be considered carefully in the light of whatever provisions are contained in the contract. Then, if some other arrangement is desired, it should be set forth clearly in the settlement agreement.

Company practices often permit payment of the accidental death benefit to a different beneficiary or in a different manner than that provided for payment of the face amount.

It may be important to consider to what extent added payments from accidental death benefits will subject the estate to federal estate tax, and what effect these payments will have on the amount of the total estate qualified for the marital deduction.

§4.15. Loans, dividends, and advance premium deposits. In general, the proceeds of a policy will be decreased by any loan outstanding at the time of the insured's death, and increased by the amount of any dividend accumulations or the face amount of paid-up dividend additions. Similarly, the stated cash surrender value of the policy usually is decreased by outstanding loans and increased by the cash value of any dividend accumulations or additions. In all cases, the amount of loan deducted includes interest to the date of death or surrender. Premiums deposited in advance, generally at a discount, are usually considered as belonging to the policyowner and are payable to him or to his estate in event of his death. Sometimes, these deposits are considered as a part of the policy proceeds and, if so, may be included with other funds under a settlement option, or may be paid in one sum to the beneficiary.

Companies appear to be almost evenly divided on the practice of permitting the beneficiary to repay a policy loan after the insured's death in order to restore the full amount of insurance that might be payable under a settlement option. This possibility may be an important point to keep in mind in planning settlements and in estimating the amount of the clean-up fund. Incidentally, the two major government insurance programs have opposite provisions in this regard. Under U.S. Government Life Insurance, the regulations have been formally interpreted to allow the beneficiary to repay loans after the insured's death. On the other hand, National Service Life Insurance regulations specifically prohibit the beneficiary from repaying loans.

C. SETTLEMENT OPTION AGREEMENT PROCEDURES

§4.16. Requests for settlement option agreements. Settlement option agreements may be requested in the application for a new policy, in a memorandum accompanying it, or as separate transactions from time to time during the life of the policy. To implement the request, the company then prepares an agreement in proper legal form for the policyowner's signature. Requests from one sum beneficiaries after death of the insured are usually handled in connection with the claim papers.

1. *Requests under new insurance.* The desired settlement plan may be specified in the application for new insurance. Some companies provide for automatic "Interest Option—all privileges" settlement in the contract or in a special rider that may be requested in the application, as mentioned in Section 2.2. Rarely, however, will the application have enough space for any but the simplest of plans, and a separate memorandum often will be preferable.

In many cases, it may be better to specify a simple beneficiary arrangement on a one sum basis until the policy is placed in force, then request the settlement option agreement as a change of beneficiary, as discussed in the following paragraph. If a valid beneficiary is not named in the policy pursuant to a request signed by the policyowner, the untimely death of the insured may require court action to determine who is entitled to payment of the policy proceeds.

2. *Requests under existing insurance.* There are two usual ways to prepare a request for a settlement option agreement. One is to write a letter for the policyowner's signature; the other is to write a letter for the life underwriter's signature, with a separate note from the policyowner directing the company to deal directly with the underwriter. A check-off form such as that shown in Appendix A may be substituted in either case.

Some underwriters feel that having the policyowner sign each request helps him realize the extent of the service rendered him. In such cases, a letter may be easier for the client to understand. On the other hand, a checklist may save valuable time and help to prevent overlooking an important point. Even where a checklist is not used as the actual request, it may be helpful as a guide in preparing request letters.

Most companies will recognize the life underwriter of another company only on written authorization from the policyowner. In a letter-request to be signed by the policyowner, this can be expressed somewhat as follows:

> Re: Policy No.
> Insured:

Gentlemen:

> Please furnish Mr. John Underwriter, 122 First Street, Green Village, New York, the necessary forms to accomplish the following with respect to the above policies in your company:

> . . . .

> You are hereby authorized and directed to give Mr. Underwriter any additional information and forms he may request in connection with this insurance. Your cooperation in this matter will be appreciated.

If the letter of request for a settlement option agreement is to be signed by the underwriter, a separate note of authorization should be attached. This can take much the same form as the two paragraphs suggested on page 124.

Some companies prepare all settlement option agreements in the home office. In such instances, when requests are directed to the local agency, an extra courtesy copy for the agency's file will speed service, because it obviates the need for copying the request for transmittal to the home office. However, the trend is to have such agreements prepared in the agency field office, or even in the insured's home or office, on simplified forms, as explained in Section 4.17. Handling requests will be expedited if the particular company's practice is ascertained so the requests may be directed to the proper office.

3. *Executing the settlement agreements.* When an insurance programing case involves more than one company, it is well to defer having any forms or agreements signed until all are received. Not only is it possible that a major change in the pattern for one policy may require modifications in the others, but it saves time to have the policyowner execute all forms at one sitting.

4. *Importance of "keeping it simple."* Despite the wide variations in practice among companies, the requirements of most policyowners and beneficiaries can be met efficiently and simply by almost any company. It is easy to be tempted into requesting all the possible privileges and special features that a company can be persuaded to grant, whether or not they are needed. As a result, many settlement option agreements are unnecessarily long and complex. There is a tendency to cover too many remote contingencies. Similarly, many beneficiary designations appear aimed at listing all the relatives of the insured, no matter how small their chances of collecting benefits.

To set up complex arrangements requires more time and correspondence. They tend to get out of date quickly and so demand frequent review and revision. All this is expensive in time and money for everyone concerned.

Most of the needs found in life insurance programing are basically simple. Most often, the settlement option agreements to provide for these needs can also be simple. Frequently, an agreement covering a single policy can take care of several needs without even the necessity of dividing the proceeds into separate funds for each need.

Of course, there is such a thing as being too simple, and this should be avoided just as carefully as undue complexity. Undoubtedly it would be "simpler" for the policyowner to leave all his insurance in one sum, or under the equivalent Interest Option with privileges of withdrawal or change, in the sense that he would thereby escape deciding now how his insurance should actually be arranged for best results. But this could prove far from simple for the beneficiary the insurance is supposed to protect, for she would inherit the full responsibility for deciding on the actual program of settlement to be put into effect.

Provided the underwriter is prepared to meet his responsibilities for continuous service, it is often better for the underwriter, the client, and his wife to work out these plans together, while the client is still alive. Changes can be made as often as necessary during the insured's lifetime to keep the plan up to date, and this approach helps to "keep it simple" on a sound basis.

§*4.17. Mechanical procedures.*   Beneficiary designations and settlement option elections, or changes in either, do not become effective until executed by the policyowner on forms acceptable to the company, and either endorsed on the policy or recorded officially by the company, as the company practice may require.

Agreements electing settlement options are made effective in one of two ways. Historically, all changes of beneficiary and elections of options were required to be endorsed physically on the policy itself, like any other amendment to the contract. This practice is still followed by a number of companies. However, there is a trend toward recording such changes in the home office and leaving it up to the policyowner to attach or file with the policy a copy of the beneficiary designation and settlement option agreement.

When the change is to be endorsed on the policy, the company will request that the policy be returned with all copies of the signed and witnessed settlement option agreement. The home office will insert the original agreement, or a photocopy, in the policy and return it to the owner or his agent. Sometimes, the entire agreement is copied or digested in the space provided in the policy for endorsements, but most agreements are too long for this to be practical.

The recording technique involves an agreement generally prepared in triplicate or quadruplicate, all copies of which must often be signed, witnessed, and returned to the home office. One copy is then returned to the policyowner or his agent, bearing a certification that the settlement plan has been recorded in the home office of the company and has been made effective as of a specified date. This method has become increasingly popular because it saves time and expense. Many companies today require that only the original copy be signed, and some have moved away from the witnessing requirement.

Economies have also been effected under both methods by the trend away from manuscript settlement option agreements to forms containing all or most of the possible settlement option arrangements printed in advance. As the name indicates, the manuscript form is, in effect, a legal instrument which is drafted and typed individually for each settlement option request. Certain of the standard paragraphs, such as the spendthrift clause, may be inserted by an automatic typewriter, but, essentially, the document and the control of the automatic paragraphs is an individual task involving a qualified key employee and a typist.

The first step away from individually prepared agreements is the kind of form which contains printed standard clauses together with blank spaces in which the beneficiary designation and distributive provisions can be typed. Obviously, the more provisions that can be incorporated in the printed sections, the shorter can be the typed sections. This procedure is now in use by a substantial number of companies.

In recent years, a number of companies have developed "block" forms for electing settlement options, thus eliminating manuscript or partially printed forms in all but a small percentage of cases. The block form seeks to cover by printed paragraphs virtually all the possible ways in which the settlement options may be used, each paragraph keyed to a box. To set up such an agreement, the policyowner needs only to fill in the names of the beneficiaries, place a check mark or X in the appropriate boxes, and sign the form. The need for special distributive instructions is kept to an absolute minimum by forms of this type. An example of a modern block form is shown in Appendix B.

Most of the companies which have not adopted a full-fledged block form agreement have adapted this idea to forms used by the policyowner to request a settlement option agreement. In these cases, the request form is checked off by the policyowner and sent to the company, where it serves as an instruction sheet and checklist in drafting the formal settlement option agreement.

As indicated above, settlement option agreements usually include a designation of beneficiaries as well. Thus, the agreement normally starts off with a revocation of previous beneficiary designations and of any previous settlement option agreement. However, separate forms may be required to designate beneficiaries on the one hand and to set up a settlement option agreement on the other. If so, the settlement option agreement often refers to the beneficiaries as primary, contingent, second contingent, and final, or by a number identified with a particular beneficiary on the separate form which names the beneficiaries and indicates priority.

Electronic data processing may produce designs of settlement option agreements and revisions in procedures for recording beneficiary designations and changes to a degree not foreseeable today. However, companies which are installing or have installed EDP seemingly have not yet felt that beneficiary and settlement designations are the kind of operation on which electronic processes can be of significant value.

Chapter 5

Legal Aspects of Settlement Options

§5.1. *Introduction.* A general knowledge of some of the more important legal aspects of settlement options will help the life underwriter to understand what companies probably will or will not do in preparing settlement agreements and in administering proceeds under those agreements. Moreover, it will also help him to understand the reasons that motivate the companies in prescribing certain rules.

Generalizations are difficult, and many questions cannot be answered precisely. Each state has the right to pass statutes setting forth "ground rules" for life insurance policies that are subject to interpretation in that state. Where there is no statute on the precise question, the rule in a particular state may result from court decisions. A body of law largely built up on the precedent of earlier decisions is known as the "common law" of a state.

A federal law sometimes enters the picture. Examples are in the laws relating to bankruptcy and the enforcement of various federal tax liens.

§5.2. *Which state law governs?* If the home office of the life insurance company is in the same state in which the policyowner and the beneficiary live and have lived since the policy was issued, only the laws of that state will apply.

Often, however, the company may be in one state, the policyowner may live in a second, and the beneficiary may live in a third. A policyowner or beneficiary often moves to another state after the policy is issued and before the last payment is made by the company under one of the settlement options. The insured may die in still another state, although the place of death does not generally determine which state law governs.

Speaking very generally, purely procedural matters will be determined by the laws of the state where the action is filed. However, in most cases, substantive rights—those that go to the heart of the transaction—will be determined under one of these three principles:

(1) The court will look to the law of the state in which the contract was *made*. Here, it is necessary to determine where the last act took place to bring a binding contract into existence.

(2) The court will look to the law of the state where the contract is to be *performed*. Here, some courts have distinguished between performance of the obligations and formation of the contract itself.

(3) The court will look to the *intention* of the parties. To avoid complex questions of conflict of laws, the contracting parties sometimes specifically agree that the laws of a particular state shall apply. Courts generally uphold such provisions.

These rules apply to settlement option agreements just as they apply to other contracts. This interesting subject is thoroughly explored in Professor Carnahan's textbook, *Conflict of Laws and Life Insurance Contracts*, listed in the Bibliography in Appendix E.

§*5.3. Nature of the settlement option agreement.* Traditionally, a contract may be enforced only by a person who signs it as a contracting party. Other persons usually cannot sue under it. Courts recognize an exception to this rule, namely, if two parties make a contract for the benefit of a third party, it may be enforced by the third-party beneficiary.

1. *Third-party beneficiary contracts.* The beneficiary provision, including settlement options, under a life insurance policy is a recognized example of such a contract. Thus, the beneficiary may sue for payment of the proceeds after the life insurance company receives proof of the insured's death.

2. *Debtor-creditor relationship.* After the insured dies, the insurance company owes the proceeds to the beneficiary. This creates a debtor-creditor relationship, whether the proceeds are payable in one sum or under a settlement option. If a settlement option agreement was elected by the policyowner during the insured's lifetime, performance of that agreement after the insured's death is regarded merely as a continuation of the third-party beneficiary arrangement. If the beneficiary of a one sum payment elects to leave the proceeds under a settlement option, some courts have decided that there is no longer a third-party beneficiary contract, but rather a direct agreement between the insurance company and such beneficiary. Of course, if that beneficiary names contingent payees to receive any remaining payments after the beneficiary's death, such contingent payees will be regarded as third-party beneficiaries.

§*5.4. The settlement option agreement distinguished from a trust.* In a trust, the trustee holds title to specific trust property for a beneficiary. Under a settlement option agreement, on the other hand, the insurance company holds no specific property. It merely owes a debt to the beneficiary as a creditor. The insurance company's obligation is absolute, no matter how much or how little income it earns on its assets. Some life insurance companies specifically negate the trust relationship by stating in their settlement option agreements that the company may mingle the proceeds of the policy with general corporate assets. Under present laws, this result seems assured without such provision.

The charters of some life insurance companies permit them to exercise trust powers in the administration of settlement options. In practice, however, these companies rarely, if ever, exercise such powers today. Instead, they usually follow the general practice of holding the policy proceeds under the debtor-creditor concept.

§5.5. *The settlement option agreement as a disposition of property.* A transfer of property by the owner at the time of his death is a "testamentary disposition." It is a fundamental principle of law that such disposition may be made only by a will that complies with the required formalities of the particular state statute of wills. As a general rule, an attempt to dispose of property at death by other means will not be upheld. The property affected by that instrument will become part of the owner's estate.

Of course, the owner of property may give it away while he lives. He may also contract to transfer his property at death. Such contract will be upheld if it is not subject to revocation while he lives. An example may be found in a deed transferring title to real property which reserves a life interest to the grantor. Such contracts have been held not to involve a testamentary disposition. The transfer is regarded as taking place during the owner's lifetime rather than at his death.

The provisions of life insurance policies for payment of proceeds at death have been upheld even though such policies are not wills, are not generally given away during lifetime, and even though the policyowner reserves the right to change the beneficiary until the insured dies. Whether the life insurance proceeds are payable in one sum or in installments, the provisions for payment are upheld as a firmly established exception to the testamentary disposition rule.

Questions of testamentary disposition are not raised when the *policyowner* elects the settlement option, because of the well-recognized exception just discussed. However, in two leading cases, the question was raised when the *beneficiary*, entitled to a one sum payment of the death proceeds, made the election. In *Mutual Benefit Life Insurance Co. v. Ellis*, 125 F.2d 127 (2d Cir. 1942), a widow as beneficiary was entitled to receive the proceeds in one sum at the insured's death. She elected the Interest Option for her benefit. She reserved the right to withdraw the proceeds at any time. She directed that at her death the remaining proceeds should be paid to the insured's sisters. After the widow's later death, the administrator of her estate attacked the validity of the settlement agreement and made claim to the fund. In awarding the proceeds to the insured's sisters in accordance with the settlement agreement, the court said the transaction was not a testamentary disposition.

In *Hall* v. *Mutual Life Insurance Co. of New York*, 306 N.Y. 909, 119 N.E.2d 598 (1954), a daughter was entitled to receive the proceeds of a policy in one sum at the death of her insured father. She elected to have these proceeds retained by the company under the Interest Option, subject to her right of withdrawal. She specified that any proceeds remaining at her death were to be paid to her husband. The daughter divorced her husband. At her death, the daughter's executors attempted to upset the provisions for payment to the ex-husband as an invalid testamentary disposition. The ex-husband won. The court said it was in the public interest to recognize the validity of such "insurance" agreements. The testamentary disposition argument was brushed aside. Section 24-a of the New York Personal Property Law, enacted in 1952 before the appeals in the *Hall* case were decided, crystallizes into a statute what was to be the final ruling of the case: settlement option agreements are not testamentary dispositions.

The testamentary disposition question was also raised in a case where the insured elected to have the endowment maturity value retained during his lifetime under the Interest Option, with a full withdrawal privilege. *Toulouse* v. *New York Life Insurance Co.*, 40 Wash. 2d 538, 245 P.2d 205 (1952). The court, by a five to four vote, decided that the nieces and nephews who were named contingent payees were entitled to the proceeds, and that no testamentary disposition was involved. Perhaps because of fear of the testamentary disposition question raised in these cases, or perhaps because of practical reasons, the rules of many companies still prohibit complete freedom of action in settlement arrangements elected by beneficiaries to whom the proceeds are payable in one sum. For example, some companies will not permit naming of a contingent payee even if a full withdrawal right is reserved to a primary payee. Many companies will not permit the primary payee to reserve the right to change the contingent payee.

§*5.6. Rule against perpetuities.* Public policy requires that property stay in circulation. Accordingly, there are rules that limit the length of time during which property owners can deny to others the full enjoyment of property. At common law, the limitations are expressed in the form of a "rule against perpetuities." The transfer of property—in fact, the creation of any interest—will be upheld only if ownership *must* absolutely vest within the permissible time limit. This common law time limit is 21 years after the deaths of persons living at the date the property is transferred or the interest is created. The common law rule has been changed to some extent by statute in a few states.

Holmes v. *John Hancock Mutual Life Insurance Co.*, 288 N.Y. 106, 41 N.E.2d 909 (1942), was apparently the first decided case on the question whether the rule against perpetuities applies to a settlement agreement. This case ruled that the New York statute did not apply. The court said if this were a trust fund, the directions would have been void under the statute. However, the court ruled that the proceeds of a life insurance policy were not a trust fund but rather a debt owing by the company to the beneficiary, and that the statute did not apply to such an obligation.

It is generally felt today that the rule against perpetuities is not applicable to settlement option agreements, because such agreements merely create a debtor-creditor relationship. However, in *First National Bank & Trust Co. v. Purcell*, 244 S.W.2d 458 (Ky. 1951), the court said such settlement option agreements do involve transfers of contract rights, and, therefore, the rule against perpetuities would apply. Under the particular facts, however, the court held that the rule was not violated.

Company practice usually avoids any possible application of the rule against perpetuities by prohibiting agreements that would postpone complete distribution of proceeds beyond the lives of two successive *classes* of beneficiaries. Family needs usually are met by providing a settlement arrangement for the insured's wife as primary beneficiary and his children as contingent beneficiaries, possibly with a provision for per stirpes distribution to children of deceased children, as explained in Section 3.16.2. As a practical matter, a well-advised policyowner will wish to distribute proceeds of his policy within such time.

§5.7. *Rule against accumulations.* This rule is somewhat allied to the rule against perpetuities, but it concerns itself only with a prohibition against accumulating income for an unreasonable period. Some states permit accumulations during the full period of time recognized as valid under the rule against perpetuities, as explained in Section 5.6. The laws of many states prohibit such accumulations except during the minority of a beneficiary entitled to the income. However, all state laws permit such accumulations during minority. In addition, the laws of some states provide that income may be accumulated during some stated period, such as 10 years, even though the beneficiary is an adult.

Laws restricting the accumulation of income are felt

to apply to life insurance settlement options. Even if a statute does not specifically refer to such options, life insurance companies will usually permit accumulations of interest under settlement options only during the minority of beneficiaries. Some companies will not permit any accumulations.

§*5.8. Payment to or for minors.* In the absence of a statute in a particular state, the age of majority for both males and females is 21. At common law, a person not of age is regarded as incapable of making a binding contract. If a minor does enter into a contract, he may repudiate it at any time before becoming of age or within a reasonable time thereafter. Otherwise, the contract is enforceable.

1. *Direct transactions with the minor.* Statutes have been passed in many states authorizing a minor of a certain age to purchase insurance on his own life and to exercise all rights under the policy, without intervention of a guardian. In some states, the authorized age is 15; in others it is 16 or 18.

Such legislation usually provides that a minor who has attained the authorized age may not only buy life insurance but may also exercise any of the policy rights without the appointment of a guardian. Under such statute, a minor may change the beneficiary or elect settlement options, although the persons to be designated usually must be within the classes specified in the statute. Many of these statutes require that the beneficiary shall be the minor's estate, or persons closely related by blood or marriage, such as father, mother, husband, wife, children, brother, or sister.

Since such statutes are designed to change firmly established principles of the common law, they will be "strictly construed" by the courts—that is, the statutes will be applied only if all the specified conditions are met. Therefore, companies must be careful that all provisions of the state law have been observed before permitting a minor to change the beneficiary or to elect a settlement option.

These statutes usually refer only to policies on *the life*

of the minor himself and do not necessarily apply to policies on *some other person's life.* If the minor is the owner or beneficiary of a policy on some other person's life, conservative practice suggests the following conclusions, except as a statute may expressly give minors greater rights:

(1) A minor owner may not exercise any policy right.

(2) A minor beneficiary cannot validly execute a release or discharge for a one sum or installment payment due him. Companies will require the appointment of a guardian before making payment, except, for example, where a statute such as Section 145 (2) of the New York Insurance Law permits payments direct to minors. This statute provides that a minor domiciled in New York who has attained age 18 may receive and give a valid release for a single payment not exceeding $3,000, or for periodic payments not exceeding $3,000 in any one year under a settlement option arrangement elected for or by him.

(3) Where proceeds are payable to a minor in one sum, he may not elect a settlement option unless he is permitted to do so under a statute such as that described in paragraph (2) above.

2. *Transactions by a guardian for the minor.* Guardians derive their power and authority from statutory and case law in the state in which the minor resides. In general, a guardian's duty is to conserve the assets of his ward. Most statutes pertaining to guardians do not specifically refer to life insurance policies.

When the proceeds of a policy are payable in one sum to a minor, insurance companies will pay the guardian on receiving a copy of the court order making the appointment. Such a payment legally discharges the insurance company.

It is generally believed that a guardian has little power to elect settlement options for the minor, except as a specific statute may give him such power. However, even without specific statutory authority, the insurance company probably assumes little risk in permitting a guardian to elect the Interest Option if a withdrawal privilege is reserved.

In *Latterman* v. *Guardian Life Insurance Co.,* 280 N.Y. 102, 19 N.E.2d 978 (1939), the court ruled that election of the Interest Option did not constitute an "investment" and that a guardian could elect such option for the benefit of a minor.

There is no indication that the court would reach the same decision if another option were involved. Companies that permit the guardian to elect settlement options often prefer the Interest Option to be selected because it tends to conserve the proceeds. However, an installment arrangement under the Fixed Period Option or Fixed Amount Option, related to the minor's maintenance needs, is permitted by some companies. Certainly, the Life Income Option would rarely be permitted because of the substantial percentage of proceeds consumed by the deferred annuity portion.

It also seems important that the guardian reserve full control of the proceeds at all times by a withdrawal or commutation privilege, and that the minor's estate be named contingent beneficiary if he dies before becoming of age.

Without statutory authority, a guardian seemingly may not designate a beneficiary under a policy owned by a minor on another's life. *California Western States Life Insurance Co.* v. *Marsters,* 145 Ore. 640, 28 P.2d 233 (1934); *Kay* v. *Erickson,* 209 Wis. 147, 244 N.W. 625 (1932). In the *Kay* case, the court pointed out that the right to change the beneficiary was the minor's property right, and the guardian had no more authority to change the beneficiary than he would have had to make a will for the minor.

However, it is logical that a guardian should have the right to change the beneficiary to the *minor's estate.* In fact, the occurrence of certain events, such as the death of one or more beneficiaries, may create a duty on the guardian to present the facts to the court for possible instructions about change of beneficiary. Since the primary purpose of the guardianship is to protect the minor's estate, the court may order a beneficiary change to the estate.

§*5.9. Effect of assignments on settlement option agreements.* Life insurance contracts are freely assignable by the insured unless some limitation is placed in the policy. Life insurance companies routinely furnish assignment forms. By an assignment, the insured transfers his rights in the policy to the assignee. The extent to which these rights are transferred depends on the provisions of the policy concerning assignments, the intention of the parties as expressed in the assignment form, and the circumstances surrounding the actual assignment.

1.   *Types of assignments.*   Assignments are conventionally of two types—"absolute" and "collateral." The absolute assignment normally is intended to make the assignee the owner of every right in the policy that the policyowner possessed before the assignment. When the transaction is completed, the original policyowner will have no further interest in the policy. Phraseology differs in absolute assignments. In essence, it is stated that the policyowner transfers to the assignee all the policyowner's right, title, and interest in the policy. Some companies suggest the use of an "ownership clause" to accomplish the assignment or transfer of ownership rights, as discussed in Section 5.10.

The collateral assignment, on the other hand, is a more limited type of transfer. It contemplates a security arrangement to protect the assignee who has lent money to the policyowner. After the indebtedness is repaid, it is contemplated that the assignee shall release his interest to the policyowner, i.e., that he shall transfer back the rights transferred by the assignment. If the collateral assignment is still in force at the death of the insured, under usual procedure the assignee certifies to the insurance company the amount of indebtedness, including interest at that time, and receives that amount in one sum. Any excess proceeds are then payable to the named beneficiary in accordance with the beneficiary designation.

2. *Collateral or absolute assignment for security trans-actions?* Even though the arrangement is merely one of security calling for a collateral assignment, many lenders insist on receiving a form called an "absolute assignment." This insistence probably stems from the practice of some life insurance companies in demanding joint signatures of the policyowner and the assignee if the assignee wishes to deal with the policy. Even the use of the absolute assignment form may not assure the assignee in every case that the company will deal with him alone. Despite the sweeping language, it may not spell out clearly the prematurity rights the assignee is intended to have. Too often, the parties to the assignment fail to make their intentions plain in this respect.

Problems such as these led to the creation of a middle-ground form of assignment by the joint efforts of the Bank Management Commission of the American Bankers Association and representatives of the Association of Life Insurance Counsel. This form states clearly five specific rights that pass to the assignee and that may be exercised by the assignee alone. Included is the sole right to collect the proceeds at the death of the insured or date of maturity of the policy, and the sole right to surrender the policy for its cash surrender value. Without impairing the right of the assignee to surrender the policy, certain rights are reserved to the policyowner. Included are the right to receive disability benefits that do not reduce the amount of insurance, and the right to designate and change the beneficiary. Also, the assignee promises not to surrender the policy without giving the policyowner notice of his intention to surrender. This so-called "ABA assignment form" is now used by many banks and is recommended by a substantial number of insurance companies. In fact, many companies have adopted it as their own standard form.

3. *Notice of assignment to the insurance company.* To protect the assignee fully, notice must be given the life insurance company that the assignment has been made. If a company with no notice of an assignment makes payment of the proceeds to an assignee under a subsequent assignment or to a named beneficiary, the majority view is that it cannot be made to pay a second time. A typical policy provision concerning assignments is: "No assignment shall be binding upon the Company until the original or a duplicate thereof is filed at its Home Office. The Company assumes no obligation as to the effect, sufficiency, or validity of any assignment. All assignments shall be subject to any indebtedness to the Company on this policy."

4. *Need the beneficiary be changed before assignment of the policy?* Some modern policies and some beneficiary forms provide, in effect, that "the rights of any revocable beneficiary will be subordinate to the rights of any assignee of record with the Company, whether the assignment was made before or after the date of the beneficiary designation." When this provision appears, most banks will accept the assignment, and most life insurance companies will record the assignment without change of beneficiary. Unless clear-cut language in the policy indicates that the beneficiary's interest is diminished by an assignment, or unless the assignment is to be made to the beneficiary named in the policy, the best practice is to change the beneficiary to the insured's estate prior to making the assignment. Frequently, a second change of beneficiary is made to be recorded immediately following the assignment, to reinstate the beneficiary designation. At least one company follows the procedure of incorporating requests for both changes of beneficiary in the assignment form itself.

If someone other than the assignee is designated as

beneficiary at the time the assignment is made, and if this possibility and its effect are not covered in the policy or the beneficiary designation form, there is a question whether the assignee or the named beneficiary will be entitled to payment of the proceeds when the insured dies. A different answer may be given in the case of an absolute assignment than in the case of a collateral assignment transaction.

In respect to absolute assignments, one view interprets the assignment either as a change of beneficiary or as destruction of the interest of the beneficiary. In this view, the assignee is entitled to receive the proceeds of the policy when the insured dies. In the opposite view, the policy specifies a definite procedure for changing the beneficiary, and this procedure must be followed. The theory in support of this view is that the named beneficiary would have received the proceeds at the insured's death had there been no assignment, and a mere change in ownership rights should not change this concept or result.

When the question has been litigated under a transaction in which an assignment was given as collateral security for money loaned, most courts have ruled that the rights of the assignee are superior to those of the beneficiary. Since assignments are used so frequently in collateral security transactions, there are compelling business reasons for a rule of law that will give maximum protection to those who lend money with policy values as security. However, some few courts have ruled that the beneficiary cannot be deprived of his interest without his consent unless a change of beneficiary is made exactly as provided in the policy.

Obviously, troublesome questions such as those just described can be avoided by a change of beneficiary prior to making the assignment, when that procedure is indicated.

Logically, settlement options should be available for election even though a policy has been assigned, and a majority of companies permit such election either by practice or by policy provisions. Under an absolute assignment intended to transfer all rights of the policyowner, an assignee should seemingly be permitted to elect the options either for beneficiaries or for himself, just as the original policyowner might have done. In an assignment given for collateral security, it would also seem proper to permit the policyowner to elect settlement options as respects proceeds in excess of the debt.

§*5.10. Ownership provisions.* Today, in many instances it is desired to place ownership in someone other than the insured. Such third-party owner may be designated from the inception of the policy, or ownership may be transferred at some later time. The vehicle for placing ownership in the third party depends on the practice of the particular company. In many cases, the absolute assignment form is used, as discussed in Section 5.9.

In other cases, owners are designated by means of an "ownership clause." Such clause resembles the absolute assignment in many respects, but it may actually be more limited in scope than the absolute assignment form. For example, the policy may refer to the rights exercisable by the "owner" of the policy. The policy may provide that the insured shall be the owner in the absence of a contrary provision. The application for the policy may request that the insured's wife or other third party be named as owner. A typical clause may be incorporated as follows:

> Ownership—The insured is the owner of this policy unless otherwise provided in the application or by later transfer. Subject to the rights of any prior assignee, and unless the owner and the Company shall agree otherwise, all rights which are available while the insured is living are vested in the owner, and may be exercised by the owner without the consent of anyone else. Proceeds payable at the insured's death are payable to the beneficiary and not to the owner unless the owner is also named as the beneficiary.

If ownership is transferred after the policy is issued, and if company practice prescribes use of an ownership clause instead of an absolute assignment form, appropriate language is embodied in an instrument of transfer. An ownership clause offers more potential flexibility than the conventional form of assignment. It is useful when it is desired to name successive owners if the first owner dies before the insured. It is also useful to name an owner for a limited period of time, such as during minority, or until a specified date, or the occurrence of a specified event, with provisions for automatic transfer of ownership thereafter.

The practice of naming a contingent or successive owner has a great deal to recommend it. It enables the owner to avoid having the policy pass through his probate estate, and it is advantageous to the insurance company to know with whom it can deal after the death of the original owner.

Gray v. *Penn Mutual Life Insurance Co.,* 5 Ill. App. 2d 541, 126 N.E. 2d 409 (1955) illustrates the use of contingent or successive owners. The insured absolutely assigned a policy on his life to his mother. Thereafter, she transferred ownership of the policy to herself under an ownership clause which read: "Edna A. Fonyo, while living, thereafter to Melvin A. Krauss, friend of the insured, while living, thereafter to the insured." The ownership clause provided that all rights of ownership in the policy were in the owners in the order specified. The mother died. Shortly thereafter, the insurance company made a policy loan to Krauss. Sometime later Krauss reassigned the policy to the insured, who on discovering the policy loan sought to have it set aside, on the theory that the attempted transfer to Krauss was an invalid testamentary disposition. The court said the transfer was not testamentary in character. The court cited with approval the *Ellis* case explained in Section 5.5.

It is important that the policy provisions be carefully examined under clauses of this type. The owner may merely "stand in the shoes" of the insured. His rights may be limited to the rights which the insured himself might have exercised during his lifetime, and those rights may expire with the death of the insured. Since the insured could not have received the death benefit payable under the policy, the third-party owner likewise may not be entitled to receive that death benefit unless he has designated himself as beneficiary.

§*5.11. Special problems in beneficiary designations.* Sometimes special problems are encountered, such as irrevocable beneficiary designations, divorce situations, and attempts to designate beneficiaries by will.

1. *Designation of an irrevocable beneficiary.* Irrevocable beneficiary designations were more popular some years ago than they are today. Their legal effect often was not clear. Sometimes, it was felt that a form of joint ownership was created between the insured and beneficiary. More usually, the designation was regarded as placing a restraint on the exercise by the insured of policy rights. Such exercise required the irrevocable beneficiary's consent. Tax and other uncertainties were created by such designation.

The irrevocable beneficiary designation was sometimes used in the mistaken belief that sole ownership would be placed in the beneficiary. However, now that the third-party ownership is so popular and its legal aspects so much better understood, as explained in Section 5.10, the use of the irrevocable beneficiary designation tends to be limited to special situations, such as placing restrictions on an insured under separation agreements and property settlement arrangements in conjunction with a divorce.

2. *Effect of divorce.* In the great majority of states, entry of a divorce decree does not of itself affect an existing beneficiary designation naming a divorced spouse. In many instances, the policyowner will voluntarily change the beneficiary. In others, the court may order the insured to maintain the policy for the benefit of his divorced spouse as a part of the property settlement arrangement. In such event,

the rights of the beneficiary can be best protected by making the designation irrevocable or by assigning the policy to the divorced spouse.

In a minority of states, a divorce decree can have an impact on the beneficiary designation. By statute, in Kentucky, Kentucky Revised Statutes Annotated, Section 403.060 (1963) and in Michigan, Michigan Statutes Annotated, Section 25.131 (1957), a divorce decree will of itself automatically revoke a beneficiary in favor of a spouse who is a party to the divorce proceedings.

In New York, where the only ground for divorce is adultery, Section 177 of the New York Domestic Relations Law provides that a beneficiary divorced for adultery forfeits his or her interest in the policy, except to the extent that the beneficiary has contributed to the premiums from the beneficiary's separate estate.

Missouri and Minnesota have unusual statutes. Section 61.15 of the Minnesota Statutes Annotated (1946) and Section 376.560 of the Annotated Missouri Statutes (1952) provide that any policy payable to the insured's wife shall inure to her separate benefit, but in event of the wife's death or divorce, the insured may designate another beneficiary. In a case construing the Missouri statute, it was held that an insured after divorce may change the beneficiary *even though the policy does not reserve this right to him,* provided the policy was issued after the effective date of the statute. *Mutual Life Insurance Co.* v. *Tuemler,* 251 S.W. 727 (Mo. App. 1923).

3. *Change of beneficiary by will.* A majority of decided cases hold that a beneficiary can be changed only as provided in the policy, and policies do not provide that the beneficiary may be changed by a will. This is the correct view. A will can speak only from the date of death of the testator, whereas the rights of a beneficiary in a life insurance policy are said to "vest" absolutely at the moment of the insured's death. In this view, a beneficiary designa-

tion or change must be made during the insured's life-time. This view is also supported by practical considerations: all sorts of problems are presented if the insurance company cannot promptly pay claims on the basis of the provisions found within the four corners of its policy. A few decisions have reached a contrary result on the theory that the intent of the insured is paramount, however that intent is expressed.

Both forms of government life insurance contracts, USGLI and NSLI, are exceptions to the general rule. Under regulations governing these policies, a beneficiary designation may be made by will, provided that no beneficiary has been designated before or that all previously designated beneficiaries predeceased the insured.

§5.12. *Rights of creditors.* There is probably no subject in this book more completely covered by statutory and case law, and on which there is more variation between laws, than that of protection of life insurance proceeds from claims of creditors. A comprehensive discussion of the subject is beyond the scope of this section. The important aspects of creditors' rights are considered here primarily as they affect proceeds payable under settlement options. To the extent that creditors satisfy their debts out of life insurance proceeds, the amount available for distribution under settlement options may be reduced materially. This fact can have an important bearing on an insurance program.

1. *Creditors of the insured.* Practically all states, by statute, grant some degree of protection to life insurance by placing it beyond the reach of creditors of the insured. This favored treatment by the various state legislatures is intentional. The social significance of life insurance in protecting a man's family rises above the normal desire of the law to see that a man pays his debts. This assurance that proceeds will go to the persons intended by the insured makes life insurance a very valuable form of property.

a. Types of exemption statutes. The rule of exemption statutes vary greatly. As a general rule, exemptions are granted only if the policy is payable to beneficiaries other than the insured's estate. Pennsylvania has the most common type of statute, Pennsylvania Statutes Annotated, title 40, Section 517 (1954). The exemption applies if the policies are payable to or for the benefit of the wife, children, or other relatives dependent on the insured. It is available even though the insured retains the right to change the beneficiary under the policy, and it is not limited to any stated amount of proceeds nor to the proceeds attributable to any amount of premium.

One variation of this common type of statute limits the exemption to a stated face amount of proceeds or to the proceeds attributable to a limited amount of premium per year. For example, Mississippi limits the exemption to $10,000 of proceeds payable at the insured's death to a beneficiary other than his estate. Mississippi 1942 Annotated Code, Section 308 (1956). California (California Code of Civil Procedure, Section 690.19) and Nevada (Nevada Revised Statutes, Section 21.090 (1957)) are but two of several states which grant the exemption to as much insurance as can be purchased by annual premiums of $500. The proceeds in these two states are exempt in the proportion that $500 bears to the total annual premiums paid. Thus, if the proceeds total $48,000 and the annual premiums are $1,200, 5/12 of the proceeds, or $20,000, would be exempt, and the remaining $28,000 would be subject to claims of the insured's creditors.

New York has a more comprehensive type of exemption statute which applies if the policy is payable to any person other than the insured. New York Insurance Law, Section 166.

b. Exemption of lifetime values. Some statutes simply say that the "proceeds" are beyond the reach of the insured's creditors. Since the philosophy of exemption laws is to render values under the policy exempt from the claims of creditors of the insured both during his lifetime and at his death, statutes have been changed in many states to exempt "proceeds and avails." The addition of the word "avails" or similar language makes it clear that the exemption applies to cash values during the insured's lifetime, in addition to proceeds payable at his death.

Another problem is the extent to which values under endowment policies are exempt. Courts have ruled that the exemption applies to cash values and death benefits, on the theory that life insurance features are a part of the endowment policy. Some statutes specifically provide that the exemption shall apply to endowment policies, but it is not clear that courts would interpret these statutes to apply to maturity values payable to the insured. In Pennsylvania, a statute specifically states that under a contract of insurance or annuity issued to a solvent citizen, income payments are exempt to an amount not exceeding $100 per month, even though the payments are made to the insured or anuitant. Pennsylvania Statutes Annotated, title 40, Section 515 (1954).

Disability benefits payable to an insured are not usually exempt from claims of the insured's creditors. In several states, however, as in Louisiana, the statute is broad enough to exempt disability and accident and health benefits from claims of the insured's creditors.

Similarly, annuity contracts do not come within the protection of the general exemption statute, except in those few states which have specific statutory provisions in favor of such contracts. Those few states have a variety of provisions. In Pennsylvania, the statute limits the exemption to payments not exceeding $100 per month. The New York statute provides that the first $400 per month of income to an annuitant may be subject to garnishment only in the same manner as wages, namely, to the extent of 10 percent. Income in excess of $400 per month is also exposed to claims of creditors of the annuitant to the extent deemed proper by the court. In a number of other states, an annuity may be exempt if it is purchased for the benefit of someone other than the purchaser.

   c. Effect of Federal Bankruptcy Act. Section 70 (a) of the Federal Bankruptcy Act provides generally that title to the bankrupt's property shall vest in the trustee in bankruptcy, except "insofar as it is property which is held to be exempt . . ." Section 6 of the Act provides that exemptions will be recognized to the extent that they are granted under the law of the state in which the bankrupt lives.

   If title to the policy does pass to the trustee in bankruptcy, Section 70 (a) (5) provides that the bankrupt may pay the trustee the cash value of the policy, obtain a release of the policy by the trustee, and then continue the policy in force for his own benefit.

   Quite aside from any question of exemption under state law, if a beneficiary is designated irrevocably, title to the policy will not pass to the trustee in bankruptcy under Section 70 (a) (5) because of the property rights vested in the beneficiary by the irrevocable designation. The trustee in bankruptcy can acquire no greater rights than the bankrupt possesses.

   2. *Creditors of the beneficiary.* There are at least three possible factual situations concerning the extent to which proceeds are protected from creditors of the beneficiary.

   (1) A state statute may provide that the proceeds of a policy are automatically exempt from claims of the beneficiary's creditors.

   (2) A state statute may specifically permit the inclusion of protective provisions—known as "spendthrift clauses"—in a settlement option agreement or in the policy itself, and if such provisions are included, the proceeds usually will be exempt from claims of the beneficiary's creditors.

   (3) There is no statute specifically permitting the in-

clusion of a spendthrift clause. In many states, if such a clause is included, it will be upheld by court decisions. However, courts in a few states consider spendthrift clause provisions to be against public policy and will not uphold them to protect the beneficiary from claims of his or her creditors.

a. *Statutes automatically exempting proceeds from claims of the beneficiary's creditors.* There are very few states in this category. Under the New York law, the proceeds and avails of a policy purchased by the wife on the life of her husband are protected against the claims of *her* creditors. New York Insurance Law, Section 166. A Wisconsin statute provides that if a policy is taken out by a married woman on the life of any person, its proceeds and avails payable to her are exempt from the claims of her creditors to the extent of $5,000. Wisconsin Statutes, Section 246.09 (1957). In Washington, a statute places beyond the reach of the beneficiary's creditors the proceeds and avails of life insurance effected by any person on his own life or on another person's life. Revised Code of Washington Annotated, Section 48.18.410 (1961). In California, exempted from claims of creditors of the beneficiary are insurance proceeds up to the amount obtainable with $500 of annual premiums on insurance inuring to the benefit of the insured's spouse or minor children. California Code of Civil Procedure, Section 690.19.

b. *Statutes specifically authorizing inclusion of spendthrift provisions.* A substantial number of states have statutes which permit the insured to include a spendthrift clause either in the settlement option agreement or in the policy. Such clause may read about as follows:

> Unless otherwise provided in this settlement agreement, no beneficiary may commute, anticipate, encumber, alienate, withdraw, or assign any portion of his share of the proceeds. To the extent permitted by law, no pay-

ments to a beneficiary will be subject to his debts, contracts or engagements, nor may they be levied upon or attached.

If such clause is incorporated, it will be effective to protect the insurance proceeds against claims of creditors of the beneficiary. It would be expected that such provision must be elected by the insured to be given effect. However, where the beneficiary herself elected the settlement option which included a spendthrift clause, the Pennyslvania Supreme Court decided that the beneficiary's creditors could not reach the proceeds. *Provident Trust Co.* v. *Rothman,* 321 Pa. 177, 183 Atl. 793 (1936).

c. *Spendthrift clauses governed by court decision.* In many states, there is no specific reference in a statute to the inclusion of spendthrift clauses in life insurance policies or in settlement option agreements under those policies, but these clauses are upheld by court decisions. These decisions recognize a public policy in favor of spendthrift *trusts,* either because of a statute or court decisions that permit inclusion of spendthrift provisions in a trust agreement or in a trust created under a will.

In a few states, spendthrift clauses are considered against the public policy of the state. In consequence, they will not be upheld to prevent claims of creditors of the beneficiary of life insurance proceeds. These states follow the old English law under which spendthrift trusts were not recognized. This rule is followed in Kentucky, *Meade* v. *Rowe's Executor and Trustee,* 298 Ky. 111, 182 S.W.2d 30 (1944), in New Hampshire, *Brahmey* v. *Rollins,* 87 N.H. 290, 179 Atl. 186 (1935), and in Rhode Island, *Petition of Smyth,* 49 R.I. 27, 139 Atl. 657 (1927). Even in these states, however, comparable results may be obtained by a so-called "discretionary trust" under which a beneficiary may receive only that portion of the income or principal as the trustee in his unfettered discretion shall see fit to give him. Another alternative might be to create an insurance trust in another state where spendthrift trust provisions are clearly recognized and by whose laws the trust would be interpreted.

An interesting question may arise as to whether those states that recognize spendthrift clauses will extend recognition to situations in which the beneficiary has a complete right of withdrawal or commutation of the proceeds held by the insurance company. Such complete control may appear to be inconsistent with the restrictions expressed in spendthrift clauses. However, at least one court has held that a spendthrift clause is valid even though the beneficiary possesses an unlimited right of withdrawal. *Genesee Valley Trust Co.* v. *Glazer,* 295 N.Y. 219, 66 N.E.2d 169 (1946).

3. *Special types of creditors.* It has been ruled that certain types of creditors are not barred by general state exemption statutes. Aside from the federal tax collector, discussed in Section 5.13, two of the more important types of special creditors are welfare officials and the wife of the insured.

a. A welfare official. Various state laws give such officials priority over other creditors to life insurance proceeds payable to the estate of an insured if the insured is indebted to the state for maintenance costs. The constitutionality of the New York law on this subject was affirmed in *Smyth* v. *City of New York,* 156 Misc. 400, 282 N.Y. Supp. 136 (Sup. Ct. 1935). In *In re Ciappei's Estate,* 159 Misc. 438, 287 N.Y. Supp. 988 (Surr. Ct. 1936), a welfare claim was given precedence over a judgment creditor of the insured. The extent of the official's priority would seem to be determined by the provisions of the applicable statute.

b. The insured's wife. An interesting situation arises when the wife is a creditor, either because she has paid premiums or because alimony or similar marital obligations are owing to her. She may seek to levy on a policy of life insurance owned by her husband and payable so as to appear to be exempt under a particular state law. Is the wife to be treated like any other creditor, or will the courts hold that the exemption statutes are designed to protect the insured's family only from claims of creditors outside the family?

Most courts reason that the exemption laws are designed to relieve the insured and his dependents from the claims of outsiders and not to relieve the insured of his own family obligations. Courts also reason that the obligation to support a wife is not an ordinary debt, but is a liability of first importance imposed by law for the protection of society. Furthermore, insurance policies are often taken out primarily for the benefit of the wife and children, and this desirable objective is accomplished when their values are devoted to the payment of alimony and child support claims. See Schwarzschild, *Rights of Creditors in Life Insurance Policies,* page 228, and cases cited therein.

§*5.13.　The federal tax collector.*　The federal government enjoys a special status as a creditor with respect to taxes owing to it.

1. *Tax deficiencies against the insured.*　As a general rule, the exemption statutes discussed in Section 5.12 do not prevent the District Director of the Internal Revenue Service from seizing the values of life insurance policies during a policyowner's lifetime to satisfy tax deficiencies owed by such a policyowner.

The District Director may place a lien against the cash value during the insured's lifetime. Such lien will prevent the insured policyowner from exercising rights or enjoying benefits under the policy. By a formal civil action against all interested parties, a surrender of the policy may be forced. *Knox* v. *Great West Life Assurance Co.,* 212 F.2d 784 (6th Cir. 1954).

If the insured dies after the lien arises by reason of a deficiency assessment, the United States Supreme Court has held that regardless of the state exemption statute, the government's lien may be enforced against the death proceeds up to the amount of the policy's cash surrender value just before the insured's death. *U.S.* v. *Bess,* 357 U.S. 51 (1958). However, if the lien does not exist until after the death of the insured, an exemption statute in favor of the beneficiary will insulate the proceeds from the lien. *Commissioner* v. *Stern,* 357 U.S. 39 (1958). Two interesting recent cases relating to this general subject are *Meyer* v. *U.S.,* 375 U.S. 233 (1963), and *Wintner* v. *U.S.,* 375 U.S. 393 (1964).

If the lien follows the proceeds after the insured's death under the rule of the *Bess* case, what happens if the death proceeds are payable under a settlement option arrangement agreed to prior to the date of the government's lien? Since the lien could have been enforced against the cash value during the insured's lifetime, and since the lien is said to follow the proceeds up to this value after death, it would seem logical that the mode of payment of the proceeds should not affect the government's right to collect its lien in one sum.

2. *Tax deficiencies against the beneficiaries.* Reported cases appear not to have decided the extent to which the District Director may proceed against the beneficiary of proceeds payable at the insured's death, for unpaid taxes of the *beneficiary.* A debt is owing by the insurance company to the beneficiary. It would seem that a lien could reach the proceeds whether payable in one sum or in installments. State exemption statutes would seem to offer no protection.

However, if the proceeds are payable in installments under a settlement option arrangement elected by the insured, the government's lien should be enforceable only against the installment payments as and when payable by the insurance company. Revenue Ruling 55-210, 1955-1 CB 544. To extend the government's rights further would permit alteration of the contract entered into between the company and the *insured* to satisfy a lien enforceable only against the *beneficiary*. See *John Hancock Mutual Life Insurance Co.* v. *Helvering,* 128 F.2d 745 (D.C. Cir. 1942).

　§5.14. Community property. The community property concept, followed in a few of our states, merits some discussion.

　1. *History.* For most purposes, states other than Louisiana follow the common law of England. Under old English law, a wife was regarded as a sheltered creature. Her husband was looked upon as her superior and protector. Accordingly, she had little or no property rights without the joinder of her husband. Some modern statutes have authorized a wife, in certain circumstances, to hold property in her own name and to dispose of it without her husband's consent. Today, in most common law states, a spouse has no property rights in personal property owned by the other spouse. It naturally follows that life insurance contracts, being personal property, belong to the spouse named as owner. In common law states, the other spouse has no interest in such policy except as the policyowner may have specifically created such an interest.

　In times past, on the continent of Europe—particularly in Spain and France—the wife shared more fully in her husband's problems. She was regarded as a partner in the marital venture, each partner having certain duties. The civil law that developed in these countries vested the wife with an interest in property acquired during marriage. In many instances, this interest equaled that of her husband. The interest of one spouse in the property of the other became known as a "community property" right.

　Louisiana follows the civil law of France and Spain. For the purpose of this section, the most significant difference between Louisiana law and the common law followed by the majority of states is this community property concept. This concept has been adopted in seven other states which in most other respects follow common law principles —Arizona, California, Idaho, Nevada, New Mexico, Texas, and Washington. Most of these states were territories subject to French or Spanish control or influence.

Three types of property must be considered in these community property states:

(1) The separate property of the husband—that which was acquired by the husband before marriage and that which he acquired after marriage by gift or inheritance.

(2) The separate property of the wife—that which was acquired by the wife before marriage and that which she acquired after marriage by gift or inheritance.

(3) Community property—property (including earnings) acquired by either spouse after and during the continuance of the marriage relationship, other than by gift or inheritance.

Under community property laws, the separate property of the husband or wife, as described in (1) and (2) above, is treated like individually owned property of a spouse in a common law state. There are no special problems with respect to life insurance and annuity contracts owned as separate property by either spouse in a community property state.

2. *Life insurance and annuity contracts acquired as community property.* There can be no special community property problems unless premiums are paid on a policy from community funds during marriage. Even then, special problems are avoided, as respects proceeds payable at the insured's death, if the spouse is named as primary beneficiary to the extent of at least half the proceeds—whether payable in one sum or in installments. They are also avoided if the interest of the spouse is released in such policy or if the spouse consents to the designation of another person as beneficiary under the policy.

A problem arises only if the spouse is not named as beneficiary to the extent of at least half the proceeds, and the interest of such spouse has not been released or the spouse has not consented to the designation of another person as beneficiary. In such circumstances, the spouse is entitled to her community property interest in the proceeds. Although there is no case directly in point, if the insurance company pays to the designated beneficiary other than the spouse, it may also be liable to the spouse for her share under community property laws. See *New York Life Insurance Co.* v. *Bank of Italy*, 60 Cal. App. 602, 214 Pac. 61 (1923). In Washington, it has been held that a husband's attempt to change the beneficiary was invalid in its entirety as contrary to community property laws. *Occidental Life Insurance Co.* v. *Powers*, 192 Wash. 475, 74 P.2d 27 (1937).

In *Tyre* v. *Aetna Life Insurance Co.*, 54 Cal. 2d 399, 353 P. 2d 725, 6 Cal. Rptr. 13 (1960), the court held that a settlement option agreement selected by the insured husband and providing a 10-year-certain life income to his wife with any remaining guaranteed payments being payable equally to three daughters could be voided by the wife who had not joined in the election. The wife was permitted to stand on her community rights and take her half of the proceeds in one sum, but since by her election she disqualified herself as a policy beneficiary, the husband's half was payable to the daughters as alternate beneficiaries.

However, if the life insurance company has no notice of the community property claim of the wife, the company has been held to be discharged from liability by payment to the beneficiary substituted for the wife. *Blethen* v. *Pacific Mutual Life Insurance Co.*, 198 Cal. 91, 243 Pac. 431 (1926). In more recent years, legislation has been enacted in most community property states to protect an insurance company which makes payment to a designated beneficiary in absence of prior written notice of an adverse community property claim. California Insurance Code, Section 10172, and Revised Code of Washington Annotated, Section 48.18.-370 (1961), are examples of such statutes.

This is a very brief picture of the types of additional

questions encountered in community property states. There are many other problems, such as recognition of certain acts performed by the husband as manager of the community property; respective rights of parties if a policy was purchased before marriage, and some premiums were paid from separate property and some from community funds; and disposition of life insurance policies on dissolution of the community by death or divorce.

Chapter 6

Tax Aspects of Settlement Options

§6.1. *Introduction.* There are numerous tax problems affecting life insurance settlement options, just as tax problems have an impact on other aspects of business and personal life. The very high, progressive rates under present-day federal income and estate tax laws may substantially reduce the amount of proceeds or income that ultimately will be left for family use. To a lesser extent, state and local taxes also enter the picture.

Rarely is it proper to make important decisions concerning the fulfillment of family needs on the basis of tax consequences alone. Intelligent programing implies that decisions on the use of settlement options will be based on an analysis of the needs in each case. However, in solving a given problem, alternate routes or approaches may be found equally attractive for meeting the need. Taxwise, one approach may ultimately produce much more net family income than another. Accordingly, a knowledge of the principles of taxation as they apply to life insurance settlement options is essential to the intelligent preparation of a life insurance program.

Historically, life insurance death proceeds—that is, amounts payable by reason of the insured's death—always have been excluded from federal *income* tax. As regards the

161

federal *estate* tax, the rules have varied from granting a limited exemption to treatment even more severe than that accorded other property, with current law purporting to result in equal taxation of both. It is socially and economically desirable that the breadwinner make provision for his family after his death. Because life insurance is the ideal vehicle to accomplish this, certain tax exemptions for death proceeds are well warranted whether paid in a single sum or under a settlement option.

Three principal taxes have an impact on the payment of life insurance proceeds—federal income tax, federal estate tax, and federal gift tax. The broad application of these taxes to life insurance and annuity contracts is beyond the scope of this chapter. The primary concern here is with an understanding of how such taxes apply to income arrangements under the settlement options.

Throughout this chapter, references to the "Code" mean the Internal Revenue Code of 1954, as amended, unless otherwise indicated. "Regulations" refer to official Regulations of the Treasury Department which interpret sections of the Code.

A. FEDERAL INCOME TAX

§6.2. General. In approaching income tax problems, it should be remembered that the tax is imposed only on "income," as defined in the Code. It is not a tax on every conceivable type of payment that may be received. There are many twilight zones. Accordingly, that which is to be regarded as income under a life insurance policy and that which is to be excluded or exempt as principal may depend on definitions in the statute, Regulations, administrative rulings, and court decisions.

For brevity, a payment which the Code considers as "includible in gross income" often is referred to in this discussion as "taxable income."

Complex "ground rules" are often involved in computing taxable income under a particular type of payment. Fortunately, however, it is not necessary for everyone to become a mathematical expert in the many possible situations. Most life insurance companies are equipped to give prompt and accurate service in making computations for particular cases, and are glad to do so on request.

Income tax problems in the area of settlement options fall into two broad categories—inclusion of *death benefits* as income to the recipient, and inclusion of *living benefits* as income to the policyowner on maturity or surrender of the contract.

§*6.3. Proceeds payable by reason of death of the insured.* Under Section 101 (a) (1) of the Code, life insurance "proceeds" payable by reason of the death of the insured are specifically excluded from gross income. Usually, the proceeds payable by reason of the insured's death consist of the face amount of the policy, increased by dividends on deposit, paid-up additions and benefits under supplementary agreements, minus loans and unpaid premiums. There are two important exceptions to the general rule. The exclusion from gross income does not apply to death proceeds of policies which have been subject to certain transfers of ownership for a valuable consideration, as discussed in Section 6.3.11, nor to payments received by a divorced or separated spouse under a policy maintained by the other spouse pursuant to certain agreements for alimony or separate maintenance, as discussed in Section 6.3.12.

1. *Proceeds payable in one sum.* With the exceptions just noted, proceeds payable in one sum are fully excluded from taxable income, regardless of the total amount. Moreover, it is immaterial that the proceeds payable at death may greatly exceed the total premium payments. That this increment is fully excluded is one of the substantial advantages of life insurance. Its exclusion is based on the broad philosophy that life insurance attempts to indemnify for a loss of human life values.

2. *Proceeds retained under the Interest Option.* If death proceeds are held by the insurance company under an agreement to pay interest, Code Section 101 (c) requires the interest payments to be included in the beneficiary's gross income, even though the proceeds themselves are fully excluded from tax. Such arrangement has been likened to a deposit in a savings account on which the bank pays or credits interest each year.

3. *Installments of principal and interest.* Installments which include both principal and interest are provided by the Fixed Period Option, the Fixed Amount Option, the Life Income Option, and certain other options derived from them. Under prior law, the entire guaranteed installments, including the interest element, were considered proceeds "payable by reason of the death of the insured" and, therefore, were excluded from taxable income. Only interest paid in excess of the interest included in the guaranteed installments was fully taxable. This rule still applies if the insured died on or before August 16, 1954, the effective date of Code Section 101.

The 1954 Code effected an important change with respect to policies on the life of an insured who dies after August 16, 1954. For the first time, the law itself specifically required a proration of principal and interest to determine the portion of the installment payments each year which is to be regarded as proceeds "payable by reason of the death of the insured" and, therefore, to be excluded from gross income. The remainder of each year's installments is fully taxable as income to the beneficiary. Code Section 101 (d) technically refers to the amount to be excluded as "the amounts held by an insurer."

The principle of seeking to tax the interest element in each year's installments is by no means illogical. In fact, the total exclusion that formerly obtained had been criticized as placing life insurance installments in an unduly favorable position compared with other assets in a decedent's estate, or with proceeds retained under the Interest Option.

Three other important aspects of the Code apply generally to all the installment options. First, the rules of exclusion and taxability are the same whether the settlement options are elected by the insured or the beneficiary. Second, the Code itself does not spell out the precise method of ascertaining the taxable portion of each year's installments. Rather, it provides that the proration of the amounts held by the insurer to determine the excludable portion of the installment payments shall be determined in accordance with the Regulations. The Regulations state that calculations shall be made by use of the mortality table (if a life income is involved) and the interest rate used by the insurer in calculating payments to be made. Third, where the beneficiary of the life insurance policy is the surviving spouse of the insured, an additional annual exclusion is allowed on installment payments to such spouse.

The spouse may exclude from income the first $1,000 of the interest portion of each year's installments. This exclusion applies in addition to the basic exclusion of proceeds "payable by reason of the death of the insured" under Code Section 101(d)(1)(B). This special statutory exclusion for the surviving spouse applies *only when the proceeds are payable in installments containing both interest and principal,* as explained fully in Section 6.3.10 below. This special exclusion is not taken into account in the examples shown in Sections 6.3.4, 6.3.5, and 6.3.6. Interest on proceeds held under the Interest Option is fully taxable, whether payable to a surviving spouse or to anyone else.

4. *Fixed Period Option.* Computation of the excludable portion of installments under the Fixed Period Option is relatively simple. The Regulations provide that the amount that would have been paid in one sum at death is divided by the number of fixed installments which are payable. The resulting figure is the portion of each install-

ment to be excluded. The balance of each installment is regarded as taxable income.

> *Example.* If the proceeds of a $75,000 policy are payable to the beneficiary in 10 equal annual installments of $8,536, the excludable portion of each installment is $7,500 ($75,000 divided by 10). The amount of each installment included in gross income is $1,036 ($8,536 minus $7,500).

5. *Fixed Amount Option.* The Fixed Amount Option is basically similar to the Fixed Period Option. The Regulations provide that the proceeds shall be divided by the number of installments of the specified amount to be produced under the *guaranteed* interest rate in the policy. The result is the amount of each installment to be excluded, and the balance of each installment is considered taxable income. If more than the calculated number of installments is paid because of excess interest credited to the policy, the additional installments are considered taxable income in their entirety. If excess interest is not used to extend the number of installments but is paid in addition to the fixed amount each year, such excess interest is currently reportable as taxable income.

> *Example.* The $20,000 death benefit under an insurance policy is payable to the beneficiary in monthly installments of $200 under the Fixed Amount Option. The policy provides that interest will be credited each year to the balance of the proceeds remaining with the company. Based on a guaranteed interest rate of 2½ percent, the $200 monthly installments would be paid for nine years and three months—a total of 111 months. The excludable portion of each monthly installment would be $180.18 ($20,000 divided by 111), and the amount of each installment to be included in taxable income during the 111 months would be $19.82 ($200 minus $180.18) or $237.84 per year ($19.82 times 12). Under such a calculation, the full amount of each installment beyond the period of 111 months would represent taxable income.

6. *Life Income Option.* If the installment payments are to continue during the lifetime of the beneficiary, instead of being limited to a fixed period, the amount of income to be excluded each year will be obtained by dividing the one sum proceeds by the years of life expectancy of the beneficiary. The number of years of life expectancy is determined by application of the mortality table used by the insurer. The excludable amount, once determined, remains constant even though the beneficiary outlives his or her life expectancy.

The Regulations, moreover, state that if there is any refund or period-certain feature, the present value of such feature must be subtracted from the one sum proceeds before the division is made. The present value of the guaranteed refund feature is to be determined by use of the mortality table and interest rate used by the insurer in determining the amount that may be paid to a contingent beneficiary. This subtraction will have the effect of increasing the taxable portion of the payments. The balance of payments in excess of the exclusion thus computed will be the taxable portion of each year's installments.

Payments to a contingent beneficiary are not taxable to the extent that such payments are made by reason of the guaranteed refund feature.

> *Example.* Assume that $25,000 of proceeds payable by reason of the insured's death are payable to his mother under the Life Income Option, 10 years certain. The monthly installments are $137 or $1,644 per year, based on her age 65. The mother's life expectancy, determined by the mortality table used for this option, is 18.9 years. The value of the period-certain feature (computed from the mortality table and interest rate used by the company) is $1,312 and must be subtracted from the proceeds ($25,000 − $1,312 = $23,688). Dividing the life expectancy figure into the adjusted one sum (18.9 into $23,688) produces the amount to be excluded each year ($1,253.33). The balance paid to the mother each year ($390.67) represents her taxable income.

7. *Joint and survivor annuity options.* If payments are to be made to two or more beneficiaries in the nature of a joint and survivor annuity, computation of the excludable portion involves substantially the same principles as under the other options. The present value of the payments to be made to all such beneficiaries is divided by the life expectancy of such beneficiaries as a group. The present value of any refund feature, operative in event of the death of all annuitants, must be subtracted from the present value of the payments to the group before the division is made. Again, these factors are determined by the interest rate and mortality table used by the insurer in determining the benefits to be paid.

8. *Family maintenance and family income policies.* If the insured dies during the family maintenance or family income period, and if the proceeds are paid out in accordance with those provisions, special rules apply. A portion of each installment is regarded as interest paid on the proceeds of the base policy. This amount is treated as an interest payment, and is fully taxable—the $1,000 annual exclusion for surviving spouse (as described in subsection 10 below) not being available. The balance of each installment is considered as received from the term insurance element under a Fixed Period Option. The regular rules relating to the Fixed Period Option apply to this element, and the special annual exclusion for a surviving spouse is available. The face amount of the base policy received at the end of the income period is tax free under this method of computation.

9. *Payments to contingent payees.* Under the Interest Option, the interest payments each year are as fully taxable to a contingent payee as to the primary payee. Installment payments under the Fixed Period Option or the Fixed Amount Option follow the general principle of law that "a second taker stands in the shoes of the first taker," and the includible and excludable portions of the installments ap-

ply to the contingent beneficiary in the same manner as to the primary beneficiary.

In the case of the Life Income Option, the Regulations, in effect, provide that the payment or payments to the contingent beneficiary are not taxable to the extent that such payments are made by reason of the guaranteed refund feature. Of course, excess interest allowed by the company in addition to the guaranteed amount would be taxable.

10. *Installment payments to a surviving spouse.* As mentioned in Section 6.3.3, a special statutory exclusion is granted by Code Section 101 (d) (1) (B). The insured's surviving spouse is not taxed on the first $1,000 of what normally would be regarded as the interest portion (including any excess interest allowed by the company) of each year's installment payment.

> *Example.* Assume that $100,000 of proceeds payable by reason of the insured's death is payable to the widow under the Fixed Period Option in 10 annual installments of $11,382 each. The prorated amount is $10,000 ($100,000 divided by 10). The widow would include only $382 in her gross income, and exclude $11,000 each year determined in the following manner:

Fixed payment	$11,382
Prorated amount	10,000
Excess over prorated amount	$ 1,382
Special exclusion in favor of payments	
to surviving spouse	1,000
Amount of taxable income	$ 382

This illustration dispels a possible misconception that the $1,000 annual exclusion applies to the *total payments* received by the surviving spouse each year rather than to the *interest portion* of those payments. Thus, a very substantial face amount may be paid *in installments* to a surviving spouse without income tax liability.

Here is another illustration of the importance of intelligent life insurance programing. Assuming that the needs of a particular family can be met equally well either by the Interest Option with the right of withdrawal or by one of the installment options, an installment option will certainly produce a much better tax picture. The $100,000 left with the life insurance company and credited with interest of, say, 4 percent would produce $4,000 of income fully taxable to the widow, without the benefit of the special $1,000 exclusion.

The special exclusion for a surviving spouse does not depend on the number of life insurance policies, but it does depend on the number of *deceased spouses*. For example, a widow whose deceased husband left five policies payable to her under one of the installment options would still be entitled to a maximum of only $1,000 of tax-free interest. However, a surviving spouse of two deceased husbands, each of whom provided policies payable in installments to her, would be entitled to $2,000 of tax-free interest.

To qualify a periodic payment to a widow as an "installment containing both interest and principal," an attempt is sometimes made to select a Fixed Amount Option only slightly in excess of the amount produced under an Interest Option. In determining whether an amount paid under an option represents an "interest only" payment or "proceeds payable in installments containing both interest and principal," the Regulations provide that the payment shall be considered interest unless each installment results in a "substantial diminution" of the principal amount held by the insurer. For example, if a monthly payment is $100, of which $99 represents interest, and $1.00 represents diminution of the principal amount, then the principal amount shall be considered held under an agreement to pay interest thereon, and the interest payment shall be included in the gross income of the recipient. This means that the special $1,000 surviving spouse exclusion would not be available, because it applies only to amounts payable in installments containing both interest and principal.

Policy provisions or company practices usually obviate this problem by requiring that the amount paid annually under the Fixed Amount Option be equal to at least 5 percent, 6 percent, or some other stated percentage of the original proceeds retained by the company.

While the discussion in this section assumes that the husband is the insured and the widow is the surviving spouse, the special statutory exclusion applies with equal force if the wife is the insured and the husband is the surviving spouse.

11. *Transfers for value.* With certain exceptions, the general rule excluding from gross income life insurance proceeds paid by reason of the death of the insured does not apply where ownership of a policy has been transferred for a valuable consideration. In that case, any amount by which the proceeds payable at death exceed the total of the consideration paid by the transferee, plus any premiums paid by him, is taxable to the transferee as ordinary income. If the proceeds are placed under an installment option, only the consideration paid for the transfer plus premiums subsequently paid may be considered as the "amount held by an insurer" for proration purposes.

> *Example.* An insured sells a policy having a face amount of $50,000 for its cash surrender value of $15,000. The purchaser thereafter pays premiums totaling $10,000 until the death of the insured. The face amount of $50,000 is then paid to the purchaser. The purchaser must report $25,000 as ordinary income, which is fully taxable to him. If the proceeds are paid under an installment option, only $25,000 may be recovered free of tax during the installment period.

For the purpose of this discussion, there is a major exception to this general rule. The adverse income tax consequences will not apply if the transfer is to the insured, to a partner of the insured, to a partnership in which the insured is a partner, to a corporation in which the insured is a shareholder or officer, or to a policy whose cost basis is determined in whole or in part by reference to the cost basis of the transferor, such as in a tax-free reorganization. Code Section 101 (a) (2). In transfers for value to other transferees, a substantial portion of the death proceeds of a policy may be subjected to income tax. Of course, the transfer of a policy as a *gift* does not bring into operation the transfer *for value* rules.

12. *Policies under agreements relating to separate maintenance or divorce.* A divorce decree or separation agreement may require the husband to pay premiums on an insurance policy on his life in which his wife or former wife is given ownership rights. In such circumstances, if the wife is absolutely and irrevocably given all the ownership rights, premium payments by the husband on the policy are taxable as income to the wife. Should the husband predecease the wife, she is taxed on that part of the proceeds of the policy which exceeds her "cost"—that is, the cash surrender value when she was given ownership rights, plus the premiums thereafter paid by her husband.

This is another exception to the general rule that proceeds payable by reason of the death of the insured are excluded from taxable income. As in the case of transfers for valuable consideration, proceeds received by a divorced or separated wife in these circumstances and subsequently paid to her under the settlement options involve tax computations different from those prescribed in the usual case.

13. *Employee benefit plans.* Various types of fringe benefits are routinely provided for employees today, often under life insurance and annuity contracts. In some cases, the settlement options are used for the employee or for members of his family. Consideration must often be given to the effect of such benefits when programing the insurance estate.

The rules governing taxation of death benefits under employee plans are frequently different from those discussed elsewhere in this chapter. Often, part or all of the premium payments made by the employer—or from funds contributed by the employer—is not taxed as income to the employee when the premium is paid. Accordingly, special rules are prescribed to tax the employee at some later time on the benefits from the premium payments. Code Section 101 (b) provides a special exclusion up to $5,000 as respects . . . "amounts . . . paid by or on behalf of an employer . . . by reason of the death of the employee." Amounts that would otherwise be taxed as income to the employee's estate or to beneficiaries named by him are excluded up to $5,000, if the payment meets certain tests prescribed in the law.

The rules concerning payments under employee benefit plans can become complex. While final Regulations have clarified many questions which arose after the 1954 Code was enacted, new problems and uncertainties have arisen in such areas as the Self-Employed Individuals Tax Retirement Act of 1962 (also known as H.R.10 or the Keogh Act) and the "tax-sheltered annuity" provisions of Code Section 403 (b). The answer in a particular case may depend on whether or not a plan is qualified under Section 401 of the Code; the extent to which an employee's interest is said to be "vested"; whether the employee has made contributions to the plan; whether the employee is an "owner-employee"; and, in many instances, whether the benefits are to be paid in one sum or in installments. Comprehensive coverage of the taxation of death benefits under employee benefit plans is beyond the scope of this chapter.

§6.4. Proceeds not payable by reason of the death of an insured—annuities, endowment maturities, surrenders. Section 72 of the Code specifies the method for determining taxable income under life insurance or annuity contracts arising from payment of surrender values, endowment maturity values, or certain annuity income.

Payment of any funds to a beneficiary under the Life Income Option is technically the payment of an "annuity." One may wonder, therefore, why such payment will be covered at times under Code Section 72 and at other times under Code Section 101. This is because Code Section 72 (a) states that amounts received as an annuity shall be taxable under Code Section 72 "except as otherwise provided" in the chapter relating to income taxes. Section 101 (d) of the income tax chapter specifically covers Life Income Option payments in the case of proceeds *payable by reason of the death of the insured.*

Generally speaking, proceeds taxable under Code Section 72 are paid for reasons other than the death of the insured. In such cases, the policyowner usually is entitled to recover tax free the amount of premiums he has paid under the contract. The manner in which he receives the proceeds, however, determines how he is to recover his premium cost.

1. *Proceeds payable in one sum.* If the policyowner receives the proceeds in one sum, he is entitled to exclude his premium cost from taxable income in the year the proceeds are received. The difference between this cost and the one sum payment is taxable as ordinary income under Code Section 72 (e) (1). The policyowner's cost will usually be the premiums he has paid. However, this total cost will be reduced by extra premiums for supplementary features such as disability and accidental death benefits. It will also be reduced by dividends he has received under the contract. This reduction of cost is designed to relate the premium only to the cost of the basic insurance or annuity policy to which the gain is normally related. Throughout this chapter, this adjusted cost will usually be referred to as "net cost" or "net premium cost."

> *Example.* An insured surrenders a policy on his life for its cash value of $5,000. He has paid total premiums of $4,800, of which $300 were for accidental

death and disability benefits. The insured had previously received $500 in dividends. His net cost of the basic insurance policy is $4,000, and his taxable income is $1,000. The same method of calculation applies at maturity of an endowment policy.

2. *Proceeds retained under the Interest Option.* Interest payments on proceeds retained by the company are fully taxable under Code Section 72 (j). If endowment maturity or surrender values are placed under the Interest Option, the 1954 Code does not state whether any amount in excess of net cost is taxable to the policyowner in the year of surrender or maturity. Obviously the proceeds are not *actually* received by the policyowner. However, if a taxpayer is given full control of a fund, he is sometimes regarded as having "constructively received" the fund, even though the control is not actually exercised.

Under prior law, if the election of the Interest Option was made *after* the maturity date of an endowment, the maturity value was considered as constructively received and the excess of the maturity value over the cost was taxable as ordinary income in the year of maturity. Even if the election was made *prior* to the maturity date, the excess of the maturity value over the policyowner's cost was seemingly regarded as constructively received if he also reserved the right to withdraw the proceeds at any time. In such circumstances, he would have complete control over the proceeds. *Constance C. Frackelton,* 46 B.T.A. 883 (1942).

On the other hand, if no right of withdrawal was reserved, or if in addition to the withdrawal privilege the policyowner had a contractual right to elect another settlement option, it has been suggested that constructive receipt was avoided. *Blum* v. *Higgins,* 150 F.2d 471, 473 (2d Cir. 1945). A policyowner who contemplates electing the Interest Option in these circumstances will be well advised to request inclusion in the settlement option agreement of the right to change to another settlement option, to preserve the maximum possible tax advantages, if his policy does not already include the contractual right to change to another option.

3. *Proceeds payable in installments of principal and interest.* "Annuities" clearly include installments payable under the Fixed Period and Fixed Amount Options, even though no life contingency is involved.

Code Section 72 (h) provides that when one elects to receive the proceeds as an annuity, instead of in one sum, under an option in the contract, and such election is made within 60 days after the day on which the one sum first became payable, no part of the one sum will be taxable under the doctrine of constructive receipt. This favorable tax result was reached under prior law only if the settlement was elected *prior* to the date the one sum became payable.

On the other hand, if the election is *not* made before the end of this 60-day period, the constructive receipt theory applies. The excess of the one sum over the taxpayer's cost will be taxable as ordinary income in the year of maturity.

> *Example.* The endowment maturity value of a contract that matured September 1, 1964, was $10,000. The aggregate net premium cost to the policyowner was $8,000. If before the date of maturity or within 60 days after that date he elected an installment option provided in the policy, the $2,000 gain would not be considered taxable income in 1964. If the election of the installment option were not made until after the end of the 60 days following the maturity date, the $2,000 gain would be taxed as ordinary income in 1964, under the constructive receipt theory.

In either case, the subsequent installment payments will be taxed in accordance with the rules pertaining to annuity payments, discussed in the following subsections. However, the "cost of the annuity" will differ. If the election is made before the end of the 60-day period, this "cost" will be the net premium cost; if it is made after the end of the 60-day period, the "cost" will be the maturity value.

4. *Fixed Period Option.* In effect, the net cost is spread out over the entire installment period, to be received free of income tax. The amount of each year's installments in excess of the prorated net cost is taxable as ordinary income. The same basic computation applies as in the case of installments under the Fixed Period Option from proceeds payable by reason of the death of the insured, except that the *net premium cost* is recovered tax-free instead of the *death proceeds.*

Regulations under Code Section 101, covering payments by reason of death of the insured, provide a relatively simple formula for ascertaining the taxable portion of fixed installments. The death proceeds are divided by the number of years during which the fixed installments are payable, to determine the excludable portion of each installment. Under Code Section 72, the theory of ascertaining the taxable portion of such installments is quite similar, but the approach is different and involves a more complicated formula.

Code Section 72 prescribes that an "exclusion ratio" shall be determined to furnish the percentage of each installment to be excluded from taxable income. The exclusion ratio is the proportion which the "investment in the contract" bears to the "expected return" under the contract, as of the "annuity starting date."

Assuming that the installment option is elected prior to the end of the prescribed 60-day period, the investment in the contract is simply the policyowner's net premium cost. The expected return is the number of dollars he expects to receive according to the policy guarantees. Under the Fixed Period Option, this is the amount of each periodic installment multiplied by the number of guaranteed installments.

The annuity starting date is the date when the first installment under the contract is payable, except in the case of annuity payments which began in a pre-1954 taxable year. In such a case, the annuity starting date is January 1, 1954. For most taxpayers, the new annuity tax treatment began with the calendar year 1954. Amounts received tax free before January 1, 1954, are subtracted from the cost figure in determining the investment in the contract.

> *Example.* The endowment maturity proceeds of a contract which matured October 1, 1964, were $10,000. The policyowner elected to have the proceeds paid to him in annual installments of $1,138.20 for 10 years under the Fixed Period Option. This election was made either before the date of maturity or within 60 days after that date. The aggregate net premium cost to the insured was $8,000, which was the investment in the contract. The expected return is $11,382—the guaranteed annual intallments multiplied by 10. The following computation is then made:
>
> $$\frac{\text{Investment in the contract}}{\text{Expected return}} = \text{Exclusion ratio}$$
>
> or
>
> $$\frac{\$8,000}{\$11,382} = 70.3\% \text{ (70.29 rounded to nearest tenth)}$$
>
> By applying this percentage to each guaranteed installment payable during the 10 years, $800.15 will be excluded from taxable income. The balance of each guaranteed installment—$338.05—will be regarded as taxable income each year, as will be all excess interest that may be payable by the life insurance company.

The $10,000 maturity value did not enter into this computation, because the installment option was elected before the expiration of 60 days after maturity. Only if the insured failed to make the election until after this time would the maturity value represent his cost. In this event, the difference between the net premium cost and the maturity value, $2,000 in this example, would be taxable as income in the year of maturity, under the constructive receipt theory. The exclusion ratio for the installment payments would then be calculated as follows:

$$\frac{\$10,000}{\$11,382} = 87.9\ \%$$

This percentage would result in excluding $1,000.48 from each of the 10 annual installments, leaving $137.72, plus any excess interest, as taxable income each year.

There may be a few cases in which the taxpayer would benefit under this second approach. By delaying his election of the installment option, he could accept a larger amount of taxable income in the year of maturity, in return for a reduced taxable amount in each subsequent year during the installment period.

However, the arrangement suggested in the example on page 178 will probably be more advantageous in most cases, because it spreads the total gain evenly over the entire installment period.

5. *Fixed Amount Option.* The method of calculating the exclusion ratio should follow the same pattern as that for the Fixed Period Option. Section 1.72-5(d) of the Regulations simply provides that, in computing the expected return with respect to an amount certain, "the expected return shall be the total amount *guaranteed.*" (Italics supplied.)

The expected return is determined by multiplying the fixed amount of each installment by the number of installments that will be produced at the guaranteed interest rate in the policy. The exclusion ratio is then determined by the formula shown in the example for the Fixed Period Option.

The exclusion ratio applies only to installments during the period projected by the guaranteed interest rate. Any payments made beyond this period from excess interest credits are taxable in full.

6. *Life Income Option or annuity payments involving one life.* As in the Fixed Period and Fixed Amount Options, an exclusion ratio must be determined. However, there are two important differences in the computation of the taxable and excludable portions.

(1) Since the specified installments are payable for life, the expected return is determined by multiplying the amount of each year's installments by the number of years in the life expectancy of the payee. The life expectancy relates to the annuity starting date or January 1, 1954, whichever is later. The life expectancy is obtained from Table I of the Regulations, which is reproduced in Appendix C.

(2) The investment in the contract is not simply the net premium cost. Rather, that cost must be reduced by the value of any refund or period-certain feature. The Congressional Committee Reports explain that this reduction avoids a double exclusion. In practical effect, guaranteed payments to the contingent payee are usually excluded from taxable income to him, as explained in Section 6.5.2. If the value of this refund feature were not subtracted from the primary payee's net premium cost, he or she would, in effect, also enjoy an exclusion intended only for the contingent payee to whom the refund will be paid.

The "percent" value of this refund feature is obtained from Table III of the Regulations, reproduced in Appendix D. This table gives a percentage at the point where the horizontal line showing the primary payee's age intersects with the vertical column showing the number of years during which payments are guaranteed.

The percentage found in Table III is then multiplied by the net premium cost or by the total amount guaranteed as of the annuity starting date, *whichever is smaller.* The value of the refund feature thus determined is subtracted from the net premium cost to determine the adjusted investment in the contract.

Example. On January 1, 1964, a husband, age 65, purchased for $15,750, an immediate installment refund annuity to provide monthly payments of $100 during his lifetime. The contract provided that if he did not live long enough to recover the full purchase price, payments were to be made to his wife until the total payments equaled the purchase price. The adjusted investment in the contract is computed as follows:

Cost of the annuity contract (investment in the contract, unadjusted)		$15,750
Amount to be received annually	$1,200	
Number of years for which payment is guaranteed ($15,750 divided by $1,200)	13.1	
Rounded to nearest whole number of years	13	
Percentage located in Table III for age 65 (age of the annuitant as of the annuity starting date) and 13 (the number of whole years)	20%	
Subtract value of the refund feature to the nearest dollar (20% of $15,750)		3,150
Investment in the contract, adjusted for the present value of the refund feature		$12,600

The taxable and excludable portions of the annual installments are then computed as follows:

Annual payments		$1,200
Life expectancy for male age 65 — from Table I	15.0	
Expected return ($1,200 times 15.0)	$18,000	
Investment in the contract (as adjusted in the preceding example)	$12,600	
Exclusion ratio $\dfrac{\$12,600}{\$18,000}$ =	70%	
Annual exclusion (70% of $1,200)		840
Taxable income		$360

The exclusion ratio, once determined, *remains constant throughout the life of the annuitant.* Accordingly, the annuitant may live long enough to receive tax free a sum in excess of the net premium cost.

7. *Annuity payments involving more than one life.* The Regulations for Code Section 72 (c) contain rules and numerous tables for determining the taxable portion of annuity payments that involve more than one life. Various types of joint and survivor annuities are discussed, including variable payment annuities. The principles involved are substantially the same as those illustrated above. However, the computations become more complex when more than one life is involved and when payments differ in specified circumstances. Space does not warrant the number of illustrations that would be needed to explain these various computations. Persons requiring calculations in a specific case will normally direct an inquiry to the home office of the particular life insurance company. Those who would pursue the study further are referred to the Regulations themselves.

8. *Employee benefit plans.* There are special rules governing taxation of payments to an employee. The reasons for the difference in tax treatment are understandably the same as those discussed in Section 6.3.13 concerning *death benefits* under employee benefit plans. It is logical that if an employee receives annuity payments set up by his employer, to which the employee has made no contributions, the annuity payments will be fully taxable to the employee as received. In these circumstances, the employee has no "investment in the contract" to recover free of income tax.

There is no $5,000 exclusion from income tax, such as is provided in the case of amounts paid by reason of the employee's death. However, there is a special exclusion under Code Section 72 (d) if the proceeds are received by an employee *as an annuity* and if he has contributed a part of the premium for it. If the employee's benefits during the first three years will equal or exceed his contributions, benefits will be entirely excluded from taxable income to the employee until he has received his premium cost. Thereafter, the annuity payments will be fully taxable to the employee.

The departure from the more usual rules of taxation quickly leads to complex and unanswered problems. A full discussion of these problems is beyond the scope of this chapter.

§*6.5. Other problems under both Code Sections 101 and 72.* The tax consequences of partial withdrawals of proceeds and of payments to contingent payees require some consideration.

1. *Effect of partial withdrawals of proceeds.* There is no problem when the proceeds are retained under the Interest Option and a partial withdrawal is made. As a practical matter, no problem is usually encountered under the Fixed Period Option or the Life Income Option, because partial withdrawals are almost universally prohibited under these options. However, under the Fixed Amount Option or a policy containing family income or family maintenance benefits, partial withdrawals could affect the payee's tax picture.

The effect of partial withdrawals is not covered under Code Section 101 nor the Regulations thereunder, except to the extent that Regulations Section 1.101-4 (f) indicates that the amount withdrawn shall not be included in gross income unless such amount and all other amounts previously received income tax free exceed the amount that was payable at the time of the death of the insured. This leaves unanswered the question of the taxation of subsequent installments after the partial withdrawal. It seems obvious, however, that the amount to be recovered tax free must be reduced by the amount withdrawn, and that the balance to be recovered tax free should be prorated over the remaining installment period.

Although Code Section 72 does not cover the effect of partial withdrawals, the Regulations issued thereunder do specifically cover the problem. A distinction is made as to the treatment to be given depending on whether subsequent installments are to be received for a different term or whether a reduced amount is to be received for the original term.

a. *Subsequent installments received for a different term after a partial withdrawal.* The one sum withdrawn is not to be treated as taxable income unless it, plus amounts received tax free in prior years, exceeds the cost basis. Regulations Section 1.72-11 (e) provides that a new exclusion ratio should be determined on the basis of the new payments. The investment in the contract should be reduced by any prior tax-free amounts received before the change and by the amount of the partial withdrawal. The expected return should be redetermined by multiplying the annual payments to be received by the term of years or life expectancy, as of the date of the change. As in other instances, the exclusion ratio is then determined by dividing the investment in the contract by the expected return.

b. *Subsequent installments received in a reduced amount for the original term after a partial withdrawal.* Regulations Section 1.72-11 (f) provides that the original "exclusion ratio" continues to apply to the new annuity payments, but a special computation must be made to determine the taxable portion of the one sum withdrawal. Any one sum withdrawn will be included in gross income, except that there shall be excluded the portion of the one sum which bears the same ratio to the aggregate premiums paid for the contract (reduced by prior tax-free amounts) as the amount of the reduction in the annuity payments to be made thereafter bears to the annuity payments originally provided for under the contract.

> *Example.* A partial withdrawal of $4,000 reduces the payments from $100 per month to $75 per month. Original cost was $20,000, and in five years before change, "A" receives $5,000 tax free. Balance of consideration is now $15,000.
>
> Ratio of reduction in monthly payment is 25/100 or ¼. Single sum received was $4,000, so that one-fourth of $15,000 (balance of consideration) or $3,750 deducted from $4,000 leaves $250 as the portion of the one sum which is includible in the payee's gross income. The amount of $250 is reportable income.

2. *Payments to contingent payees.* In the case of the Interest Option, the interest payments each year are as fully taxable to a contingent payee as to the primary payee.

Payments under the Fixed Period Option or the Fixed Amount Option follow the general principle of law that "a second taker stands in the shoes of the first taker." The includible and excludable portions of the periodic installment payments, as determined when the payments commence, apply to the contingent payee whether the installment payments are covered by Code Section 101 or by Section 72.

Slightly different considerations are presented under the Life Income Option with a period-certain or refund feature. The Regulations under Code Section 72 provide that refund payments to a contingent payee are not taxable until the total received, together with any other excluded amounts received under the contract, exceeds the net premium cost. The Regulations under Code Section 101 provide that payments to a contingent payee are not taxable to the extent that such payments are made by reason of the guaranteed refund feature. In practice, this usually results in no taxable income to the contingent payee.

B. FEDERAL ESTATE TAX

§6.6. Background. The federal estate tax is, in effect, an excise tax on the privilege of making a transfer at death. In general, the tax is imposed on all property in which the decedent owns an interest at the time of his death, on property transferred within three years of his death and "in contemplation of death," or on property concerning which he may have transferred something less than an absolute ownership in principal and income while he lived.

Accordingly, there is included in a decedent's gross estate, for federal estate tax purposes:

(1) property in which he has an ownership interest at the time of his death (Code Section 2033); (2) property that he may have transferred by way of gift, in contemplation of his death (Code Section 2035); (3) property that he may have transferred but in which he has retained the right to the income or the right to designate who shall enjoy the income (Code Section 2036); (4) transfers which do not in fact take effect until his death (Code Section 2037); (5) certain revocable transfers which are subject to the decedent's power to alter, amend, revoke, or terminate (Code Section 2038); (6) property owned by the decedent jointly with other persons, including his spouse (Code Section 2040); and (7) certain property which he does not in fact own but over which he has a "power of appointment" (Code Section 2041).

The list of specific types of property also includes the two which are of principal concern in this chapter—annuities (Code Section 2039) and proceeds of life insurance (Code Section 2042). It is apparent that many forms of property will be included in the gross estate for tax purposes, even though they do not, in fact, pass through the hands of the executor.

A number of items are deductible from the gross estate for tax purposes. Code Section 2053 provides for the following usual deductions in arriving at the taxable estate:

(1) funeral expenses; (2) administration expenses; (3) claims against the estate; (4) unpaid mortgages or other indebtedness on property included in the gross estate.

Special provisions of the Code also permit deduction for certain transfers to charity (Section 2055), deduction for specified losses incurred during settlement of the estate (Section 2054), and credit or deduction for certain state death taxes (Section 2053).

A special "marital deduction" was added by the Revenue Act of 1948. In general, property includible in the gross estate which is transferred at death to a surviving spouse in such a way as to give the spouse complete control while she lives may be deducted up to the total amount of one half the "adjusted gross estate." The adjusted gross estate is the gross estate less the above deductions other than the deduction for certain transfers to charity.

The marital deduction also applies to property which, though not subject to the spouse's control while she lives, will pass to her estate when she dies or is subject to her right to make it pass to her estate. Code Section 2056 specifies the precise requirements that must be met to qualify assets for the marital deduction. To the extent that such assets are not taxed in the decedent's estate because of the marital deduction, they may be taxed in the estate of the surviving spouse at his or her later death.

Finally, after all deductions have been taken, including the marital deduction, a personal exemption of $60,000 is allowed in determining the "taxable estate." The estate tax is then applied on a graduated rate basis. At one time, federal estate tax laws gave preferential treatment to life insurance payable to named beneficiaries in the form of a specific exemption of a stated amount. Today, life insurance policies as well as annuity contracts are generally includible in the gross estate of the policyowner, at their value on the date of his death, on much the same basis as any other form of property reached by the statute.

Example.

Gross estate	$230,000
Less deductions	30,000
Adjusted gross estate	$200,000
Marital deduction	100,000
	$100,000
Exemption	60,000
Taxable estate	$ 40,000

The estate tax aspects of life insurance and annuity contracts are discussed separately below, because the tax consequences differ in some particulars. Life insurance is considered primarily with respect to proceeds payable under the settlement options, in the following three categories: (1) policies owned by the insured on his own life; (2) policies owned by someone other than the insured; (3) proceeds at the death of a payee after the insured's death.

§6.7. *Life insurance policies owned by the insured on his own life.* Here is a brief summary of the rules concerning the taxability of such policies and qualification of the proceeds for the marital deduction.

1. *Rules for determining includibility in the gross estate.* Proceeds payable to the *insured's estate* or used for the economic benefit of his estate are includible in the gross estate regardless of who owned the policy. On the other hand, proceeds payable to *named beneficiaries* other than the insured's estate are included in the gross estate only if the insured possessed any "incidents of ownership" at the time of his death or had transferred ownership as a gift "in contemplation of death."

Many pages could be devoted to the refinements of what constitutes incidents of ownership within the meaning of Code Section 2042. In general, they are the contractual rights and privileges of the policyowner, such as the rights to change the beneficiary, to elect settlement options, and to surrender or borrow against the contract. For the purposes of this discussion, the phrase may be viewed as including actual ownership of the policy, or a transfer of ownership in such a way that the insured retains a 5 percent or better chance that he or his estate will regain ownership. The latter situation is technically described in the law as a "reversionary interest."

As in the case of other transfers of property, a transfer of ownership of a life insurance policy within three years prior to the death of the insured may be regarded as a gift made "in contemplation of death." Unless the executor can prove that the gift was not so made, the proceeds will be included in the insured's gross estate just as if he had owned the policy at his death.

These tax consequences apply with equal force whether the proceeds are payable in one sum or under a settlement option. If a settlement option is elected before the insured's death, the amount includible in the gross estate is the amount that would have been paid had no settlement option been elected.

2. *Qualifying proceeds for marital deduction.* In estates of more than $60,000—the present specific federal estate tax exemption—the policyowner will want to consider qualifying the proceeds of one or more life insurance policies for the marital deduction under Code Section 2056 (b) (6).

The marital deduction rules pertaining to proceeds of a life insurance policy or an annuity contract specify that such proceeds may be qualified for this deduction in any one of these ways:

(1) If the proceeds are payable to the wife in one sum, even though contingent beneficiaries are named (provided there is no possibility under the policy that someone other than the wife or her estate could become entitled to receive the proceeds following the insured's death, as when a pol-

icy provides that the beneficiary must be alive when proofs are filed or payment of the proceeds is made to be entitled to the proceeds of the policy).

(2) If the wife is named as primary beneficiary, and the only contingent beneficiary is her estate, even though a settlement option is specified which gives the wife no right to withdraw or commute the proceeds.

(3) If the proceeds are payable to the wife as primary beneficiary under a settlement option, and a contingent beneficiary other than her estate is named, the proceeds will qualify if she is given either: (a) the full right to withdraw or commute the proceeds while she lives, *or* (b) the power to appoint her estate as contingent beneficiary.

With respect to the third method, the surviving spouse need never *exercise* either power. It is sufficient that she possess one power or the other.

The provisions of some companies' policies create a "terminable interest" which disqualifies for the marital deduction, as described in (1) above. These provisions would also disqualify the arrangement described in (3) (a) above. Disqualification in either case may be avoided by including in the beneficiary designation the power described in (3) (b), *exercisable from the moment of the insured's death,* even though the beneficiary is not entitled to receive the proceeds because of the policy requirement that she be alive when proofs are filed or when payment is made.

Policies in many companies place administrative restrictions and limitations on a right of withdrawal, such as the number of withdrawals permitted or minimum amounts. Such restrictions raise a question as to whether the right of withdrawal can be exercised "in all events," and this may lead to a disqualification for marital deduction purposes. Accordingly, when proceeds are to be qualified for the marital deduction, it would appear advisable to "put an extra bolt on the door" by including in the beneficiary designation a power of appointment clause of the type described in (3) (b) above, and not to rely solely on a right of withdrawal, or on the fact that the proceeds are payable to the wife in one sum.

The following sample clause represents an acceptable power of appointment:

> Said wife, by a writing (other than by a will or by a codicil to a will) executed subsequent to the death of the insured and during her lifetime, shall have the power to direct the Company to pay in one sum to the executors or administrators of the estate of said wife, or to such other contingent beneficiaries as she may designate, the proceeds undistributed at the death of said wife, notwithstanding any contrary provision of the policy or this settlement option agreement.

While this discussion refers to the surviving spouse as the "wife," the marital deduction is, of course, equally applicable as respects the surviving husband.

Whether one or more life insurance policies should be qualified for the marital deduction often involves complex estate planning considerations. The relative size of the estates owned by both spouses may be a factor. For example, if the wife has a large estate, full use of the marital deduction by the husband's estate may result in the total tax on both estates being increased rather than decreased. There may be many factors other than tax reduction that have a bearing on the degree of control of the estate which should be given to the surviving spouse.

If it is decided to take advantage of the marital deduction, there is also the question of which assets to qualify for this purpose. Normally, under the policies of most companies, insurance proceeds intended to be available in cash to the spouse can be made to qualify, either as a one sum payment or under the Interest Option subject to unlimited withdrawal. In addition, proceeds payable under installment options may be more logical to qualify than other assets of equivalent value. Because principal is being ex-

pended each year under the installment options, there may
be much less principal, if any, exposed to tax at the subsequent death of the surviving spouse.

These are but a few of the many considerations involved in deciding on the use of the marital deduction. An
attorney familiar with the various aspects of estate planning should be consulted regarding this decision. Obviously, he should be conversant with the estates of both
spouses.

§6.8. *Policies owned by someone other than the insured.* In the case of a policy owned by a third party, there
may be tax consequences on the death of the owner as well
as on the death of the insured.

1. *Death of insured during lifetime of owner.* If the
insured dies during the owner's lifetime, and the beneficiary is other than the estate of the insured, the proceeds in
most circumstances will not be included in the insured's
gross estate for federal estate tax purposes. This is particularly true if the policy was applied for and owned by a third-
party owner at the outset. It may also be true of a policy
transferred by the insured to another, by assignment or
otherwise.

The proceeds of a policy originally owned by the insured but transferred by him to another owner may still be
included in his gross estate: (1) if the transfer was made in
such a way that the insured retained an incident of ownership within the meaning of Code Section 2042; or (2) if the
transfer is held to be a gift in contemplation of death, under
Code Section 2035.

2. *Death of owner during lifetime of the insured.*
Where a policy is owned by a person other than the insured,
and the owner predeceases the insured, the value of the
policy will be includible in the gross estate of the owner
for federal estate tax purposes, under Code Section 2033,
as property in which the decedent had an interest. This re-

sult will follow whether the third-party ownership was established in the original application for the policy or by later assignment.

A question is presented as to the method of valuing the policy in the deceased owner's gross estate. Regulations Section 20.2031-8 provides that the value of a policy on the life of a person other than the decedent is the cost of a comparable contract sold by the issuing company. If such cost is not readily ascertainable, and if further premiums are to be paid, the value may be approximated by using the interpolated terminal reserve plus any premiums paid for a period beyond the insured's death. This principle was upheld in *Estate of Richard C. du Pont* v. *Commissioner,* 233 F.2d 210 (3d Cir. 1956). The estate in that case contended unsuccessfully that the lower cash surrender value was the amount properly includible.

§6.9. *Proceeds payable at the death of a payee after the insured's death.* The following principles apply whether the policies were owned by the insured at the time of his death or by some other person. The question is what part of the proceeds, if any, is includible in the gross estate of a beneficiary who dies after the insured.

1. *Settlement option elected by beneficiary.* If the proceeds payable by reason of the insured's death were payable to the beneficiary in one sum, but the beneficiary elected one of the settlement options, with income payable to herself for her lifetime, any balance of proceeds payable at the beneficiary's death will be includible in that beneficiary's gross estate. This rule will seemingly apply whether or not the beneficiary has reserved any control over the proceeds.

If the beneficiary's right is limited to the receipt of interest or installment income, he or she will be regarded as having made a transfer intended to take effect at death, or as having retained the life income under transferred property. In either case, any proceeds remaining at the beneficiary's death will be taxable under one or more of Code Sections 2036 through 2038.

2. *Settlement option elected by insured or other owner.* Under a settlement option agreement elected before the insured's death, if the primary beneficiary's rights are confined to receiving interest or installment payments as they become due, i.e., if only a life estate is given, and if any remaining proceeds at the primary beneficiary's death are payable otherwise than to the primary beneficiary's estate, no part of the proceeds should be includible in the primary beneficiary's gross estate for federal estate tax purposes.

On the other hand, where the primary beneficiary is given a complete right of withdrawal or commutation, or a power to appoint her estate as contingent beneficiary, she will be deemed to possess a general power of appointment over the proceeds, under Code Section 2041(b). If the beneficiary's right to withdraw the proceeds was created after October 21, 1942, the value of any balance remaining with the life insurance company at the time of her death will be includible in her gross estate under Code Section 2041(a)(2).

If the primary beneficiary's right to withdraw principal is limited, there is a question as to what portion of the remaining proceeds may be included in the beneficiary's gross estate at her death. A popular arrangement is to provide that a beneficiary may withdraw up to a specified amount of principal each year, for example, not in excess of $1,000 per year. To the extent that the full permissible amount is not withdrawn in any one year, the right to make withdrawals for that year lapses.

Code Section 2041(b)(2) provides that if a power of appointment created after October 21, 1942 lapses during the life of the individual possessing the power, this will generally be considered a release of such power. Release of a power of appointment created after that date will make the property over which the power was exercisable includible in the gross estate of the one who may exercise the power. However, the general rule that a lapse is considered a release of a power will not apply to the extent that the value of the property over which the right could have been exercised does not exceed $5,000 or 5 percent of the then value of proceeds, whichever is greater.

Accordingly, if the beneficiary of life insurance proceeds retained by the insurance company is given annual withdrawal rights not in excess of the greater of these limits, there will be included in her gross estate at her death only the unwithdrawn balance of the permissible amount *for the year in which her death occurs.*

> *Example.* The insured died in 1955. The proceeds of a $100,000 life insurance policy on his life are retained under the Interest Option for his wife, who is given the right to withdraw $5,000 per year. Children of the insured are named as contingent beneficiaries. The wife dies in 1965, having withdrawn no part of the principal amount. There will be included in her gross estate, for federal estate tax purposes, only $5,000—the amount of principal she might have withdrawn in the year of her death.

§6.10. Annuity contracts. At death of the purchaser of an annuity contract purchased after March 3, 1931, the value of any payments to be made under the contract after his death is includible in his gross estate under Code Section 2039, whether payable to a named beneficiary or to his estate. In general, the rules and principles which apply to life insurance proceeds are applicable to annuities, except that Code Section 2042 will not apply to the death benefit under an annuity contract because "life insurance" is not involved.

1. *Value to be included in gross estate.* Of course, payments under a straight life annuity cease at the death

of the annuitant, and there is no estate tax liability. Under a cash refund or retirement annuity, the death benefit payable in one sum is the amount to be included in the gross estate. In an installment refund or period-certain annuity, the commuted value of the unpaid guaranteed payments at the death of the purchaser-annuitant is includible.

Under a joint and survivor annuity, if all the purchase price was contributed by the decedent, the value for estate tax purposes is the cost of a comparable annuity at the survivor's attained age when the decedent died. Regulations Section 20.2031-8.

On the other hand, if the decedent did not contribute to the purchase price, or if the contract was purchased before March 4, 1931, the decedent's gross estate would not include any value for the contract. Finally, if part of the purchase price was contributed by the decedent and part by the surviving annuitant, only a proportionate amount of the replacement cost value would be included in the decedent's estate.

2. *Employee annuities.* Frequently, life insurance policies are used to fund qualified pension or profit-sharing plans. These policies are often of the retirement income type with insurance, or retirement annuities may be used. Under Code Section 2039 (c), the proceeds are entirely exempt from estate tax if the plan is noncontributory and if the proceeds are payable to the employee's beneficiary, other than his estate. If the plan is contributory and the proceeds are payable to the employee's beneficiary, other than his estate, the proceeds are taxable in the employee's estate only to the extent that they are attributable to the employee's contributions.

If the pension or profit-sharing plan is not qualified under Code Section 401 (a), death benefits attributable to an employee's contributions are includible in the employee's gross estate, and any contributions made by the employer are also considered as contributions of the employee for this purpose, if made by reason of his employment.

C. Federal Gift Tax

§6.11. Introduction. This is the third major federal tax that may affect life insurance and annuity contracts. Like the estate tax, the gift tax is imposed, on a progressive rate basis, on the privilege of transferring property. However, it applies to transfers during life and involves a somewhat different method of determining tax liability by providing both annual exclusions and a lifetime exemption. The federal gift tax law provides for a marital deduction corresponding to the marital deduction allowed under the federal estate tax law.

There are relatively few gift tax problems concerning payment of proceeds of life insurance or annuity contracts under settlement options.

§6.12. Taxable transfers generally. As indicated in Section 6.8, the proceeds of a policy may not be subject to estate tax in certain instances if ownership has been transferred to someone other than the insured. However, such transfers may constitute a taxable gift, whether made by absolute assignment or otherwise.

One example of a taxable transfer "otherwise" than by absolute assignment is the designation of an irrevocable beneficiary. Such designations are specifically ruled to be gifts under Regulations Section 25.2511-1 (h) (8). On the other hand, the mere designation of a *revocable* beneficiary is not considered a taxable gift.

Where a policy is transferred as a gift, the value for tax purposes is normally determined in the same manner as for cases involving the death of a third-party owner before the insured. (See Section 6.8.2.) The payment of premiums by someone other than the owner of the policy constitutes a gift to the owner in the amount of the premium paid each year. Regulations Section 25.2511-1 (h) (8).

§6.13. Gift tax on certain death proceeds. Proceeds of a policy owned by an insured, and paid by reason of his death, are not a "transfer" subject to gift tax. The same result follows if a third-party owner himself receives the proceeds as beneficiary when the insured dies.

However, if the owner designates someone other than himself as beneficiary, an adverse gift tax consequence can result. In *Goodman* v. *Commissioner*, 156 F.2d 218 (2d Cir. 1946), the wife owned a half million dollars of insurance on the life of her husband. She named her children as primary beneficiaries, subject to her right to change the beneficiary designation. The insured died. The court held that there was a taxable gift from the mother to her children at the moment of the insured's death. The value of the gift was the entire proceeds and not merely the value of the policies immediately prior to death.

This situation is easily overlooked in the designation of beneficiaries by owners other than the insured. The unfavorable tax consequence can be avoided if the owner designates himself as beneficiary. If the owner designates someone else as beneficiary, the principle of the *Goodman* case will apply whether the proceeds are payable in one sum or in installments. Presumably, the same gift tax result would also follow the naming of a beneficiary other than the owner under the various types of annuity contracts involving refund features.

In a settlement option elected by an owner-beneficiary, *if no right of withdrawal or power to change contingent beneficiaries is retained,* there may be a taxable gift from such owner-beneficiary to the contingents, at the moment of the insured's death. While there are apparently no decided cases on this question, the Treasury Department could contend that an interest vests in the *contingent* beneficiaries at the moment of the insured's death, following the reasoning of the *Goodman* case. The value of such a gift may be significant or negligible, depending on the actuarial value of the primary beneficiary's interest in income during his or her lifetime.

Normally, such an arrangement would also be subject

to federal *estate* tax in the estate of the owner who names himself as primary beneficiary, whether or not there is a right to withdraw proceeds or a power to designate or change contingent beneficiaries. Inclusion of such a power, if desired, will have no unfavorable estate tax consequences, and it should avoid any possibility of gift tax liability.

§*6.14. Gifts of endowment contracts at maturity.* If prior to maturity the owner of an endowment policy irrevocably designates someone else as the payee to receive the maturity value in one sum or in installments, there is a taxable gift in the amount of the maturity value. Any income tax on the gain at maturity or on settlement option installments as they are received is payable by the donee and is determined in the same manner as it would have been for the donor.

If the maturity proceeds of an endowment policy are made payable under a joint and survivor annuity option, the irrevocable designation of a survivor annuitant constitutes a taxable gift by the owner. The value of the gift is the cost of a comparable annuity to provide similar payments to the donee-annuitant. Regulations Section 25.-2512-6.

D. TAXES IMPOSED BY THE STATES

§*6.15. State death taxes.* All states except Nevada have some form of inheritance or estate tax levied on assets of a decedent. In general, the state inheritance tax is levied on the privilege of inheriting. The rate of tax may depend on the relationship of the recipient to the decedent. The rate may be constant or graduated. It may also depend on the type of property involved. In any event, the amount of tax will depend on the share of the estate received by a particular person.

Most states also have an "estate" tax designed to absorb the maximum credit allowed under the federal estate tax law for death taxes paid to the states. A few states have a true estate tax, usually in lieu of the more common inheritance tax. In either case, estate taxes levied by the states are based on the same philosophy as is the federal estate tax. In effect, they represent a tax on the privilege of transferring property. The amount of the tax is based on the total value of the estate, after deductions and exemptions, rather than on the values of individual shares.

The concept of taxable property under state inheritance tax laws usually differs greatly from the comprehensive scope of the federal estate tax law. An example of the much more limited application of state laws is property jointly held by husband and wife. Although under the federal estate tax law the full value of such property may be included in the gross estate of the spouse first to die, such property is wholly exempt under state inheritance tax laws in about one-fourth of the states.

Generally, life insurance proceeds payable to the insured's estate are fully taxable under state laws. Life insurance proceeds payable to named beneficiaries are wholly or partially exempt in many states, and this is true even though the insured owns the policy. In a number of states, there are special exemptions for life insurance proceeds varying in amounts from $10,000 to $100,000. In some instances, the exemption for life insurance proceeds depends on whether the beneficiary is within a limited class, such as wife or children.

Generally, annuity death benefits are not considered insurance and are not entitled to the special tax treatment granted life insurance. Annuity death benefits would normally be taxed in the same manner as other property owned by the decedent.

§6.16. **State income and personal property taxes.** Almost three-fourths of the states have income tax laws for individuals. Many of the states now follow the pattern of the 1954 Code. In the future, more states may be expected to change over to this or a similar pattern. However, no generalization can be made, and the laws and regulations of each state must be carefully examined to determine the extent to which insurance proceeds may be exposed to income taxes.

Some states, like Michigan and Ohio, do not have individual income tax laws, but impose taxes on income from intangible property under a personal property tax law. The tax on income from intangible property in such states is often broad enough to reach the interest or income element of life insurance proceeds payable in installments.

Chapter 7

Other Aspects of Settlement Options

§*7.1. Synchronizing proceeds of several policies.* A client frequently will own policies taken out at different times. These policies may be in the same company; more usually they will be spread among several companies. The quality of the programing job will depend on proper use of the various policies, and the extent to which they have been synchronized to provide a unified distributive pattern.

Essentially, this means arranging income payments to run concurrently from all policies allocated to this purpose, insofar as practicable. If separate policies are used to provide successive periods of income, a policy which is lapsed or heavily borrowed against when death occurs may cause an entire "block" of income to be eliminated or sharply reduced. With concurrent installments, by way of contrast, the effect of such a situation would be a small reduction in income spread over a longer period of time.

Obviously, this is not a rule which can be followed in every case. For example, income for the Social Security gap period usually must be arranged to start when the youngest child is 18 and to end when the widow reaches age 62. However, it is a good principle to keep in mind, especially when planning the settlement of dependency period income.

§7.2. Combining policies in the same company. Often, proceeds of two or more policies in the same company may be combined under one settlement option agreement, where appropriate, to achieve greater simplicity. Some companies will not permit such arrangements where the policies contain different income guarantees under the settlement options. Where such a plan is permitted despite income differentials between the policies, care should be taken that any withdrawable funds are not deemed to come from the contracts having the higher interest guarantees.

§7.3. Using older policies for long periods of income. Where it is desired to provide long periods of income, whether for a term of years or during the lifetime of the beneficiary, older policies will usually give the better return. Conversely, newer policies and small contracts whenever issued should be used to provide income for short periods of time and for cash funds.

Where proceeds are to be payable over a long period of time, such as 20 years or more, the interest rate becomes an important consideration. The installment options use the principle of compound interest. Accordingly, the longer the specified income period, the larger will be the interest element in proportion to the total payments.

On the other hand, the rate of interest is of minor concern in setting up funds that are expected to be withdrawn within a relatively short time after the insured's death, such as clean-up, mortgage cancellation, or emergency funds.

Older policies give better settlement option income for two reasons. First, these policies provide higher *guaranteed* interest rates and installments based on these rates than do policies issued during the past 20 years or so. In practical effect, since actual distributive rates are higher today than the guaranteed rates in most instances, the higher guarantees in older policies are not as meaningful, so long as these higher distributive rates continue. Second, the bet-

ter return under Life Income Options in older policies results in large part from the more favorable annuity rates
attributable to higher mortality assumptions in the older
policies. Advances in medical science and other factors have
resulted in an increase in the span of human life. This has
been as true of annuitants as of others. The lengthening of
their life spans has necessitated lower annuity returns in
policies issued in recent years. Thus, the Life Income Option with a 10-year-certain period, in a policy issued in 1934
by a typical life insurance company, provided for a male
annuitant age 65 a guaranteed monthly annuity of $7.32 per
thousand of proceeds. The corresponding figure in a policy
issued by the same company 30 years later is $6.24.

These two factors account for the difference in income
rates guaranteed in policies issued at different times, especially under the various Life Income Options. In connection with these options, a third factor may accentuate the
difference. Most policies issued in the last 30 years or so provide smaller life income returns for female beneficiaries or
annuitants than for males of the same age, because, on the
average, women live longer than men. Frequently, this differential is absent in older contracts. This differential is
also absent in Life Income Options in U.S. Government
and regular (participating) National Service Life Insurance policies.

Older policies cannot always be used to provide long-
period income. This is particularly true of small policies,
unless they can be combined with other contracts in the
same company to form a reasonably workable fund. Although many companies will accept as little as $1,000 of
proceeds under an option, it is usually impractical to settle
such small amounts in this way, unless the proceeds are to
be paid out over a short period of time, such as one to three
years. The minimum installment provision in the policy
may require the use of relatively inconvenient quarterly or
semiannual installments. An outstanding loan at the time

of claim may reduce proceeds below the required minimum and result in a cash payment anyway.

§7.4. *Making sure each policy contains all available options.* Chapter 4 explains why practices of companies differ in the extent to which settlement options are made available for the benefit of an insured or for beneficiaries designated by the insured. These variations are particularly noticeable when the request is one which the company is not obligated to grant under the terms of its contract with the policyowner. For example, some settlement options, such as those providing joint and survivorship life income, are attached by some companies only on special request. Another example is the denial by a few companies of an *insured's* request to apply the cash surrender value under the options in the contract for his own benefit, as respects policies issued some years ago.

It is well to learn the practices on these points of each company represented in a client's program. If certain options are included only on request, such request may easily be inserted in the application for a new policy. For existing policies, the appropriate request form is readily obtainable from the company.

The settlement option provisions of the policy will often give the answers concerning the extent to which settlement options are available, particularly the extent to which they may be used by the insured at the time of surrender or at the date of endowment maturity. However, in some cases, the policy is silent or is not entirely clear on this point. Some life underwriters use something like the following paragraph in letters prepared for an insured's signature:

> It is my desire that at retirement I have the right to settle the cash value of this contract under any of the settlement options, including joint and survivorship life income. Please endorse the policy so as to add such of these privileges as may be available and not already a

part of the contract. If the joint and survivorship option is available, please furnish the monthly income rates for at least my ages 55, 60, and 65; on the other hand, if I must specify a particular age at this time, this would be age 65 for myself, and age 62 for my wife.

§*7.5. Trusts versus settlement options.* When should the insurance proceeds be administered by a corporate trustee rather than under the settlement options? An intelligent answer to this question will depend on a number of factors, which will vary in each case. The decision should be reached only after consultation with the insured's attorney. Several motivating factors should be considered.

1. *Degree of discretion required.* If the needs of the beneficiaries can be met by a fixed schedule of payments—at definite times to specified individuals—requiring little or no discretion as to the times or amounts of payments, the settlement options probably will be the more attractive. Proceeds designed for emergency funds, dependency period income, and other basic family needs can frequently be well covered by an interest or installment option combined with withdrawal privileges. This is particularly true in the small or medium-sized estate, which consists principally of the home, modest savings in the form of cash or its equivalent, and the life insurance policies. Even a fixed schedule of payments is not necessary in the case of minor children. As suggested in Section 3.15.5, proceeds can be retained under the Interest Option, with a trustee given full withdrawal privileges and the right to elect other options. On the other hand, if judgment, discretion, or flexibility to a greater degree is required, the proceeds may be better administered under a formal trust arrangement.

For example, an insured may wish to make principal available for the benefit of a mentally or physically handicapped child, even though funds may be expended that would otherwise be payable to the other children. In such case, the skilled services of an experienced corporate trustee furnishes the only complete solution.

2. *Size of the estate.* In substantial estates, trust arrangements are often more appealing than the use of settlement options. The discretionary aspect assumes added importance. Such estates are usually composed of many types of property and frequently include closely held business interests, which present special problems of a continuing nature. The estate owner may feel that payment of the insurance proceeds to the trustee will result in a more synchronized arrangement to conserve general estate assets and will implement what is often an elaborate estate plan.

In the smaller estate, where life insurance is the principal asset except for the home and the modest savings, the life insurance company with its settlement options generally provides the ideal solution. However, there may be instances where a life insurance trust can be both useful and practical. Often, the various cash funds set up under the life insurance program aggregate a substantial sum. Though a large portion of these proceeds may be needed at once for clean-up or mortgage cancellation purposes, the total to be held intact for some years to cover emergency and educational expenses might be large enough to justify a trust as primary beneficiary.

Discretionary common trust funds have become increasingly popular for administering relatively small trusts. Sometimes called combined or general trust funds, such plans for investing assets of trusts are offered by many trust companies in most of the states. The common trust fund is essentially a means of pooling or commingling funds from a number of small trusts to afford such trusts wider diversification, greater stability of income, and more economical administration than would be possible if they were separate investment entities. If available through local trust companies, such common trust funds may prove very useful for administering emergency and educational funds, as well as mortgage and estate clearance funds provided by life insurance.

If a trust is feasible in such smaller estate, it might

also constitute an ideal contingent beneficiary for unpaid balances under policies used to provide income for the widow, in event of her death before the children are grown. Even when the estate owner feels that the settlement options can fulfill all anticipated needs of his widow, he frequently prefers to designate a trustee as contingent beneficiary to administer the funds for his children and grandchildren. This arrangement is a popular compromise between the exclusive use of a trust and the exclusive use of settlement options.

3. *Safety of principal.* When settlement options are used, the entire assets of the insurance company stand behind the proceeds of a policy to assure certainty of income and safety of principal. In the case of a trust, any loss of trust assets is borne by the individual trust, though this loss may be minimized when a common trust fund is used. This problem has been academic for more than two decades of good business and continued inflation, but it may again assume importance if the business pendulum swings the other way.

4. *Cost of administering the trust.* Proper trust administration requires much skill and experience and merits compensatory fees. On the other hand, the use of settlement options involves no direct charge to the insured or his beneficiaries. The administrative cost of the settlement option service is borne by the entire group of policyowners.

5. *Rate of return.* Figures have been produced to show that a better rate of return is realized under a trust than under settlement options, and vice versa. If the proceeds are payable to a surviving spouse under an installment option, the interest element will be tax free to the extent of $1,000 each year. Under the Internal Revenue Code, the net return to the beneficiary will usually compare most favorably with the net return under a trust after payment of income taxes. Regardless of which plan shows a higher estimated return, this is just one of the factors

that must be weighed in formulating the overall decision in a particular case. The security of a guarantee is quite important to many insureds. Such a guarantee is provided under the settlement options, whereas there is none in the trust.

6. *Need for annuity income.* If a life income must be provided in a particular case, with a maximum dollar return to the beneficiary by use of both principal and income, an annuity settlement is the only practicable solution. This can be provided only through the life insurance company; it cannot be made available under a trust. A trust can distribute income and principal only until the principal is exhausted.

7. *Corporate or individual trustee?* If the decision is in favor of using a trustee, a corporate trustee usually will be indicated. With present-day complexities of trust law and trust administration, legal requirements that must be met, and periodic tax and other returns that must be completed, there is a need for continuity of trust administration that can usually be furnished best by the corporate trustee. Corporations do not die, do not take extended vacations, and are not absent on business trips when important decisions are to be made. Experience gleaned in the daily administration of trusts and the handling of trust problems constantly tends to improve the skills of the corporate trust department.

The naming of one or more individual cotrustees is a popular practice, particularly when the principal beneficiary is the surviving spouse or when there are business interests to be administered. For example, when the surviving spouse is to receive income while she lives, together with such payments of principal as the trustee may deem necessary and proper for her maintenance and support from time to time, she may be named as individual cotrustee. She will then be in a position of sharing responsibility for important decisions in trust management and trust administration. A "we" rather than a "they" attitude is likely to be engendered.

When a business interest is to be administered in some fashion by the trustees, the naming of one or more business associates, with full individual responsibility for making business decisions, is another common arrangement.

8. *Other factors.* It may be said that, as a general rule, settlement options will solve most of the family needs in modest and medium-sized estates, whereas trusts will be more appealing to the very substantial estate owner, and to those who have unusual family or personal problems. Trusts may be particularly attractive where it is desired to provide luxuries according to a pattern followed when the estate owner was alive. There will be many instances where a predominance of the considerations will not be in one direction, and where the decision can well go either way.

Settlement options and trusts are rarely, in a strict sense, in competition with each other. Each has its particular advantages and its limitations. The best service can be rendered the estate owner by development and consideration of all pertinent facts, and by making certain that he understands how each method applies in his particular case.

§7.6.   *Other trust problems concerning beneficiary designations.* The use of a trust arrangement in connection with life insurance raises certain other problems which merit consideration.

1. *Funded and unfunded life insurance trusts.* Discussion of all the various types of trusts that may be created is beyond the scope of this book. However, two terms should be understood because they are frequently encountered in designating trustees under life insurance policies. These terms are "unfunded trusts" and "funded trusts."

The designation of trustees under life insurance policies usually involves an unfunded life insurance trust. This is one in which the creator (frequently referred to as the "settlor") of the trust makes the insurance payable to the trustee by a beneficiary designation, with provisions in the trust instrument concerning administration and distribution of the policy proceeds at death, but without imposing active duties on the trustee concerning maintenance of the policy while the insured lives.

A funded life insurance trust, on the other hand, is one in which the settlor not only makes the insurance payable to the trustee and specifies how the proceeds shall be handled after his death, but also delivers to the trustee cash or other property, such as securities, from which to make payment of premiums. Under such a trust, the trustee is charged with the active duty of supervising the maintenance of the policies during the insured's lifetime.

A funded or unfunded life insurance trust is also called an *inter vivos* or "living" trust—that is, one created during the lifetime of the settlor.

The unfunded insurance trust is generally, but not necessarily, *revocable,* whereas the funded insurance trust is often, but likewise not necessarily, *irrevocable.* A revocable trust is one under which the settlor reserves the right to alter, amend or revoke the trust at any time, whereas these rights are not reserved in the case of the irrevocable trust. The latter is principally used to make living gifts of property without placing full legal title and management responsibility in the hands of the donee.

2. *Designation of testamentary trustees.* Instead of designating as beneficiaries the trustees under an *inter vivos* life insurance trust, an insured at times requests that trustees under his will be so designated. Since a trust created by will is known as a testamentary trust, this is known as a "testamentary trustee" designation. Quite frequently the wife or some other person is named as primary beneficiary with the trustees under the will as contingent beneficiaries. Under such an arrangement, the trust provisions are incorporated in the insured's will rather than in a trust

agreement. The trust created under the will has no more effect during the lifetime of the settlor than does the will itself. Its existence after his death depends on probate and enforcement of the will. Should the will fail to qualify for probate or be declared invalid for any reason, the testamentary trust in that will would fail also.

There is a danger that the insured may change his will and forget to make a change in the beneficiary designation that ties into the provisions of the will. A new will may name no trustee. Even if a trustee is so named, the insured may no longer desire the proceeds of the particular life insurance policy or policies to be payable to the trustees under his will. Certainly notations should be kept with both the will and the beneficiary papers so that both instruments will be considered together when a change is contemplated in either.

Obviously the designation as beneficiaries of trustees under an insured's will can be hazardous. Certainly it should not be attempted without careful and thorough study by a competent attorney.

It is interesting to observe that statutes have been enacted in a number of states, including New York and Pennsylvania, specifically exempting life insurance proceeds payable to testamentary trustees from claims of creditors and state inheritance taxes.

In wills prepared today, more than one trust often is created. This is particularly true since passage of the Revenue Act of 1948 which introduced the marital deduction explained in Section 6.6. The estate tax minimizing principle of the marital deduction applies to trusts that meet the qualifying rules of Section 2056 (b) (5) of the Internal Revenue Code. Two trusts are often set up in a will for the benefit of the insured's surviving spouse. These trusts may be designated "Trust A" and "Trust B." The wife will be the income beneficiary under both trusts. One trust contains provisions to qualify it for the marital deduction under the Code section just mentioned, and it is frequently called the "marital deduction trust." The other trust does not contain qualifying provisions, and it is called the "bypassing trust"—so named because it is designed to bypass the surviving spouse's taxable estate at death. In such cases, there may be valid reasons for having the proceeds specifically paid to the trustees under one or the other trust in the balancing of assets for marital deduction purposes. Despite the compelling reasons that may exist for this designation, it should be requested only on the advice of an attorney who has considered the entire estate picture. The following example of a clause used illustrates the many contingencies inherent in such designation:

> The proceeds shall be paid to the trustees under "Trust A" designated under the insured's will, or to their successor or successors in trust, without any responsibility on the part of the XYZ Life Insurance Company to see to the proper discharge of any part of said trust; but if the Company receives written evidence satisfactory to it that:
>
> > (1) the trustees for any reason fail to serve and no successor trustee was appointed; or
> >
> > (2) a will of the insured, which was admitted to probate, made no provision for "Trust A"; or
> >
> > (3) a personal representative of the insured has been appointed in intestacy;
>
> then, in any such event, the proceeds shall be paid to the executors or administrators of the insured; provided, however, that the Company shall be fully discharged for any payment made to said trustees before receipt of written evidence satisfactory to it that said trustees are not entitled to payment under the provisions of this Designation.

In most instances, it will be sufficient simply to designate as beneficiaries the trustees under the will without referring to a specific trust, because the will usually provides that estate assets shall be allocated to one trust or the other to obtain the maximum marital deduction.

§7.7. *Common disaster provisions.* Discussion of "common disaster" in life insurance policies usually refers to the contingency that the insured and his wife may die in such circumstances that the insurance proceeds will pass in a manner inconsistent with the wishes of the insured. Common disaster clauses are designed to prevent this adverse result.

Assume that the insured and his wife are riding in an automobile and that they are fatally injured as the result of an accident. Assume further that the insured is killed instantly and that his wife survives for an hour or two and then dies. Finally, assume that the proceeds of a policy on the life of the husband are payable "to my wife, if she be living at my death, otherwise to my surviving children equally." In these circumstances, the proceeds of the policy would not be payable to the children because the wife was actually living at the death of the insured. Accordingly, the wife's estate would be entitled to the proceeds. In turn, these proceeds would pass to those people who were named as beneficiaries under her will or to her heirs under the intestate laws if she left no will.

The danger of improper distribution of proceeds in event of common disaster is often more fancied than real. In the first place, the possibility that one person will die as the result of accidental means is remote; the possibility that a person and his wife will both die in the same accident or disaster is even more remote. And if the contingency does occur, and if children survive, the life insurance proceeds will usually pass to them through the estate of the parent who lives longer if they do not pass under the beneficiary designation itself. However, costs of administration, fees and expenses, and inheritance taxes are usually saved if the distribution is made under the beneficiary designation rather than the estate. Therefore, no matter how remote the contingency, when husband and wife frequently travel together, and especially when they travel in such circumstances that a common accident could occur, the desirability of covering this contingency merits discussion. Appropriate provisions can be incorporated easily in beneficiary agreements. In fact, the contingency is often covered automatically by use of interest or installment arrangements.

To emphasize the remoteness of the common accident or common disaster hazard, no problem is presented if the insured and his wife are fatally injured, and if there is evidence that the wife predeceased the insured. If a contingent beneficiary has been named under the policy, the contingent beneficiary will be entitled to the proceeds, because the wife as primary beneficiary will not be living at the death of the insured. Again, if the insured and his wife are killed in such circumstances that there is no evidence that she survived him, the Uniform Simultaneous Death Act, now in force in some form in almost all the states, enters the picture. Under this act, the proceeds of the insurance policy are distributed as if the insured had survived the beneficiary. Of course, the circumstances of the death of the insured and beneficiary must be such that "there is no sufficient evidence that they have died otherwise than simultaneously."

1. *Common accident or common disaster clauses.* If there is proof that the wife of the insured, named as beneficiary in the policy, did survive the insured by a few moments or hours, her executors or administrators will be entitled to the proceeds. A true common disaster clause does not prevent this undesirable result, because the clause provides in substance that proceeds shall be paid to the contingent beneficiary *only* if the insured and his beneficiary are killed in such circumstances that it cannot readily be determined who died first. Such clause really does no more than to reiterate the provisions of the Uniform Simultaneous Death Act which applies in most states without such clause. For that reason, a "delayed payment provision," as

described in the following paragraph, is more generally requested than a true common disaster clause.

2. *Delayed payment provisions.* Under a delayed payment provision, the proceeds are made payable to the beneficiary—the wife, for example—only if she is living at some stated time after the insured's death, such as 10, 30 or 60 days. Such a clause provides that if the wife is not living at the stated time, the proceeds will be paid to the named contingent beneficiary, rather than to the wife's estate.

3. *Disadvantages of delayed payment provisions.* There are several objections to a delayed payment provision. First, it is difficult—without the proverbial crystal ball—to determine how long the period of delay should be. Second, if the proceeds of the particular policy are to be qualified for the marital deduction, as discussed in Section 6.7.2, the marital deduction will be lost if the contingency expressed in such a provision actually occurs. Third, such a delayed payment provision does not cover the much more common danger of "short-term survivorship." The insured may die from natural causes, and his wife may die within a few months, also as the result of natural causes. If for any reason the life insurance company has not yet paid the proceeds of the policy to the wife as beneficiary, or if payment has been made and the funds have not been spent by her, the proceeds will form a part of her estate.

4. *Use of the Interest Option.* All the objections just mentioned are avoided by a provision for retention of the proceeds under the Interest Option, subject to the beneficiary's full right of withdrawal. Should the beneficiary and the insured be killed in a common accident, not even the first interest payment will be payable, assuming that the beneficiary dies within one month and that interest will be payable monthly. Certainly, the beneficiary will have no opportunity to exercise her withdrawal privilege. The proceeds can be specifically payable to a contingent beneficiary if the primary beneficiary dies either before or after the

insured. Such arrangement automatically covers the common accident contingency without any special clauses. If qualification for marital deduction under the federal estate tax law is desired, this arrangement may meet the qualifying rules explained in Section 6.7.2. Of more importance, if a common accident does occur, the full withdrawal privilege will preserve marital deduction qualification, as compared with its possible loss under a delayed payment provision. The withdrawal will not be exercised if the common accident does occur, and the proceeds will be paid exactly as desired by the insured.

5. *Use of installment options.* The common accident contingency is also covered automatically if one of the installment options is specified, with certain exceptions. Since most policies provide that the first installment is payable immediately on the insured's death, the first installment may be payable to the estate of the beneficiary who dies within, say, one month of the insured's death. The remaining proceeds will be payable to named contingent beneficiaries under the terms of the beneficiary designation. Of course, if installments are payable annually, the initial installment to be paid to the beneficiary's estate in event of her death shortly after the insured's death could be a more sizable amount. Here again, if the insured and the beneficiary die in such circumstances that there is no evidence of death otherwise than simultaneously, the Uniform Simultaneous Death Act will prevent even the first installment payment from passing to the estate of the beneficiary.

A potentially more serious problem is presented if installments are payable under the Life Income Option. As explained in Section 3.10.2, a significant percentage of the policy proceeds is consumed by the life annuity feature on which there is no refund for contingent beneficiaries. If the primary beneficiary dies soon after the insured, the proceeds may shrink by as much as two-thirds because of this fact. A delayed payment provision, preceding the commencement of payments under the Life Income Option, will prevent such a result. This adverse result may also be prevented by a provision that the proceeds shall be retained at interest for a short period after the insured's death, before the life income payments commence.

6. *Marital deduction qualification.* It is observed in Section 7.7.4 that retention of the proceeds under the Interest Option with full withdrawal privileges may meet the qualifying rules for marital deduction under the federal estate tax law. If it is desired to qualify the proceeds for marital deduction under an installment option, the surviving spouse must be given the power either to take down the commuted value of the proceeds while living, or to appoint his or her estate as contingent beneficiary at death.

In the enthusiasm to preserve the fullest possible benefit of marital deduction qualification, companies have been requested to incorporate "reverse common disaster presumptions." This expression refers to a provision that if the insured and his spouse—the primary beneficiary under the policy—die in such circumstances that it cannot be determined who died first, *it will be presumed that the beneficiary survived the insured.* The Treasury Regulations imply that the presumption created by such clause will generally be recognized.

§7.8. **Designation of children and grandchildren as beneficiaries—class designations.** It is sometimes desired to designate a group of persons without identifying the individual members of the group. This is known as a class designation. The designation of "children of the insured" is a common example of such a class designation. The beneficiaries actually entitled to receive the proceeds at the death of the insured will be determined by the members of the class in existence at that time. Such a designation automatically includes members of the class who may be

born after the date of the beneficiary designation, and before the insured's death. Companies tend to limit the designation of this type of beneficiary to classes of people
closely related to the insured, and in which the members
of the class are easily identified. It is unusual for company
practices to permit class beneficiary designations for other
than children, grandchildren, brothers and sisters; and
some companies have limitations even within those groups.

When it is desired to name children as beneficiaries, the
simplest and usually the safest way is to designate "children of the insured" as a class. If the children are designated by name, as "John Doe and Susan Doe, children of
the insured," then children born after the date of the beneficiary designation will be excluded. If the insured wishes
his living children to be designated by name and also
wishes to include after-born children, the designation may
be made to read, "children of the insured, including John
Doe and Susan Doe."

A class designation sometimes observed, but with
much less frequency than formerly, is "children born of
the marriage of the insured and his said wife." Such designation will exclude as beneficiaries the insured's own children born of an earlier or later marriage, and all children
born to his wife by a former marriage. All adopted children
will also be excluded under such limited designation. The
request for payment to children born of the marriage
seemingly stems from a desire to eliminate alleged illegitimate children as beneficiaries. Such children, however, are
generally eliminated by the routine provisions of beneficiary and settlement option agreements prepared by companies today which provide, for example, that " 'child'
or 'children' as used herein shall include only lawful
and legally adopted sons and daughters." An alleged
illegitimate child of the husband-insured probably would
have no valid claim as beneficiary even without such an
express provision. Of course, provision may be made for an

illegitimate child whom the insured acknowledges by simply designating him as beneficiary by name.

The safer procedure again is to use "children of the
insured," or "children of the insured, including John Doe
and Susan Doe." If there are children by a former marriage
of the insured's wife, they must be specifically named to
be included under the beneficiary designation. Usually,
this is done by some phraseology such as "children of the
insured, and John Smith and Margaret Smith, children of
the insured's wife."

§*7.9. Final payees.* Companies are frequently asked
to provide that if all beneficiaries die before completely
exhausting proceeds retained by the life insurance company, any remaining proceeds will revert to the estate of
the insured. Such a provision may pose complications.
There may be legal barriers to opening an estate on which
administration is long since closed. There may also be difficulty in determining who are the insured's heirs, and in
locating and identifying them to make payment. There
may be a very few dollars left to be distributed.

Life insurance companies routinely provide that at
the death of all the beneficiaries who survived the insured,
any remaining proceeds will be paid to the estate of the
last surviving beneficiary. If such distribution is inconsistent with the insured's wishes in this remote contingency,
the problem can easily be solved by naming a charity or
group of charities as final payees.

There are some instances when the insured's estate is
quite properly named as final payee. One such instance is
the reversion to the insured's estate of clean-up funds discussed in Section 3.3.1. Such reversion is on a short-term
basis. Essentially, it is designed to provide cash to the insured's estate if the wife dies before having opportunity to
clear its obligations.

Another such instance is a larger estate where federal
estate taxes against the husband's estate may be materially

increased if his wife dies before him, because of loss of the marital deduction. Some policy proceeds that would normally be used to provide income for the wife and children may have to be paid to the insured's estate, if his wife dies first, to cover the increased tax liability resulting from loss of the marital deduction.

§*7.10.   Qualification for Veterans Administration compensation or pension benefits.*   Many cases will be encountered in which veterans benefits must be considered. In some cases, the settlement plans adopted for commercial insurance may affect the right of a beneficiary to receive payments from the Veterans Administration.

1. *Dependency compensation for service-connected death.* If the insured is in the armed forces or is a veteran, his dependents may be entitled to death benefits from the Veterans Administration. If death occurs while he is in the service, or later as a result of such service, the widow, children, and dependent parents will normally be entitled to monthly dependency compensation. This is payable to the widow or children without regard to outside income, and to dependent parents if their income does not exceed stated amounts. Such payments pose no special problems in designing settlement plans for life insurance.

2. *Non-service-connected death pension.* Veterans of World War I, World War II, or the Korean conflict, who die as a result of causes *not* traceable to their military service may leave their widows or children entitled to pension benefits.

Prior to July 1, 1960, dependents of World War II and Korean veterans were not eligible for non-service-connected death pension benefits unless the veteran had a "definitely ascertainable service-connected disability of compensable type." This disability requirement is not in the present law. However, families of any veteran who died prior to July 1, 1960, but who would be eligible under the present law, may now apply for benefits under the current law. Any person receiving income for non-service-connected death under the old law may change to new benefits if it is advantageous.

Benefits are payable under the following tables:

WIDOW, NO CHILD			WIDOW, ONE CHILD		
Annual Income			*Annual Income*		
More Than	*But equal to or less than*	*Monthly Pension*	*More Than*	*But equal to or less than*	*Monthly Pension*
	$ 600	$64		$1,000	$80
$ 600	1,200	48	$1,000	2,000	64
1,200	1,800	27	2,000	3,000	43
			Plus $15 for each additional child.		

NO WIDOW, ONE OR MORE CHILDREN	
Annual income equal to or less than (earned income excluded)	*Monthly Pension*
$1,800	$38 for one child
	$15 for each additional child

Annual income under the current law includes all income except a few specific items. Commercial life insurance payments received by a beneficiary will be considered as income in the calendar year in which they are received. This applies to income under any settlement option, even where the beneficiary has the right to elect a one sum payment or to withdraw principal. If the beneficiary has the right to withdraw all or any part of the principal, such principal will not be considered income until actually withdrawn, but it will be counted in determining the beneficiary's "net worth." The "net worth" section of the new law provides in substance that the Veterans Administration may deny pension in cases where the net worth of the claimant's real and personal property is such that in all the circumstances, including consideration of income, it is reasonable that some part of the estate be consumed for maintenance.

If there is no qualified widow, then children may qualify directly under the table above entitled "No Widow, One or More Children." Where a widow is disqualified by reason of other income or net worth, these will not be considered in determining eligibility of dependent children for direct pension benefits. Obviously, this situation provides an unusual opportunity for life underwriters to be of service to their clients.

Eligibility for any particular benefit can be finally determined only by the proper government agency, based on the facts in a given case. Whenever there appears to be any possibility that servicemen, veterans, or their dependents may be entitled to a government benefit, the nearest office of the Veterans Administration or other appropriate agency should be consulted without delay.

§7.11.   *Remarriage clauses.* Life insurance companies are often requested to include in beneficiary agreements a provision that if the surviving spouse remarries, no further payments will be made to her, and that payments will then be made to contingent beneficiaries in the same manner as if the spouse had died. A majority of companies will not permit the incorporation of such a provision because of the potential complications and administrative burdens. Even those companies whose rules permit such clauses will often deny the request if the proceeds are payable under the Life Income Option. If the surviving spouse survives the guaranteed period, payments under the deferred annuity feature must be payable to someone. It would not be practicable to make those payments to anyone other than the surviving spouse herself even though she might be remarried.

Whether the surviving spouse is remarried depends, of course, on a determination of whether she is again legally married. Under the laws of a particular state, this question is sometimes difficult to answer. This is particularly true in those states where so-called common law marriages are recognized. Common law marriages are those in which two people legally able to marry live together as man and wife without complying with the usual marriage formalities.

Another difficulty in administering a remarriage clause is that there is no assurance that the life insurance company will be promptly notified of the subsequent remarriage of the surviving spouse. Therefore, the company may be unwilling to incorporate a remarriage clause even though such clause includes phraseology that will protect the company for payments made to the spouse after her remarriage but before notice to the company. Certainly the presence of a remarriage clause in the beneficiary designation would be a great temptation to a surviving spouse to conceal the fact of her remarriage, or to choose other undesirable alternatives to prevent loss of benefits under the beneficiary agreement. Even where company practice permits the inclusion of a remarriage clause, its suitability is extremely doubtful.

§*7.12. Endowment maturity proceeds.* Normally, a settlement option agreement will relate to the proceeds payable on the death of the insured. However, if the particular policy is written on some form of endowment plan, consideration may be given to disposition of the endowment maturity value should the insured survive the date of maturity.

Some companies permit the maturity value to be disposed of in the same settlement option agreement that provides for disposition of the proceeds in event of the insured's death before maturity. This may complicate a settlement plan in that a separate set of contingencies must be expressly covered. The insured's circumstances and ideas concerning the disposition of the endowment maturity value may change materially before the maturity date. Since he will be in full control of the maturity value right up to the date of maturity, there is no apparent reason why he should make a declaration of intention years in advance of this date. Of course, if the endowment policy is owned by a third party, such as a father on the life of his son, a request may properly be made to dispose of the maturity value in a settlement option agreement, because the father may not be alive on the date of endowment maturity.

§*7.13. Consulting an attorney.* Although life insurance programs are customarily discussed with and arranged by the life underwriter, an insured is well advised to review the suggested settlement arrangement with his lawyer. Such discussion may lead to a revision of his will or an analysis of his general estate, resulting in its orderly planning and distribution. The complexity of present-day laws relating to administration and distribution of estates and the high rates of inheritance and estate taxation make consultation with the lawyer and obtaining proper legal advice profitable at every turn.

Chapter 8

Programing in Action

§*8.1. Variation in philosophies and techniques.* Individual philosophies and techniques of programing vary
a good deal among life underwriters, especially as to the
manner of offering this service and of presenting final recommendations. For example, the service may be described
verbally or with the aid of illustrations. Such illustrations
may range from sketches penciled during the interview to
comprehensive presentation kits.

Often, charts based on the results of actual, though
anonymous, cases help the prospective client gain a clear
picture of how programing can benefit him. Some life
underwriters use their own programs or estate plans for
this purpose in the belief that this is more effective than
a hypothetical or composite case, and also that it involves
no hint of betraying the confidences of other clients.

Many life underwriters offer the service primarily on
the basis of improving or increasing family benefits from
present life insurance without any obligation on the part
of the client. Others prefer to establish more clearly in advance the client's seriousness of purpose regarding his financial objectives. Thus, they emphasize that if additional insurance is indicated by the facts, they will certainly recommend it, though the decision as to any purchase is obviously

up to the client. With this approach, there may be an express or implied obligation on the client's part to place with the life underwriter who performed the service any insurance which might result from the analysis. Underwriters who use this approach contend that it is in the client's interest as well as their own. They feel they are able to devote more time to doing a good job for clients whose purchases provide their living, by eliminating at the start most of the time wasted with those who are not serious.

Similarly, there is a variation in the degree of information required before analyzing a case. Sometimes a case is accepted in which the client has refused to state his income or the value of his general estate; sometimes this information is not specifically requested. On the other hand, many underwriters insist that complete confidence is essential to sound programing, and will accept a case only when the client is willing to reveal all the facts.

In this connection, a few programers obtain a medical examination in advance, believing that knowledge of the client's insurability is just as important as any other fact in the case. If life insurance is needed and the client happens to be a substandard risk, the recommendation can be exact as to amount and required premium. Disappointment may be avoided, as well as extensive revision of the original program. An advance medical examination can be of considerable importance if the substandard rating is high or the client is completely uninsurable.

§8.2. *Presenting the recommended program.* Here again, there is much variation in technique. Programing can be and often is completed during a single interview. Usually, however, at least two interviews are employed— one for offering the service and for fact-finding, and the other for presenting the recommended program. In either case, service calls will normally follow. Obviously, the more complex cases may require several interviews, including conferences with the client's attorney and other advisers.

Broadly speaking, presentation of the final recommendations may be classified under two general approaches. These might be called "report and analysis" on the one hand and "completed staff action" on the other.

In the first approach, the client's existing financial situation is compared in detail with his stated objectives. The client is led through a logical process to recognize the need for each recommendation in the plan, including any suggested additional insurance. Obviously, there is considerable motivation in this approach. On the other hand, some life underwriters feel there is also a hazard of unduly criticizing the client's past efforts to build and distribute his estate. Such implied criticism has been known to backfire, particularly where the analysis goes into detail as to inappropriate distributive provisions in existing policies. It is apt to loom more important when the analysis is reviewed in the presence of the client's wife or attorney, either or both of whom may not have been present at the fact-finding interview. As a rule, therefore, life underwriters who use this technique successfully take pains to keep the presentation objective and factual, thereby enhancing its effectiveness.

The second approach is similar in a general way to the completed staff action concept applied to military and business decisions. The new program is presented as it will appear if all the life underwriter's recommendations are adopted. Reference is made to the existing situation only as may be necessary to clarify the need for one or more features of the plan. Often, this type of presentation is used when the first interview employs hypothetical cases or the underwriter's own program to describe the service.

Proponents of this approach hold that the client has made his own comparison between his present estate and an ideal plan during the first interview, and particularly during the fact-finding process. They feel he should be allowed to make this comparison in private, just as he observes the shortcomings of his old car after a thrilling ride in a new model. It must be noted that good car salesmen count on such a private comparison and carefully avoid criticizing the old car, no matter how decrepit or how low its value may be.

Obviously, neither approach can insure that the client will clearly understand and adopt all recommendations in every case. Compromises are inevitable in any activity and must be expected in a certain proportion of program cases. Regardless of the techniques used by the underwriter, compromises can be kept to a minimum if he will prescribe objectively in the light of all the facts, and test each recommendation against all possible objections before making the presentation.

§8.3. Mechanics of programing. Irrespective of the varied philosophies and techniques which influence how clients are obtained and recommendations presented, the mechanics of programing are fairly uniform, and follow one of two general patterns. In the first or conventional method, objectives are reduced to specific family needs, which can be readily classified on a chart or graph. Income from Social Security and other sources is then plotted, after which present life insurance can be applied under tentative settlement options and the resulting income added to the chart.

Needs for additional income and capital sums are similarly plotted to determine the amount of new life insurance needed to complete the program. Charts or graphs are also helpful in developing the retirement income and disability benefits picture.

The second approach to determining needs, a comparatively recent development, is the capitalization and discount method. After objectives have been translated into specific family needs, all requirements for cash and income are reduced to lump sums by means of capitalization or discount tables. Similarly, all present resources, including life insurance, Social Security, and income from other sources, are also capitalized and lumped together. When the total capital value of such resources is deducted from the value of the requirements, the problem appears as a capital amount. The purpose is to do a measuring job and arrive at this capital amount quickly and simply, avoiding as many detailed calculations and complications as possible.

Obviously, figures will vary widely among different cases, because no two family situations are alike. Thus, the simplest way to illustrate the mechanics of programing may be in terms of a specific case. Such a case, involving principles discussed in preceding chapters, is presented below, first using the conventional settlement option approach and then using the capitalization and discount method of determining the problem. In this connection, it may be helpful to review Sections 1.11 through 1.17 which outline the programing process.

§8.4. *An illustrative case.* The following case is merely illustrative of the use of settlement options in programing. The final recommendations are not necessarily the only ones that might be made. Given the same facts, another life underwriter might arrive at a different, though equally practical, solution. Obviously, it is impossible to reproduce all the intangible factors and impressions arising out of personal interviews with the client. Yet these factors have a strong influence on the proper solution of any case problem.

Assume a man of 31, a Korean conflict veteran, now a junior executive in a moderate-sized corporation. His wife is 28, and they have a son age six months. The client's salary has averaged more than $4,800 annually long enough to assure maximum Social Security benefits, and is currently $8,000. Assets include a recently purchased home worth about $23,000, subject to a $15,000 FHA mortgage payable over a 20-year period, with interest at 5½ percent.

The home is owned jointly by husband and wife, as

are savings bonds having a value of $1,000 and household furnishings estimated at $5,000. The husband currently receives about $33 per month from a $10,000 trust under his late uncle's will. This will continue to the wife at the client's death, and, ultimately, the trust will terminate in favor of any children he may leave, subject, of course, to legal limitations on the duration of the trust. A year-old car worth about $2,000 completes the list of assets. The car is titled in the husband's name and is not encumbered.

The following life insurance is owned:

$10,000	National Service, ordinary life, converted at age 25
10,000	group life insurance
2,500	20-payment life, age 20
5,000	ordinary life, age 28
$27,500	total, plus $2,500 ordinary life on client's wife

Specific objectives are:

$ 5,000	for clean-up
4,000	to be set aside for emergencies
15,000	for retirement of mortgage
350	per month while son is dependent, followed by as large a life income for widow as practicable
8,000	for son's college education
350	per month retirement income, including Social Security

When these needs are put down on a worksheet designed for measuring how much money will be required, and also for determining how the funds should be arranged, the worksheet might look like the one on page 232.

§8.5. Plotting objectives and present resources. It appears from the facts that $450 monthly is about the level of current family living expenses. It is important to continue this level for at least a year or two, if possible, especially where there is a child or children in the picture. The underwriter in this case has, therefore, decided to recommend such an arrangement.

PROGRAMING WORKSHEET

CLIENT: *John Doe* DATE: *January 2, 1964*

CASH NEEDS

	Amount
Clean-up fund	$ 5,000
Emergency fund	4,000
Mortgage retirement	15,000
Education	8,000
Tax fund	
Other	
Total cash and monthly income requirements	$32,000

FAMILY INCOME NEEDS

	Readjustment 2 Years	Dependency Period 16 Years To 1982	Years To 19	Years To 19	Post Dependency 16 Years To 1998	For Life After Age 62
Total cash and monthly income requirements	$450.00	$350.00			$175.00	$175.00

SOURCES OF FUNDS AND HOW PAYABLE

	Amount	Readjustment 2 Years	Dependency 16 Years To 1982	Years To 19	Years To 19	Post Dependency 16 Years To 1998	For Life After Age 62
Social Security	$ 255	$190.60	$190.60				$104.80
Veterans Benefits	250						
Other: Trust ($10,000)	1,000	33.00	33.00			$33.00	33.00
Savings Bonds							

Life Insurance Provisions

Amount	Company & Plan	Settlement	Readjustment 2 Years	Dependency 16 Years To 1982	Years To 19	Years To 19	Post Dependency 16 Years To 1998	For Life After Age 62
$10,000	NSLI: Ord. Life	Ref. Life Income	37.10	37.10			37.10	37.10
10,000	Group: Term	Cash or Interest	108.60					
2,500	Co. "A", 20-Pay.	2 Yrs. Instal.	10.30	10.30			31.50	
5,000	Co. "B" Ord. Life	Int. to 1982, then 16 Yrs. Instal.	24.10	24.10			73.70	
11,700	New: Ord. Life	Same as Co. "B"						
12,400	New: Ord. Life	Int., right of w/d	16.50	16.50				
8,000	New: Ord. Life	Educ. Int., w/d	33.80	33.80				
5,900	New: Ord. Life	18 Yrs. Instal.						
$65,500	Total Provisions		$454.00	$345.40			$175.30	$174.90

Family ages:	Readjustment	Dependency	Post Dependency	For Life
Wife: 28	28-30	30-46	46-62	62-Life
Child: 0	0-2	2-18	18-34	
Child:				
Child:				

Similarly, a minimum objective of $175 per month has been established for the widow's life income after the dependency period. While this may seem low in relation to the other objectives, it is obvious from the facts that even on this basis, considerable new insurance will be needed— probably more than the client feels he can presently afford. The life income objective is also in line with a widely used formula recommended as a guide by one programing authority. For a client in the income bracket of the illustrative case, this formula suggests a minimum income during the dependency period of one-half the client's salary, with a minimum of one-fifth the salary for the widow's later life income, and more if possible.

Sometimes, the underwriter will establish dollar amounts for all the specific objectives rather than having them specified by the client. As indicated in Section 1.13, this can be done by a reasonably scientific process of translating the client's general objectives into specific figures, based on the facts.

Obviously, Social Security and Veterans benefits should be the first payments entered on the chart, since they are not subject to the client's control. The National Service proceeds are next "spent" under the Refund Life Income Option 4. This option is used despite the wife's young age because of the unusually liberal rate and because the Interest Option is not available for deferring commencement of the life annuity. At age 28, the standard NSLI Option 4 guarantees 270 monthly installments certain, which will protect the client's son in event of his mother's death before he matures.

Next, the $33 monthly income from the trust may be entered, also on a life income basis. The $10,000 group policy can cover two-thirds of the mortgage fund in this case. Because of the amount, it is possible that the Interest Option can be used for settlement, along the lines discussed in Section 3.4. If not, proceeds may be payable to the wife, with the estate of the last survivor as contingent beneficiary.

The 20-payment life policy has a face amount of only $2,500. If set up to provide income during the entire dependency period, or for life income thereafter, income would probably have to be paid quarterly to meet company minimum payment rules. Hence, it is tentatively assigned the job of providing extra income during a two-year readjustment period.

Due to space limitations, the retirement income objective does not appear on the illustrative worksheet. A separate graph may be used for this purpose, possibly on the reverse side of the worksheet. Objectives for disability income may be similarly plotted.

Also not shown is the possible benefit for the son from the Veterans Administration non-service-connected death pension. Because of total income and available cash, the widow will probably be disqualified for pension benefits, but her son might well be eligible for a child's benefit of $38 per month, assuming he does not have unearned income in his own right exceeding $1,800 annually. Depending on circumstances, such child's benefit may be available for his support or education, or may be required to be accumulated during his minority. Veterans Administration benefits are explained in Section 7.10.

§8.6. *Developing a tentative solution.* Recommendations for needed additional insurance may be formulated in various ways. It may be obvious that only a limited amount can be set aside for new premiums, though the need is great. Thus, as much as can be afforded on a relatively low premium plan might be set up on the program worksheet to go as far as possible toward meeting the most critical needs.

On the other hand, there is merit in setting up the program to meet all the specific objectives and then, if necessary, cutting the suit to fit the cloth. As a rule, few clients can add more than one or two "packages" of insurance at a time to cover specific needs revealed by the program. A complete program, though not adopted all at once, is a helpful guide to future steps as earnings permit.

The case under discussion has been developed to cover all needs. Ordinary life has been selected tentatively as the plan for new insurance, because its fairly equal balance between retirement benefits and protection fits the basic requirements of this case. An argument could be made for increasing the protection through the use of some term insurance, so as to increase the widow's life income. Conversely, life paid up at 65 might be considered because of its substantially higher retirement values at a relatively slight increase in premium over ordinary life, if the facts warrant.

In developing a tentative solution, requirements for additional income normally should be considered for the purpose of computation on the worksheet from *right to left* on the chart. This is because funds held to produce income for the widow in later life will earn interest in the interim.

In cases involving Social Security, a logical first step is to fill the gap in income between the youngest child's age 18 and the widow's age 62, when her share of benefits will resume. After the children reach 18, this will provide a level floor upon which additional life income may be built. The gap in this case extends for 16 years, from 1982 to 1998. At least $104.80 per month is needed during this gap, to match the Social Security life income payable after age 62.

The existing $5,000 ordinary life policy can provide interest payments of $10.30 per month during the dependency period, followed by $31.50 per month during the 16-year gap, under the Fixed Period Option. This leaves $73.30 to be furnished during the gap by new insurance.

Assuming that under the Fixed Period Option $1,588 is required to pay $10 monthly during the 16-year gap (see

Table III on page 40), $11,700 of proceeds will provide approximately $73.70 per month for this period ($1,588 × 7.4 = $11,751). The proceeds will also earn interest during the dependency period. The chart indicates this will run to 1982. At 2½ percent, the interest on $11,700 would be $24.10 per month.

The clean-up, emergency, and mortgage retirement needs account for $24,000 of the $32,000 total cash requirements. Social Security, Veterans benefits, savings bonds, and group insurance will provide a total of $11,505 toward these basic cash needs, leaving a deficit of approximately $12,400 to be covered by new insurance. As indicated on the chart, the new proceeds would normally be set up under the Interest Option, as explained in Sections 3.2 through 3.5. However, since it is expected that most or all of these proceeds will be spent in a short time after the insured's death, no interest from this source is shown in the income sections of the chart.

$8,000 is required for educational funds, which will normally be retained under the Interest Option until the son reaches college age. In this case, if the client should die immediately, this fund will produce about $16.50 per month at 2½ percent for 18 years, until 1982.

There remains the problem of rounding out the basic $350 monthly income desired for the dependency period. It must be assumed that the client's death could occur immediately, which would fix the minimum dependency period at a little less than 18 years. It may well be argued that the son will be dependent for considerably longer. However, since reasonably adequate clean-up, emergency, and educational funds have been tentatively scheduled, the 18-year period was used.

Again, the table of amounts needed under the Fixed Period Option to provide $10 per month is consulted (see Table III on page 40). The income shortage is about $33.50

per month, which will require slightly less than $5,900 of proceeds ($1,746 × 3.35 = $5,849). $5,900 is recommended to produce $33.80 per month.

The final step is to recheck the cash requirements, particularly the clean-up fund, for any additional estate tax needs resulting from the proposed new insurance. It is apparent that none have been created, since the total gross estate is still well under $120,000, and adequate use of the marital deduction may be assured by following the procedures suggested in Section 6.7.2.

Although a number of separate steps have been required to develop the illustrated program, the actual distributive pattern under the settlement options can be extremely simple. Moreover, a great deal of flexibility can be given the beneficiaries, if desired.

The tentative settlement plans for present life insurance are not complicated. The $38,000 of new life insurance needed could be written as a single policy to cover the $20,400 proposed for cash requirements including education, the $11,700 allocated to filling the Social Security gap, and the $5,900 needed for dependency period income. The entire proceeds could be placed under the Interest Option with the right to withdraw principal or elect other options. Or the agreement could direct that the appropriate portion be applied under the Fixed Period Option in 1982 ($11,700) to provide the 16-year gap income, with $5,900 placed immediately under this option to provide $33.80 monthly for the dependency period. The Fixed Amount Option may be used, if desired, not only for filling the gap but also for the dependency period income from the $5,900 portion.

Alternatively, two policies could be used—one for $19,-700 to cover the gap ($11,700) and educational funds ($8,-000), the other for $18,300 to cover the $12,400 cash deficit and the $5,900 dependency income fund. Or separate policies could be purchased for each need. Many companies base their rates per $1,000 on policy size, which would be an important factor in deciding how many separate policies to recommend.

Under the more or less ideal plan set forth on the completed worksheet, there are also some "self-correcting" features. For example, the longer the client lives, the larger will be the income from NSLI. Similarly, the dependency period item of $33.80 provided by new insurance will extend to a later date. The longer the client lives, the smaller his mortgage will be, which will release increasing sums from the level mortgage fund. Such funds could be used to augment the widow's life income or for other purposes.

The tentative program also works out well with regard to the client's retirement objective of about $350 per month. Though this objective will undoubtedly be raised in the future as earnings increase, it is logical to aim at about half of current earnings at a given point.

National Service cash surrender values cannot be placed under a settlement option. Even if this policy were changed eventually to an endowment, only the Fixed Period Option could be used for the maturity value. Moreover, at advanced ages the life income rates for a beneficiary exceed those in commercial policies by extreme margins. Therefore, the NSLI contract is one that should be kept as insurance after retirement. It can readily be changed to a limited payment life plan when the client can afford to do so, in order to eliminate premiums after he retires. Or, if necessary, he could take reduced paid-up insurance.

The proposed new insurance and the $5,000 ordinary life policy will develop enough value at age 65 to provide about $160 monthly on a life income, 10-year-certain basis. Social Security will add $190.50 if the wife's share of this benefit commences at her age 65, slightly less if it starts when she is 62 and the client is 65. Thus, total income of more than the desired $350 per month is assured. If the trust fund continues to produce at least $33 per month, there may be more than $380 in all.

If all ordinary life insurance except NSLI is settled at retirement under a level joint and survivorship option, total income should be about $360 per month, including Social Security. In view of the substantial income protection afforded the wife by keeping NSLI in force as insurance after retirement, a joint and two-thirds survivorship option might be in order, which would increase the income while both husband and wife are living.

The $2,500 policy, by then fully paid up, might logically be kept for clean-up purposes. However, its cash value might be settled on an income basis to produce around $10 monthly. Of course, many variations are possible, and no decisions are necessary until retirement age nears. The point is that the tentative program does appear to produce enough raw material by age 65 to meet the current retirement objective.

So much for the tentative planning process. It remains to be seen how far the client can afford to progress toward completing the program at this time. In all, $38,000 of new life insurance is indicated. On the ordinary life plan, the gross premium will be over $775 on a participating basis. Disability income provisions, if available, would increase this amount by over $100, though much of this additional cost would be absorbed by dividends on the basic contract. If the life insurance is purchased on a nonparticipating basis, much the same effect will obtain.

§8.7. *What can the client afford?* A little over $400 annually is going into present life insurance, after deducting estimated dividends, plus nearly $180 in Social Security taxes. New insurance indicated by the tentative program would result in total premium payments of more than $1,300, which is over 16 percent of present gross earnings. At this point, it is well to recapitulate the client's income and expenses, as follows:

Gross annual income, including	
the trust	$8,400
Less estimated income and	
Social Security taxes	1,100
Net income	$7,300
Estimated living expenses	5,800
Gross discretionary income	$1,500
Present life insurance premiums	400
Net spread	$1,100

Theoretically, the net spread might be considered available for additional life and health insurance, but this may be unrealistic. For one thing, no matter how carefully the facts have been obtained, expenses are rarely pinpointed exactly. For another, if all the "free" money is allocated to insurance, there is a hazard that the program will come to be viewed as a burden rather than a source of peace of mind, and so defeat its own purpose. It would also preclude savings for emergencies or other purposes until increased earnings became available.

Experience has shown that about 20 percent of net income after taxes is a practical upper limit for life insurance premiums unless the income is very substantial. In the present case, this would be a little less than $1,500. Premiums for new insurance should also be considered in relationship to the net spread. New premiums totaling 50 to 75 percent of the net spread will often represent a practical maximum. Based on these figures, a limit of $550 to $825 on new premiums would be indicated, making the total outlay for life insurance about $950 to $1,225.

Obviously, the nature of the client's spending habits must be considered in relation to the mathematical factors. This family is apparently thrifty, as evidenced by the unencumbered automobile, the conversion of the NSLI policy, and the substantial equity in the home. While this may indicate receptivity to the idea of substantial life insurance purchases, it also points to a strong desire to save up for cars and other equipment and thus avoid large installment commitments.

§8.8.　The final recommendations.　It is apparent from the foregoing that some modifications in the tentative program are in order. Certainly, a reducing term rider can be used for the mortgage fund in place of the ordinary life. Reducing term can also be used effectively for dependency period income by substituting a family income policy or rider for some of the permanent insurance tentatively allocated for this purpose.

Considering the relatively substantial amount of proceeds available in cash under the tentative plan and the $1,000 in savings bonds, perhaps the emergency fund can be reduced to $3,500. Any surplus from the clean-up fund can be used by the widow to restore all or part of this cut. However, it may not prove necessary to use a family income plan in the illustrative case.

Modifications of this nature will, of course, reduce the projected retirement income. However, this is not too vital in view of the client's relatively young age and his evident progress in business. He can improve this side of the program as he goes along. Should he become uninsurable, the remaining part of any reducing term insurance may be converted to increase retirement values and stabilize protection. A guaranteed insurability rider incorporated in part or all of the new policies to be issued would also assure the client of the ability to improve the program without question of insurability. In view of the growing use of pension plans for employees, it is entirely likely that the employer in this case may establish such a plan before many years have elapsed.

Based on all these factors, considered in relationship to what the client can reasonably be expected to put into new life insurance, the final recommended program might take the form shown on page 243. It should be borne in mind that figures in this chart are based on guarantees under the various settlement options. Income actually paid may be higher, since excess interest may be declared by the company, as explained in Chapter 2.

This program is based on adding the following two new policies, at the indicated *approximate* premium cost, including disability income benefits:

Description	Amount	Premium
Ordinary life policy	$ 5,000	
with 20-year reducing mortgage rider	15,000	$170
Ordinary life policy	17,600	410
Total initial insurance	$37,600	$580
Total permanent amount	$22,600	
Net premiums for present insurance		400
Total premiums, first year		$980
Percentage of gross income		11.7
Percentage of net income after taxes		13.4

Essential features of the settlement plans for both old and new policies to provide for distribution in accordance with the recommended program are outlined below.

(1) *New $5,000 ordinary life with $15,000 mortgage rider (Use: mortgage and educational funds).* Retain proceeds under the Interest Option, with interest payable monthly to the wife, if living, otherwise to surviving children equally, with the right of unlimited withdrawal and the further right to elect any other option in the policy at any time (subject to company rules, especially those related to Life Income Options).

In some few cases, it may be desirable to have the mortgage fund go to the estate of the survivor of husband and wife, if the home is owned jointly and it is probable that it will be retained by the executor or trustee for the children.

(2) *New $17,600 ordinary life policy (Use: dependency period and "gap" income).*

(a) Place $5,900, or the proceeds if less, under the Fixed Period Option for 18 years, monthly installments payable to the wife, if living, otherwise to the children. Or if it is desired to permit full or partial withdrawals of principal during the dependency period, the Fixed Amount Option could be specified, with payments at the rate of $34 monthly.

RECOMMENDED PROGRAM FOR JOHN DOE
January 9, 1964

Clean-up	Emergency	Mortgage	Education
$ 5,000	$ 3,505	$ 15,000	$ 8,000

SOURCES OF FUNDS

Cash

Clean-up:	Group Insurance	$ 5,000
Emergency:	Group Insurance	$2,000
	Social Security	255
	Veterans Benefit	250
	Bonds	1,000
		3,505
Mortgage:	New Term Rider	15,000
Education:	Group Insurance	$3,000
	New Insurance	5,000
		8,000
		$31,505

Income

	Mortgage	Education	Until 1998	For Life
	16.50	16.50		
Company "A" $2,500, 20-Payment Life	108.60	–	–	–
Company "B" $5,000 Ordinary Life	10.30	10.30	31.50	–
New $5,900 Ordinary Life	33.80	33.80	–	–
New $11,700 Ordinary Life	24.10	24.10	73.70	–
Social Security	190.60	190.60	–	104.80
NSLI $10,000 Ordinary Life	37.10	37.10	37.10	37.10
Trust Fund ($10,000)	33.00	33.00	33.00	33.00
Total	**$454.00**	**$345.40**	**$175.30**	**$174.90**
	2 Years	Until 1982	Until 1998	For Life

Family Ages: Wife: 28 Child: 0

Period	2 Years	Until 1982	Until 1998	62
Wife	30	46	62	
Child	2	18		

NOTE: Sources of funds for income and cash purposes are shown for illustrative purposes in connection with text discussion. Various types of charts are used in presenting the program. Often detail as to sources appears elsewhere in the presentation, and only totals are shown on the income chart.

(b) Retain any balance of proceeds ($11,700 in the absence of any outstanding loan or dividend accumulations or additions) under the Interest Option until 1982, then place under the Fixed Period Option for 16 years or under the Fixed Amount Option at $74 monthly. Of course, the change from the Interest Option to either installment option can be made automatic or left to the discretion of the widow. Also, the client may wish to permit full or limited withdrawal of principal before 1982 or thereafter. If withdrawals are to be permitted during the Social Security gap (1982-98), the Fixed Amount Option should be used for payments after 1982.

(c) Any balance remaining in either fund at the wife's death may, of course, be retained at interest for the children, with rights to withdraw or elect other options. Or such remainders may be settled as suggested in Sections 3.15 and 3.16.

(3) *$10,000 group policy (Use: clean-up, emergency, and educational funds).* Retain proceeds under the Interest Option, as outlined for policy (1) above, provided that if the wife predeceases the insured or survives him and dies within six months after his death, $5,000 of the proceeds, or any remainder if less, will be paid to the insured's estate instead of to children. (If her death occurs after this period, the full proceeds or any remainder would be held for children).

Some other period, such as one year, might be preferred to six months. If this option is not available, then payment in cash to the widow, if living 30 days after the insured's death, otherwise $5,000, or the remainder if less, to his estate and any balance to the children would be satisfactory. The portion allocated to education could then be reinvested by the widow, perhaps in a savings account, to produce interest.

(4) *$10,000 NSLI ordinary life policy (Use: life income from date of insured's death).* Pay to the wife, if liv-

ing, under Refund Life Income Option 4, otherwise under Fixed Period Option 2 for 20 years to surviving children equally. Option 4 installments will be continued to children if the wife dies after commencing to receive them.

An alternate plan would be to specify Option 2 for 36 months for the widow or children, inasmuch as the beneficiary could then elect any other arrangement except one sum after the insured's death. However, Option 4 is so valuable to the widow that any other choice should normally be avoided. In this case, dependency period income is reasonably adequate, and there should be no need to use NSLI proceeds faster than Option 4 will provide.

(5) *$2,500 20-payment life policy, Company A (Use: readjustment income).* Pay to the wife, if living, otherwise to surviving children equally, under the Fixed Period Option for two years.

The Fixed Amount Option at $100 or $110 per month would serve equally well, of course, and would permit inclusion of the right to withdraw additional sums as needed. Similarly, the Interest Option could be used, as outlined above for policy (1).

(6) *$5,000 ordinary life policy, Company B (Use: dependency period and gap income).* Retain under the Interest Option until 1982, then place under the Fixed Period Option for 16 years, or the Fixed Amount Option at the rate of $32 monthly, as outlined above for policy (2), paragraph (b).

(7) *$2,500 ordinary life policy on the wife (Use: cleanup fund for wife's estate).* Retain under the Interest Option, as outlined for the first $5,000 of the group policy (3) above, husband primary beneficiary.

(8) *Retirement and disability income.* Obviously, retirement income under this plan will be slightly less than under the tentative solution. However, the final program will produce about $270 per month at age 65 from Social Security and the life insurance.

A reasonable amount of income may also be produced in event of total disability. Estimated premiums for the new insurance are based on providing up to $226 per month of disability income, either by means of riders on the life policies or under separate contracts. In addition, the premium for the National Service policy includes the cost of a disability income rider providing $100 of monthly income.

§*8.9. Capitalization and discount method.* As suggested in Section 8.3, the capitalization and discount method of fixing the problem can save a great deal of time in determining the amount of additional life insurance required for family needs. Also, it will normally prove accurate within one or two thousand dollars of the amount developed through the conventional approach described in Sections 8.4 through 8.8. Often, the difference will be much less, perhaps as low as 1 to 1½ percent. This will be true whether the client's present resources consist entirely of life insurance and Social Security or include other income-producing assets, such as securities or trust funds.

In the following illustration, it should be borne in mind that the settlement option tables in Chapter 2 are used for illustrative purposes only and are not intended to represent any particular company rates, nor are they to be considered as typical of the industry. Similar tables in the underwriter's own rate book may be employed just as effectively.

The Capitalization and Discount Worksheet on page 247 shows how the amount of additional life insurance needed in the illustrative case discussed in Sections 8.4 through 8.8 may be determined by this simple, streamlined method, usually in less than half an hour. The worksheet is filled out as follows:

Capital Value of Estate Requirements

1. *Clean-up fund.* This is always shown in the full amount—$5,000 in the illustrative case. Even though the

fund may be placed under the Interest Option, it cannot be counted on for income.

CAPITALIZATION AND DISCOUNT WORKSHEET

CAPITAL VALUE OF ESTATE REQUIREMENTS:

1. Clean-up Fund $5,000

2. Balance of Mortgage 15,000

3. Emergency Fund 4,000

4. Life Income to Wife, Age 28 $175 per month . 58,528

5. Additional Income until Children are Grown
   $175 per month   for 18 years 30,555

6. Educational Funds:
   Amount $ 8,000 needed in 18 years . . . 5,130
   Amount $_____ needed _____ . . .

7. Other Needs (Readjustment income: $100 per mo. 2yrs) 2,344

8. Total Capital Value Required (Add lines 1 through 7). $120,557

CAPITAL VALUE OF OFFSETS TO ESTATE REQUIREMENTS:

9. Total Life Insurance (Including decreasing term, family maintenance and commuted value of family income) . . $27,500

10. Social Security:
    Cash . . . . $ 255
    $191 per mo. for 18 years 33,349
    $____ per mo. additional for ____ years . _____
    $____ per mo. additional for ____ years . _____
    $105 per mo. to Wife at age 62 8,276
    Total Social Security 41,880

11. Non-Income-Producing Liquid Assets (VA and Bonds) 1,250

12. Inheritance yielding $33 per month for Life (Trust) . 11,040

13. Income from Other Sources:
    $_____ per month for _____ . . . . . . _____
    $_____ per month for _____ . . . . . . _____

14. Total Capital Value Available (Add lines 9 through 13) 81,670

Deficit, if any $38,885

---

2. *Balance of mortgage.* The mortgage balance is also shown at the full amount, as a non-income-producing fund, though it, too, may be settled under the Interest Option.

3. *Emergency fund.* Again, emergency funds are entered at full value, rather than being discounted, because it is impossible to predict when they may have to be used.

4. *Life income to wife.* In conventional programing, this item is usually planned to commence after the children are grown. Normally, proceeds would not be placed under a Life Income Option for a beneficiary only 28 years old, except for government life insurance, as explained in Section 8.5. However, the purpose here is merely to measure capital needs. Therefore, the sum needed to produce the minimum life income requirement is calculated first, because it forms the base income throughout.

Based on the same mortality and interest factors underlying Table V, page 48, $1,000 of proceeds will pay $2.99 per month to a female age 28, for life, 20 years certain (age 28 not shown in Table V). Hence, $58,528 will be required to produce $175 per month for life ($175 ÷ $2.99 = $58,528), and this sum is entered on line 4 of the worksheet.

5. *Additional income until children are grown.* Since the dependency period income objective in the illustrative case is $350 per month, $175 of which will be provided by the basic life income, an additional $175 is needed for at least 18 years. Table III, page 40, indicates that $1,746 is required to pay $10 per month for 216 months, or 18 years. Therefore, $30,555 will provide $175 monthly ($1,746 × 17.5 = $30,555).

6. *Educational funds.* $8,000 is needed for this client's son, now six months old, to be available 18 years from now. The standard 2½ percent compound discount table found in many rate books and compends shows that $1.00 due 18 years hence has a present value of $.6412. Thus, $5,130 set aside today at 2½ percent will provide $8,000 in 18 years ($8,000 × .6412 = $5,129.60).

In practice, of course, the discounted value usually cannot be set up in the program, because the wife normally is named beneficiary, and interest cannot be accumulated for an adult. But the full sum—$8,000 in the illustrative case—would normally be placed under the Interest Option and so produce part of the dependency period income, thus reducing capital requirements for this period. The discount method is simply a quick way of measuring capital needed today to fill the educational need some years hence.

7. *Other needs.* Depending on the individual case, there could be many other needs, or none. In the illustrative case, the extra $100 per month recommended during a two-year readjustment period is considered under this heading. Table III, page 40, indicates that $2,344 of proceeds will provide this extra income, based on a 2½ percent guaranteed interest assumption.

8. *Total capital value required.* The amounts entered on lines 1 through 7 are simply added. In the illustrative case, capital requirements add up to $120,557.

Capital Value of Offsets to Estate Requirements

Continuing with the second part of the worksheet, lines 9 through 14 comprise the heart of this technique. Here the problem is fixed, at a tremendous saving of time and detail work in comparison with conventional methods.

9. *Total life insurance* (including decreasing term, family maintenance, commuted value of family income). In the illustrative case, the client owns $27,500 of life insurance.

10. *Social Security.* The cash item will usually be $255, though sometimes it might be less. In determining the value of income payments, the first step is to measure the capital value of income payable until the youngest child is 18. The income in this case is $190.60 per month, or in round numbers, $191. The one child is considered age zero, and Table III, page 40, shows that $1,746 will produce $10 per month for 18 years. This means the first Social Se-

curity income benefit on the worksheet is worth $33,349 ($1,746 × 19.1 = $33,348.60).

On the last line of item 10, it is noted that $105 ($104.80 to be exact) will be paid the widow for life, beginning at age 62. Table V, page 48, indicates that $5.48 per month will be paid to a female age 62, for each $1,000 of proceeds, for life with *no* certain period. Thus, $19,161 is needed for $105 per month ($105 ÷ $5.48 = $19,160.58). However, this figure would be unrealistically high for use on the worksheet, because the income will not become due until age 62, or 34 years from the wife's present age 28. Accordingly, it is necessary to determine the present value of this sum payable 34 years hence. The standard 2½ percent compound discount table referred to in item 6 above shows a present value of $.4319 for $1.00 due 34 years hence. On this basis, the widow's life income from Social Security after age 62 is presently worth $8,276 ($19,161 × .4319 = $8,-275.64). Adding the present value of cash and income items, the total capital value of Social Security payments in the illustrative case is found to be $41,880.

11. *Non-income-producing liquid assets.* Such assets as government savings bonds and savings and checking account balances should be included under this heading.

A business interest might also be listed here, if covered by a funded buy-and-sell agreement. If not so covered, a definite problem might be indicated which can be solved by life insurance. If it is expected that the home will be sold, a conservative estimate of the equity in it could be included in item 11, though a home is not really a liquid asset.

In the case under discussion, the entry comprises only the $1,000 in savings bonds and the $250 Veterans burial benefit, a total of $1,250.

12. *Inheritance.* Future inheritances are pleasant to contemplate, but seldom can one estimate their value or the time they might be received. This item is intended for

inheritances already received, particularly income from trusts. An inheritance not in trust might well appear under item 11 or item 13. If an income-producing trust is involved, the amount and duration of income should be entered under item 12. Table III, page 40, may be used to capitalize income payable for a limited period, or Table V, page 48, for a life income (20-years-certain column).

In this case, the client is receiving about $33 per month from a trust, which will be continued to his wife in event of his death. It is not necessary to know or enter the market value of the trust or other assets, because the purpose is to measure needs. If the $33 monthly income were not in the picture, $11,040 of life insurance would be required to produce this income for life, payable to a 28-year-old widow, 20 years certain ($33 ÷ $2.99 = $11,040, based on Table V).

13. *Income from other sources.* Income from real estate, securities, a business insurance agreement, or other assets may be entered here. Again, depending on whether the income is limited to a specific period or may be expected for life, it can be capitalized by Tables III or V. It should be remembered, however, that such capitalized values may not be valid for estimating death taxes, but only for determining possible needs for additional income-producing life insurance.

14. *Total capital value available.* Here, lines 9 through 13 are added, and in the illustrative case, the value is $81,670.

Deficit, if any

The deficit is simply line 8 minus line 14—in this case, $38,887. This compares with the $38,000 deficit developed by the conventional approach in the tentative solution to the illustrative case (Section 8.6).

Thus, the capitalization and discount deficit is $887 more than that revealed by conventional methods. However, the two approaches are not based on exactly the same figures. For example, the readjustment income in the conventional program charted on page 232 is $4.00 per month higher than the rounded $450 used in the discount example, the dependency period income is less than $350, and the life income after 1982 is about the same as used in the capitalization and discount example. An exact, to-the-penny comparison would produce almost identical deficits.

After the deficit has been ascertained, the next step is to determine how much the client can and will put into new insurance, and, in turn, the appropriate amount and type of insurance to recommend. In the illustrative case, both the conventional and capitalization methods of diagnosis have revealed approximately the same total need. Whichever method is used, the final recommendations for the illustrative case might appear as outlined in Section 8.8 and charted on page 243 in that section.

To summarize, from the standpoint of practicality, the capitalization and discount estimate of the overall need is close enough when the time and effort saved are considered. Normally, the Capitalization and Discount Worksheet can be completed in 15 or 20 minutes, in the client's presence or at the underwriter's office. Its purpose is not to plan distribution of assets. That will have to be done anyway after the sale is made, and the newer method makes it unnecessary to do this twice. Frequently, due to the usual variables and the compromises that often must be made, the actual distribution may have to be quite different from the original tentative plan.

The main purpose is to arrive as quickly and easily as possible and with reasonable accuracy at any shortage in assets that may exist. Then, attention may be turned to consideration of the appropriate amount and type of life insurance to recommend, consistent with the client's income and needs for protection, savings, and retirement income.

By saving time in the initial diagnosis step, the capitalization and discount method can help the underwriter arrive more quickly at sound recommendations for his clients.

§*8.10.   Post-delivery service.*   Regardless of which method is used to determine needs, when agreement has been reached with the client as to the scope and arrangement of the program, it is up to the life underwriter to follow through on all details. The job is not complete until the new insurance is in force and all necessary changes have been made in the settlement plans to fit the program.

Any errors found in old policies should be corrected at this time. Desirable optional features should be requested, such as joint and survivorship income options and disability riders, which might not have been included at the time of issue.

In the case discussed in this chapter, no mention was made of existing wills for the client or his wife. Though the life underwriter does not practice law, it is entirely proper and desirable that he urge the client to consult an attorney in this regard. No matter how small the general estate, a will almost always represents cheap insurance in that it can save many times its cost in reducing administration expense and expediting transfer of property. Though most such property in the illustrative case is jointly owned, some $10,000 to $20,000 of assets will eventually pass through the estate of the client or of his wife, and the amount may increase as time goes on.

Generally, it is considered highly desirable to give the client a summary of the program in final form. This should include at least a record of family names, with dates of birth, marriage, divorce, and the like, a family income chart, an outline of how each source of funds will provide what the chart describes, a summary of retirement and disability benefits, and a premium deposit calendar.

A statement of yearly cash values, dividend accumulations, and paid-up additions can be extremely helpful to the client as a record of progress toward his goal. While this may take a little time to prepare initially, it is relatively easy to keep up-to-date as the program is reviewed periodically.

Other features are often incorporated in the summary. A page indicating the location of wills and other pertinent documents can be invaluable in event of death. Similarly, a statement as to how frequently the underwriter plans to review the program will be helpful. This might well include a list of the more common events that should prompt the client to contact the underwriter at once, without waiting for the next regular review.

Finally, the life underwriter should be sure that his own records on the case are complete and up-to-date. Not only will this save him considerable time in future dealings with the client, but it will also prove of great importance at the client's death, disability, or retirement. Many underwriters retain certified copies of birth, marriage, adoption, and other appropriate records in their files. Sometimes, it takes several weeks or months to obtain correct copies of this sort, and it is obviously preferable to avoid such delays at the time of a claim by securing the records while all concerned are alive.

The life underwriter must also realize that he is mortal as well as the client. Either of them may move to another city, or the underwriter may accept a management position that would preclude serving his old clients effectively. Someone else may have to take over. An adequate and up-to-date summary in the client's hands, plus accurate records in the life underwriter's files, will help to insure that the important purposes of each life insurance program will be carried out.

§8.11. *Every case has a future.* In this chapter, a specific case has been developed to illustrate the application of principles governing the use of settlement options, and a relatively simple case was chosen for this purpose.

However, the same principles of diagnosis, prescription, and follow-through apply to all cases, regardless of size or complexity. Moreover, the program finally recommended for this particular case represents only the beginning for the client.

Looking ahead a year or two, a number of changes will have occurred in this client's situation. There may be another child, earnings probably will have increased, and a pension plan might be in force, to name but a few. These will be reflected by corresponding changes in objectives.

Yet, the original tentative program may still serve as a general guide to specific objectives. The distribution finally adopted when the program was first completed will probably remain basically sound, though requiring some minor adjustments. On the other hand, a second child would automatically increase Social Security benefits by more than $60 monthly, which might cover most of the adjustment needed in dependency period income.

Increased earnings will normally permit the client to strengthen provisions that had to be compromised in the initial program, such as the life income and the emergency fund. With additional children and a corresponding increase in educational needs, an added opportunity for improving distribution presents itself, particularly in respect to funds that might become payable to minor secondary beneficiaries.

Mention is made in Chapters 3 and 7 of the life insurance trust as a possible vehicle for administering proceeds. While for some time the illustrative case might not grow to the point that a trust is indicated for major income needs of the wife, use of a trustee could be extremely helpful if the children should become payees.

As emergency and educational funds are increased, a point may soon be reached where the total of such funds to be held intact for some years would justify a living or *inter vivos* trust as primary beneficiary. This might be especially true if a discretionary common trust fund is available.

All funds in the program intended to be held at interest and available in cash could be paid to such a trust as primary beneficiary, including clean-up, mortgage, and tax funds. The trustee, assuming he is also named executor or coexecutor, could then handle the major chore of settling the estate for the widow, after which emergency and educational funds would be retained in the trust for future use. Of greater importance is the fact that the existence of such a trust provides an ideal repository for remainders from other policies should the widow die before the children are grown.

Thus, the trust would be named contingent beneficiary under policies allocated for income to the widow. In many states, it might also be designated as beneficiary of the residuary estate under the wills of both husband and wife. Thus, any general estate property may be "poured over" into the living insurance trust to bring together all the funds of children who become orphaned, for efficient administration in their best interest.

Of course, these are only a few of the possibilities. Future developments in a given case can be infinite in number and variety. This is why the successful, conscientious life underwriter often finds that his clientele will tend to stabilize itself at somewhere between 150 and 250 families who look to him for advice over the years. He will lose some along the way and gain others, but a group of this size, their descendants, and their friends will keep him fully occupied if he keeps alert to their changing needs.

Moreover, such service will bring the life underwriter substantial rewards, not only in the form of a comfortable living, but also in the psychic pay of personal satisfaction and recognition.

§8.12.   *Responsibility for periodic review.*   Finally,

there is a *continuing responsibility* on the life underwriter's part to review the insurance program periodically. This obviously implies a further duty to keep abreast of new ideas for covering contingencies, changes in the law, new tax statutes, rulings, and regulations. All these may have to be taken into account in revising a program from time to time.

Trade publications and loose-leaf services help to keep the life underwriter's knowledge of these matters up-to-date. The *Journal of the American Society of Chartered Life Underwriters* frequently contains helpful articles. The life underwriter's study is also implemented by organized educational and training groups, such as those conducted by his own company, local life underwriter associations, training schools and courses on college campuses, the Life Underwriter Training Council, and the American College of Life Underwriters. The annual American Society Institutes are excellent refreshers for Chartered Life Underwriters.

Comprehensive instruction offered by these various educational sources makes for a well-rounded life underwriter who, in turn, will build a real clientele. An understanding of settlement options is only one segment of this process, but it is essential to a successful career in professional life underwriting.

Appendixes

Appendix A

Specifications for Beneficiary Designation and for Manner of Payment

To: _____
(life insurance company)

Please forward the proper beneficiary papers, to be executed by the owner, to put into effect under each policy listed below the following designation of beneficiary and manner of payment of proceeds:

Policies No._____ No._____ If this request applies to less than the entire proceeds, indicate the fraction_____or fixed amount $_____ to which it applies. *(Please use SEPARATE request for EACH fraction or fixed amount.)*

ARTICLE 1—DESIGNATION OF BENEFICIARY

Full Name	Relationship to Insured	Date of Birth

Primary

Contingent

☐ and any children of the insured hereafter born.
☐ The children of a deceased child shall receive his or her parent's share.

Second Contingent _____

ARTICLE 2—"CLEAN-UP FUND"

☐ Pay $_____ (or entire proceeds, if less) in one sum to the Primary Beneficiary, if living, otherwise to the executors or administrators of the insured.

☐ Hold $_____ (or entire proceeds, if less) under the Interest Option for Primary and First Contingent Beneficiary, except that if the Primary Beneficiary predeceases the insured or dies within _____ months after the insured's death, proceeds or remaining funds on deposit shall be paid in one sum to insured's estate. Primary and First Contingent Beneficiaries shall have the unlimited right to withdraw proceeds or to elect any other option in the policy at any time (subject to company rules).

ARTICLE 3—MODE OF SETTLEMENT (For entire proceeds, or for balance of proceeds not payable under "Clean-up Fund" if elected under Article 2.)

TO PRIMARY BENEFICIARY	Please "X" appropriate blocks and fill in necessary information for Options and Privileges desired	TO FIRST CONTINGENT BENEFICIARY
	One Sum Payment.............. ☐	
	Interest Option.............. ☐	
_____years	Fixed Period Option.............. ☐	_____years
_____years certain	Life Income Option.............. ☐	_____years certain
	Life Income "until proceeds are refunded" Option ☐	
$_____to **EACH** beneficiary	Fixed Amount Option.............. ☐	$_____to **EACH** beneficiary

All interest or instalment payments shall be paid:

☐ Annually
☐ Semiannually
☐ Quarterly
☐ Monthly

Option_____
on_____
On_____

☐ Automatic change to Option indicated on date specified   ☐ Option_____
☐ Pay proceeds in one sum on date specified   ☐ On_____

Beneficiary may change from Interest Option or Fixed Amount Option to:

☐ Fixed Period Option..............
☐ Fixed Amount Option..............
☐ Life Income Option..............

This change may be made subject to company rules:

☐ At any time..............
☐ At any time after date specified..............

After_____

261

Appendix A (Continued)

The Beneficiary may withdraw or commute:

☐ Entire proceeds, at any time.

☐ Entire proceeds, after date specified.............

☐ A limited part of the proceeds (Available only under Interest Option or Fixed Amount Option)

After_____
Each Primary Beneficiary
may withdraw
_____
_____

After_____
Each First Contingent
Beneficiary may withdraw
_____
_____

If the Primary Beneficiary dies while receiving payments ☐ under the Fixed Period or Life Income Options, continue remaining installments certain to First Contingent Beneficiary.

ARTICLE 4—FAMILY MAINTENANCE OF FAMILY INCOME POLICIES:

If policy provides Family Maintenance or Family Income Benefits fill out applicable blocks below:

☐ Make monthly payments as provided in the policy and pay amount due at end of Family Maintenance or Family Income Period under Mode of Settlement designated above.

NOTE: If Income payments are elected, check proper box to grant or to negative the right of commutation during such income period.

☐ The beneficiary may at any time during said Period commute all future benefits.

☐ The beneficiary shall have no right of commutation during said Period

☐ Commute all benefits and pay entire proceeds under Mode of Settlement designated above

If this portion of the Designation is not completed and if a policy provides Family Maintenance or Family Income Benefits, it will be presumed such Benefits are to be commuted at the death of the insured and such commuted value, together with the face amount of the policy, shall be paid under Mode of Settlement designated above.

ARTICLE 5—COMMON DISASTER

☐ Payment will not be made to any beneficiary until thirty days after the insured's death. If a beneficiary dies during that period, payment will be made as though he had died before the insured.

ARTICLE 6—ACCIDENTAL DEATH BENEFIT

☐ Include with and pay in same manner as policy proceeds. (Under the Fixed Period or Life Income Options, the installments are to be increased. Under the Fixed Amount Option, the installment period will be lengthened.)

262

ARTICLE 7—ADDITIONAL REQUESTS

☐ Spendthrift or creditor's clause.

☐ Joint and Last Survivor Annuity Option.

☐ Automatic Premium Loan Provision.

☐ Give wife power to appoint to her estate at her death any proceeds remaining with the Company to qualify policy for the marital deduction under the Federal Estate Tax Law.

☐ Please furnish cost and requirements for adding disability benefits:

  ☐ Waiver of premium.

  ☐ Monthly income.

Please furnish the following dividend information:

☐ Amount of accumulations or paid-up additions to date.

☐ Apply future dividends under the _____ dividend option.

☐ Advise whether current dividend accumulations can be applied to purchase paid-up additions at insured's attained age, and if so, furnish requirements.

ARTICLE 8—REMARKS (If any part of this request violates your company practice, please conform to the request as closely as your regulations will permit.)

Mail Agreement (TOGETHER WITH ANY ADDITIONAL INFORMATION AND FORMS HE MAY REQUEST) to:

Name _____

Street Address _____

City and State _____

Date _____   _____
                                       Insured or Owner

263

Appendix B

Designation of Beneficiary and Mode of Settlement

Policy Number (s) _____

Life of _____

ARTICLE 1—This Designation cancels all prior beneficiary and mode of settlement designations under these policies. Proceeds will be paid as designated below. Proceeds shall not include amounts payable upon the death of a wife or child under a Family Plan Policy, under a Family Benefit or under Children's Insurance Benefit. The owner of the policy may change this Designation.

DESIGNATION OF BENEFICIARY | Please type or print each beneficiary's full given name and relationship to insured |

CLASS A—PRIMARY BENEFICIARY (Proceeds will be paid under mode of settlement designated below)

CLASS B—FIRST CONTINGENT BENEFICIARY (Proceeds will be paid under mode of settlement designated below)

☐ Pay to children of each deceased Class B beneficiary as provided in Article 5

CLASS C—SECOND CONTINGENT BENEFICIARY (Proceeds will be paid in one sum)

☐ Pay to children of each deceased Class C beneficiary as provided in Article 5

CLASS D—FINAL BENEFICIARY—Proceeds will be paid in one sum to the owner of the policy, if living, otherwise the executors or administrators of the last to die of the owner, the primary beneficiary and the first contingent beneficiary.

MODE OF SETTLEMENT

☐ "CLEAN-UP FUND"—Pay $ _____ (or entire proceeds, if less) in one sum to the Primary Beneficiary, if living, otherwise to the executors or administrators of the insured, and pay the balance of proceeds as follows:

TO PRIMARY BENEFICIARY	Please "X" appropriate blocks and fill in necessary information for Options and Privileges desired	**TO FIRST CONTINGENT BENEFICIARY**
☐	One Sum Payment	☐
☐	Interest - Option 1	☐
☐ _____ years	Fixed Period - Option 2	☐ _____ years
☐ _____ years certain	Life Income - Option 3	☐ _____ years certain
☐	Life Income - Option 3 "until proceeds are refunded" (Available on policies above #570000)	☐
$ _____ to **EACH** individual	Fixed Amount - Option 4	$ _____ to **EACH** individual
	All interest or installment payments shall be paid:	
☐	Annually	☐
☐	Semiannually	☐
☐	Quarterly	☐
☐	Monthly	☐
Option _____ on _____ On _____	☐ Automatic change to Option indicated on date specified	Option _____ on _____ On _____
☐	Pay proceeds in one sum on date specified	☐
☐	Beneficiary may change from Option 1 or Option 4 to: Option 2, at any time	☐

□ Option 4, at any time.____

Option 3: (Use first block if policy number is below #570000)

□ Within two years after date specified.____

□ □ At any time ____ } (Available for
□ □ At any time after date specified ____ } policies above
{ #570000)

After____

After____

The Beneficiary may withdraw or commute:

□ □ Entire proceeds, at any time.____

□ Entire proceeds, after date specified ____   After____

□ A limited part of the proceeds, as specified for each
beneficiary in each Class (Available only under
Option 1 or Option 4)

After____

After____

□ If the Primary Beneficiary dies while receiving payments
under Option 2 or Option 3, continue remaining installments certain to First Contingent Beneficiary

If policy provides Family Maintenance or Family Income Benefits fill out applicable blocks below:

□ Make monthly payments as provided in the policy and □
pay amount due at end of Family Maintenance or Family
Income Period under Mode of Settlement designated above.

□ The beneficiary may at any time during said
Period commute all future benefits

□ The beneficiary shall have no right of
commutation during said Period.

□ Commute all benefits and pay entire proceeds under □
Mode of Settlement designated above

NOTE: If Income payments are elected, check proper box to grant or to negative the right of commutation during such Income period.

If this portion of the Designation is not completed and if a policy provides Family Maintenance or Family Income Benefits, it will be presumed such Benefits are to be commuted at the death of the insured and such commuted value, together with the face amount of the policy, shall be paid under Mode of Settlement designated above.

□ **ARTICLE 2**—COMMON DISASTER: Payment will not be made to any beneficiary until thirty days after the insured's death. If a beneficiary dies during that period, payment will be made as though he had died before the insured.

ARTICLE 3—The provisions appearing on the other side of this form are incorporated in this Designation.

Only the
Original
copy should
be signed

DO NOT WRITE BELOW THIS LINE

Dated ____ 19____   filed with ____   Company on ____.

Original signed copy dated ____   By ____   Registrar

____ Policyowner

265

Appendix B (Continued)

(Articles 4 through 19 appear on the reverse side of the "Designation of Beneficiary and Mode of Settlement" form reproduced on pages 264-265.)

☐ ARTICLE 4—ADDITIONAL REQUEST: Regardless of any provision herein to the contrary,

ARTICLE 5—PAYMENT TO CHILDREN OF A DECEASED BENEFICIARY: If this Article has been elected under "Designation of Beneficiary" on the other side, and if a beneficiary in a Class is deceased at the time a share would have become available for payment or retention for his benefit had he been living, such share will be paid in one sum equally to his then living children. If a beneficiary in a Class dies after his share has become available for payment or retention for his benefit, the unpaid portion of his share, if any, will be paid in one sum equally to his children living at the time of his death.

ARTICLE 6—BENEFICIARY: The beneficiaries of each Class will receive payment in the order designated in Article 1. No payment will be made to any Class of beneficiary until all beneficiaries in all preceding Classes have died. Payments specified in Article 1 will be paid to the beneficiary if living as each payment becomes due, and when a beneficiary dies, any interest or instalment accrued since the last payment will be added to the next beneficiary's share. Unless otherwise specified, if two or more beneficiaries are designated in any one Class, a separate and equal share will be provided for each member of such Class.

When two or more beneficiaries have been designated in a Class, and one or more dies:

(a) BEFORE his share has become available for payment or retention for his benefit, such share will be paid to the beneficiaries of that Class who are living at said time for payment or retention, in the proportion that their shares as set forth in Article 1 bear to each other, and in the manner specified in that Article.

(b) AFTER his share has become available for payment or retention for his benefit, the unpaid portion of his share will be paid in one sum to the then living beneficiaries of that Class, in the proportion that their shares as set forth in Article 1 bear to each other.

(c) The provisions of Paragraphs (a) and (b) are subject to any applicable contrary provisions of Article 4 or 5.

ARTICLE 7—ASSIGNMENT: The rights of every beneficiary of each policy are subordinate to the rights of any assignee who has filed a written assignment at the Home Office of the Company, whether the assignment was made before or after the date of this Designation. If such assignment is in effect at the insured's death, the Company may, at its option, pay the entire proceeds to the assignee or may deduct from the proceeds and pay to the assignee the amount owed to the assignee, as certified in writing by the assignee or any officer or partner of the assignee, and pay only the remaining proceeds to the beneficiary.

Appendix B (Continued)

ARTICLE 8—MINOR BENEFICIARIES: Unless provision is made by statute, or a provision is made in Article 4 for the designation of an informal trustee to act for a minor beneficiary, any payment becoming due a minor beneficiary will be made only to his legally appointed guardian, and any right, option or privilege given to the minor may be exercised only by such guardian.

ARTICLE 9—RELIANCE ON AFFIDAVIT AS TO BENEFICIARIES: The Company may rely on an affidavit by any beneficiary relating to the dates of birth, death, marriage or remarriage, names and addresses and other facts concerning all beneficiaries, and the Company is hereby released from all liability in relying and acting upon the statements contained in such affidavit.

ARTICLE 10—SPENDTHRIFT CLAUSE—PROHIBITION OF COMMUTATION AND ALIENATION: Unless provided in this Designation, no beneficiary may commute, anticipate, encumber, alienate, withdraw or assign any portion of his share of the proceeds. To the extent permitted by law, no payments to a beneficiary will be subject to his debts, contracts or engagements, nor may they be levied upon or attached.

ARTICLE 11—DISTRIBUTION WHEN PAYMENTS ARE LESS THAN $10 OR PROCEEDS ARE LESS THAN $1,000: If the specified payments would amount to less than $10 each, the Company may make equivalent payments less frequently. If any share of the proceeds to be retained under an Option is less than $1,000, or if any share is reduced to less than $1,000 because of withdrawals, the Company will pay that share in one sum, regardless of any provision for payment under an Option.

ARTICLE 12—MISSTATEMENT OF AGE OF BENEFICIARIES: If the age of any beneficiary has been misstated, and if Option 3 has been elected for that beneficiary, the instalments payable will be the amount that his share of the proceeds would have provided at his correct age. The Company may adjust future payments as necessary.

ARTICLE 13—EXTENSION OF TIME FOR CERTAIN PAYMENTS AND PRIVILEGES: If a date for beginning of payments (or for the exercise of a privilege) occurs during the lifetime of a person who must die before such payments can be made (or such privilege exercised), the beginning date for such payments (or for the exercise of such privilege) shall be the date of death of such person rather than the earlier date specified.

ARTICLE 14—EFFECT OF CHANGE OF BENEFICIARY UNDER ANY POLICY: A future change of beneficiary of any policy in this Designation shall terminate the Designation with regard to that policy.

ARTICLE 15—CANCELLATION OF POLICY ENDORSEMENT REQUIREMENT: The Company is requested to waive all provisions of any policy under this Designation requiring endorsement of beneficiary changes, and to endorse any such policy as follows:

"The beneficiary of this policy has been changed according to written request filed with the Company.

"Every request for change of beneficiary shall be in writing on a form satisfactory to the Company. No change of beneficiary will take effect until the request has been filed at the Home Office of the Com-

Appendix *B* *(Continued)*

pany, but when filed will take effect as of the date of the request, whether or not the insured is living at the time the request is filed, but without prejudice to the Company because of any payment made by it before receipt of the request at its Home Office. All provisions of the policy requiring endorsement of change of beneficiary are canceled."

ARTICLE 16—"PROCEEDS" DEFINED: The proceeds of a policy shall be:

(a) At the death of the insured, all amounts payable by reason of the insured's death under the provisions of the policy (including the commuted value of any guaranteed deferred payments).

(b) After the death of the insured, the balance of amounts under Paragraph (a) remaining with the Company, or the then commuted value of unpaid guaranteed instalments.

Proceeds shall not include surrender values, amounts payable at maturity of the policy during the insured's lifetime or any refund payable under a Receipt for Advanced Premiums. Specific amounts referred to in this Designation shall apply to the aggregate proceeds of all said policies and not to each policy separately.

ARTICLE 17—DEFINITIONS AND CONSTRUCTION OF TERMS: "Child" and "children" as used herein shall include both lawful and legally adopted sons and daughters, but not grandchildren or other descendents. "Brothers" and "Sisters" shall include half-brothers and half-sisters. Masculine terms shall apply to either sex and the singular shall include the plural. "Insured" shall mean "annuitant" when such meaning applies.

ARTICLE 18—DEFINITION OF TERM "OPTION": CONDITIONS OF WITHDRAWAL PRIVILEGES; AND PRIVILEGES TO ELECT OTHER OPTIONS: The terms "Option 1," "Option 2," "Option 3," or "Option 4" used in this Designation refer to the corresponding Option number appearing in the policy under the heading "Optional Modes of Settlement" or "Modes of Settlement at Maturity." Where any share of the proceeds is to be retained under Option 1, the interest will be paid at the rate provided in the policy. If Article 1 or Article 4 provides for more than one interest payment each year, the periodic payments shall be discounted so as to be the equivalent of interest payable at the end of the year.

No beneficiary may withdraw or commute the proceeds unless expressly provided in Article 1 or Article 4. Payment of any withdrawal or commutation may be deferred by the Company for the period permitted in the policy. The minimum amount that may be withdrawn under Option 1 or Option 4 is $100. Only the entire unpaid guaranteed instalments may be commuted under Option 2 or Option 3. Any privilege granted in this Designation to a beneficiary to elect other settlement options shall apply to the entire proceeds, or to any part of such proceeds in multiples of $1,000 or more.

Payments under Options are subject to all the terms and conditions appearing in the policy.

ARTICLE 19—MISCELLANEOUS: The furnishing by the Company or the filing with the Company of this form shall not constitute an admission that any policy under this Designation is in full force or is in effect under a Non-Forfeiture Option. Any provision or direction in this Designation which is immediately preceded or followed by a box □ will not be a part of this Designation unless the box is marked in such manner as to indicate clearly the election of the particular provision or direction.

Appendix C

Treasury Regulations—Section 72

TABLE I.

ORDINARY LIFE ANNUITIES—ONE LIFE—EXPECTED RETURN
MULTIPLES*

Ages Male	Ages Female	Multiples	Ages Male	Ages Female	Multiples
6	11	65.0	37	42	36.5
7	12	64.1	38	43	35.6
8	13	63.2	39	44	34.7
9	14	62.3	40	45	33.8
10	15	61.4	41	46	33.0
11	16	60.4	42	47	32.1
12	17	59.5	43	48	31.2
13	18	58.6	44	49	30.4
14	19	57.7	45	50	29.6
15	20	56.7	46	51	28.7
16	21	55.8	47	52	27.9
17	22	54.9	48	53	27.1
18	23	53.9	49	54	26.3
19	24	53.0	50	55	25.5
20	25	52.1	51	56	24.7
21	26	51.1	52	57	24.0
22	27	50.2	53	58	23.2
23	28	49.3	54	59	22.4
24	29	48.3	55	60	21.7
25	30	47.4	56	61	21.0
26	31	46.5	57	62	20.3
27	32	45.6	58	63	19.6
28	33	44.6	59	64	18.9
29	34	43.7	60	65	18.2
30	35	42.8	61	66	17.5
31	36	41.9	62	67	16.9
32	37	41.0	63	68	16.2
33	38	40.0	64	69	15.6
34	39	39.1	65	70	15.0
35	40	38.2	66	71	14.4
36	41	37.3	67	72	13.8

*U.S. Treas. Reg. §1.72-9. This table is to be used in connection with computations under Code §72 and the Regulations thereunder.

Appendix C (Continued)

Ages Male	Female	Multiples	Ages Male	Female	Multiples
68	73	13.2	90	95	4.2
69	74	12.6	91	96	4.0
70	75	12.1	92	97	3.7
71	76	11.6	93	98	3.5
72	77	11.0	94	99	3.3
73	78	10.5	95	100	3.1
74	79	10.1	96	101	2.9
75	80	9.6	97	102	2.7
76	81	9.1	98	103	2.5
77	82	8.7	99	104	2.3
78	83	8.3	100	105	2.1
79	84	7.8	101	106	1.9
80	85	7.5	102	107	1.7
81	86	7.1	103	108	1.5
82	87	6.7	104	109	1.3
83	88	6.3	105	110	1.2
84	89	6.0	106	111	1.0
85	90	5.7	107	112	.8
86	91	5.4	108	113	.7
87	92	5.1	109	114	.6
88	93	4.8	110	115	.5
89	94	4.5	111	116	0

Appendix D

Treasury Regulations—Section 72

TABLE III.

PERCENT VALUE OF REFUND FEATURE*

Male	Ages Female	10 yrs.	11 yrs.	12 yrs.	13 yrs.	14 yrs.	15 yrs.	16 yrs.	17 yrs.	18 yrs.	19 yrs.	20 yrs.
		%	%	%	%	%	%	%	%	%	%	%
40	45	3	3	3	4	4	4	5	5	6	6	7
41	46	3	3	3	4	4	5	5	6	6	7	7
42	47	3	3	4	4	5	5	5	6	6	7	8
43	48	3	4	4	4	5	5	6	6	7	8	8
44	49	3	4	4	5	5	6	6	7	7	8	9
45	50	4	4	5	5	6	6	7	7	8	9	9
46	51	4	4	5	5	6	7	7	8	9	9	10
47	52	4	5	5	6	7	7	8	9	9	10	11
48	53	5	5	6	6	7	8	8	9	10	11	12
49	54	5	5	6	7	8	8	9	10	11	11	12
50	55	5	6	7	7	8	9	10	11	11	12	13
51	56	6	6	7	8	9	9	10	11	12	13	14
52	57	6	7	8	8	9	10	11	12	13	14	15
53	58	7	7	8	9	10	11	12	13	14	15	16
54	59	7	8	9	10	11	12	13	14	15	16	17
55	60	8	8	9	10	11	13	14	15	16	17	18
56	61	8	9	10	11	12	13	15	16	17	18	20
57	62	9	10	11	12	13	14	16	17	18	20	21
58	63	9	10	12	13	14	15	17	18	19	21	22
59	64	10	11	12	14	15	16	18	19	21	22	24
60	65	11	12	13	15	16	18	19	20	22	24	25
61	66	12	13	14	16	17	19	20	22	23	25	27
62	67	12	14	15	17	18	20	22	23	25	27	28
63	68	13	15	16	18	20	21	23	25	26	28	30
64	69	14	16	17	19	21	23	24	26	28	30	32
65	70	15	17	19	20	22	24	26	28	30	32	33
66	71	16	18	20	22	24	26	28	29	31	33	35
67	72	17	19	21	23	25	27	29	31	33	35	37
68	73	18	21	23	25	27	29	31	33	35	37	39

The heading "Duration of guaranteed amount" spans columns 10 yrs. through 20 yrs.

*U.S. Treas. Reg. §1.72-9. This table, reproduced in part, is to be used in connection with computations under Code §72 and the Regulations thereunder. The full table shows a more complete range of ages and durations.

271

Appendix D (Continued)

Male	Ages Female	Duration of guaranteed amount										
		10 yrs.	11 yrs.	12 yrs.	13 yrs.	14 yrs.	15 yrs.	16 yrs.	17 yrs.	18 yrs.	19 yrs.	20 yrs.
		%	%	%	%	%	%	%	%	%	%	%
69	74	20	22	24	26	28	30	33	35	37	39	41
70	75	21	23	26	28	30	32	34	37	39	41	43
71	76	22	25	27	29	32	34	36	39	41	43	45
72	77	24	26	29	31	34	36	38	41	43	45	47
73	78	25	28	30	33	35	38	40	43	45	47	49
74	79	27	30	32	35	37	40	42	45	47	49	51
75	80	29	31	34	37	39	42	44	47	49	51	53
76	81	30	33	36	39	41	44	46	49	51	53	55
77	82	32	35	38	41	43	46	48	51	53	55	57
78	83	34	37	40	43	45	48	50	53	55	57	59
79	84	36	39	42	45	48	50	53	55	57	59	61
80	85	38	41	44	47	50	52	55	57	59	61	63
81	86	40	43	46	49	52	54	57	59	61	63	65
82	87	42	45	48	51	54	56	59	61	63	65	66
83	88	44	47	50	53	56	58	61	63	65	66	68
84	89	46	49	52	55	58	60	63	65	67	68	70
85	90	48	51	55	57	60	62	65	67	68	70	71

Appendix E

Bibliography

BOOKS

CARNAHAN, CHARLES W. *Conflict of Laws and Life Insurance Contracts*. 2d. ed. Chicago, Dennis, 1958. 768 pp.

CLARK, ROGER W. *Life Insurance Income Settlements*. Cincinnati, National Underwriter Company, 1947. 163 pp.

FIDELITY MUTUAL LIFE INSURANCE COMPANY. *Settlement Options and How to Use Them*. Philadelphia, 1955. 40 pp.

GARDINER, HAROLD W. *The Practice of Life Underwriting: A Text, Case Book, and Readings*. Philadelphia, American College of Life Underwriters, 1960. 400 pp.

HUEBNER, SOLOMON S., AND BLACK, KENNETH, JR. *Life Insurance*. 5th ed. New York, Appleton-Century-Crofts, Inc., 1958. 582 pp.

JAQUA, A. R. *Basic Life Insurance*. New York, Gregg Publishing Company, Business Education Division, McGraw Hill, Inc., 1951. 366 pp.

_____. *Formula Programing*. 2d ed. Dallas, Southern Methodist University Bookstore, 1955. 96 pp.

KRUEGER, HARRY, AND WAGGONER, LELAND T. (eds.). *The Life Insurance Policy Contract*. Boston, Little, Brown and Company, 1953. 417 pp.

LIFE INSURANCE AGENCY MANAGEMENT ASSOCIATION. *The How of Settlement Options: The Key to Career Underwriting*. Rev. ed. Hartford, 1958. 84 pp.

_____. *Introduction to Programing*. Rev. ed. Hartford, 1964. 91 pp.

MCCAHAN, DAVID (ed.). *The Beneficiary in Life Insurance*. S. S. Huebner Foundation for Insurance Education Lectures. Philadelphia, University of Pennsylvania Press, 1948. 250 pp. Rev. ed. by Dan M. McGill. Homewood, Illinois, Richard D. Irwin, Inc., 1956. 314 pp.

_____. *Fundamentals of Life Insurance Settlement Options*. Philadelphia, American College of Life Underwriters, 1949. Brochure, 9 pp.

MACLEAN, JOSEPH B. *Life Insurance*. 9th ed. New York, McGraw-Hill Book Company, Inc., 1962. 617 pp.

Appendix E (Continued)

MAGEE, JOHN H. *Life Insurance.* 3rd ed. Chicago, Richard D. Irwin, Inc., 1958. 819 pp.

MEHR, ROBERT IRWIN, AND OSLER, ROBERT W. *Modern Life Insurance: A Textbook of Income Insurance.* 3rd ed. New York, The Macmillan Company, 1961. 745 pp.

NUTT, HAL L. *Marketing Life Insurance.* Louisville, The Insurance Field, 1952. 92 pp.

OWEN, HENRY T. *Fundamentals of Life Insurance.* New York, Prentice-Hall, Inc., 1951. 424 pp.

————. *Life Insurance Case Analysis, Methods and Materials* (Supplement to *Fundamentals of Life Insurance*). New York, Prentice-Hall, Inc., 1952. 109 pp.

SHATTUCK, MAYO A., AND FARR, JAMES F. *An Estate Planner's Handbook.* 2d ed. Boston, Little, Brown and Company, 1953. 610 pp.

SHULTZ, GLADYS DENNY. *Widows Wise and Otherwise: A Practical Guide for the Woman Who Has Lost Her Husband.* Philadelphia, J. B. Lippincott Company, 1949. 285 pp.

SCHWARZSCHILD, STUART. *Rights of Creditors in Life Insurance Policies.* Homewood, Illinois, Richard D. Irwin, Inc., 1963. 381 pp.

WASHINGTON, LAWRENCE. *How to Plan Your Financial Security.* New York, McGraw-Hill Book Company, Inc., 1949. 288 pp.

WHEELER, W. J., AND TODD, T. L. *Safeguarding Life Insurance Proceeds.* New York, McGraw-Hill Book Company, Inc., 1940. 193 pp.

ANNUAL AND LOOSE-LEAF SERVICES

Advanced Underwriting Service, and other publications. Insurance Research & Review Service, Inc., 123 West North Street, Indianapolis 9, Indiana.

Compend, 77th ann. ed. Flitcraft, Inc., 75 Fulton Street, New York 38, New York, 1964. 768 pp.

Diamond Life Bulletins, and other publications. National Underwriter Company, 420 East Fourth Street, Cincinnati, Ohio.

Insurance Law Reporter, and other publications. Commerce Clearing House, Inc., 214 North Michigan Avenue, Chicago, Illinois.

Insurance Underwriters Service, and other publications. Prentice-Hall, Inc., 70 Fifth Avenue, New York 11, New York.

Little Gem Life Chart, 62nd ann. ed. National Underwriter Company, 420 East Fourth Street, Cincinnati 2, Ohio, 1964. 768 pp.

Appendix E (Continued)

Settlement Options, 23rd ann. ed. Flitcraft, Inc., 75 Fulton Street, New York 38, New York, 1964. 799 pp.

The Spectator Handy Guide. 72nd ann. ed. Chilton Co., Inc., Chestnut and 56th Streets, Philadelphia 39, Pennsylvania, 1963. 1276 pp.

Index

Index

*This book has been set on the Linotype in 12
and 10 point Baskerville Light, leaded 2 points.
Chapter numbers are in 24 point Caslon Swash
and chapter titles in 18 point English Caslon,
Cap and lower case. The size of the type page is
25 by 44 picas.*